D1074852

Also by Harry Golden

ONLY IN AMERICA

Published in a PERMABOOK edition.

# Harry Golden

## For 2¢ Plain

FOREWORD BY *Carl Sandburg*

PERMABOOKS · NEW YORK

## FOR 2¢ PLAIN

World Publishing edition published July, 1959

PERMABOOK edition published September, 1960
1st printing.........................July, 1960

"A Son of Dixie and Some Daughters" and "A Pulpit in the South" appeared in *Commentary*, February, 1954, and November, 1955, and are reprinted here by permission of *Commentary*.

Two of the essays have appeared in a syndicated column, distributed by The McClure Newspaper Syndicate, copyright, ©, 1959, by Harry Golden.

L

PERMABOOK editions are distributed in the U.S. by Affiliated Publishers, Inc., 630 Fifth Avenue, New York 20, N.Y.

PERMABOOK editions are published in the United States by Pocket Books, Inc., and in Canada by Pocket Books of Canada, Ltd.—the world's largest publishers of low-priced adult books.

To the late James Street,

Tar Heel writer,

and the late Noel Houston,

teacher of Tar Heel writers

*My champions*

*My friends*

## ACKNOWLEDGMENT

I am again indebted to Harry Golden, Jr., of the *Detroit Free Press* for this new selection of essays from my writings and for editing the manuscript

# Contents

## 3. *We're on a Single Ball of Twine*

## 6. *To Mae West and Truck Drivers*

## 7. *The Vertical Negro Opens a Second Front*

## 8. *More Complaints and Free Advice*

# Contents

# Foreword

ONE TIME I heard Harry Golden say, in talking about his home town in North Carolina, "I landed in Charlotte with only a cigar and a prayer." I know he still likes his long cigars and he says long and short prayers morning, noon, and night, and is a true praying man. Between prayers, sometimes, he laughs. Often he writes about what he is laughing at and when it is printed in *The Carolina Israelite* or a book, we read and we laugh with him. This is a very curious and important kind of sanity, this mingling of the utterly solemn and the irresistibly witty. I have spoken and written of Harry Golden as an apostle of freedom, a friend and a voice of "those who love liberty, unselfishly, for all men everywhere." His *For 2¢ Plain* stands freshly and sweetly alongside of *Only in America*. He is a fascinating entertainer, telling a good story for the story's sake. Then he shifts to be a reporter or current historian of "man's inhumanity to man" and telling the world what to do about it. Golden says with John Donne, "I am involved in mankind." He speaks to a vast American audience. The response to *Only in America* is a sign to some of us that the American Dream is alive and moving in many good hearts in this our day and time. Give him room there in Charlotte with his long cigars and his short abrupt compulsive prayers for the Humanity he loves.

CARL SANDBURG

# Introduction

I WRITE, edit, and publish *The Carolina Israelite*. Nineteen years ago I started with 600 subscribers, now I have almost 45,000. Recently people have begun to ask me to what I attribute the success of my little personal journal. The answer is a simple one: I waited.

Waited not for the national recognition both the paper and myself have fallen heir to, nor for money. Nor even, for that matter, for national advertisers. I waited for the respect of other working newspapermen, waited to see what kind of an effect my paper might have on the community where I live, waited to see if I could spend my life as a useful citizen. Often I wondered if I would see the fruition of these hopes. I was like the general who has only one given moment in which to commit the short supply of troops and materiel he commands and must wonder for the rest of the battle if he chose the right moment. Thus I waited and worked and wrote my paper in Charlotte, North Carolina.

Then came 1958. A year of trouble and joy. Yet I count my life doubly blessed for 1958.

In February, all the planes were grounded because of a blizzard and I was ten hours late for a lecture I was to give in Passaic, New Jersey. When my train finally arrived in Pennsylvania Station, I called the program chairman to announce I was here. She had to tell me that a fire had gutted my home and office back in Charlotte.

The stationmaster advised me: "Take the first train to

Washington, even if you have to stand all the way. Get to Washington and everything from there on is open to the South." During the nine and a half hours I stood on the train, I had a long conversation with a young Marine. He had a car meeting him in Washington and he risked going AWOL in order to ferry me to the airport just in time to catch the plane.

My home and office were gone, burned to the ground.

Since I have been an active integrationist, I found the Charlotte city police there on the scene, alert for any possibility of crackpot violence. After three days of exhaustive study both the police and I were convinced, beyond any shadow of a doubt, that the fire was an accident. Having once proved this, the chief of the Charlotte police, who had once caught the Touhy mob after an armored car holdup, began to worry about the loss of my subscriber list. The seven hundred sheets of paper were charred, water-soaked, and frozen. By ultraviolet and the judicious use of chemical techniques, the Charlotte police chief restored these lists to me in two days. This police chief restored these lists to a Jewish editor so he could mail his paper to a Baptist clergyman in Decatur, a rabbi in Boston, and a high-school teacher in Portland. This could happen only in America.

In the meantime, news of the fire was reported in the press throughout the South and even nationally. The response stunned me. Hundreds of Southern clergymen expressed their concern and asked how they could be of genuine help. Eminent citizens sent me telegrams and from every corner of the world I received sympathy and good wishes.

My library, which consisted of over two thousand volumes, had been destroyed, and what surprised me most was to receive replacements from the two "opposites" of our American culture: Dr. Rankin, the head of the Duke Foundation of North Carolina, sent me books and so did Mr. Dubinsky of the International Ladies' Garment Workers' Union of New York.

One thing I *had* salvaged from the fire. Only the week before I had mailed off to The World Publishing Company the manuscript of a book compiled from the many essays I had written for my paper. I was hopeful about this book. I had some clues about its merit. My good friend, Carl Sandburg, gave me permission to use his picture on the cover and he said to me after he had written the Foreword, "This is a famous book." When Joseph Wood Krutch, himself a famous essayist, reviewed the book in the *Saturday Review,* he compared it to the essays of Montaigne. The review in *The New York Times* said, ". . . it restores one's faith in the human race," and the reviewer in the *New York Herald Tribune* wrote, "It's nice to live in the same country with Harry Golden." Adlai Stevenson said, "I recommend this book to all those who seek light and joy."

Within the week of its publication, my book, *Only in America,* reached the best-seller lists. A month later it was Number 1.

There the book stayed for many weeks, and in the fall CBS asked me to appear on a television program about racial integration, along with Harry Ashmore, the Pulitzer Prize-winning editor of Little Rock, and Governor Orval Faubus. When I arrived in New York the afternoon of the telecast, however, I learned that an anonymous letter had been sent to a New York newspaper revealing a secret I had guarded for many years. The secret was that I had served a prison sentence in 1929.

I knew I owed an obligation to CBS and I showed a copy of the letter to Mr. Howard K. Smith of the network staff. I told him it was true. He urged me to go on the air anyway. But after a long discussion, several other CBS directors and I agreed that I would not be at my best, and considering the emotionally packed issue of racial segregation, the revelation of my past might obscure this basic and important problem. I did not appear on the program.

The story, handled sympathetically, broke the next morning in the *Herald Tribune* and throughout the country as I prepared to return to Charlotte. It was a lonely and somewhat terrifying trip. My work, I thought, now ends. But on my return I was greeted with warmth and affection by the press of North Carolina, Tennessee, Virginia, and Georgia. Bernard M. Baruch, Billy Graham, Fannie Hurst, Carl Sandburg, and Adlai Stevenson, and many others gave out highhearted statements to the wire services and newspapers; the leading Protestant clergymen of my city, the Catholic Bishop of the North Carolina Diocese, and practically the entire rabbinate of America offered expressions of fellowship; all of which indicated that I might continue to publish my paper.

In fact, after the incident became known, I received almost four hundred requests for speeches around the country, and in fulfilling some of these I have had the pride of standing before the entire Congregation of Temple Emanu-El on Fifth Avenue in New York City, before many Christian fellowships throughout the South, and before the Rotary Club of Charlotte, which represents the "power structure" in my home town. I was the guest speaker at the Annual Dinner of the Alumni Association of C.C.N.Y. where I was photographed in fellowship and mutual respect with a fellow guest, The Honorable Charles H. Tuttle, who was the prosecutor in my case. But what impressed me most is that the students of the leading high schools of Charlotte and Chapel Hill chose me to deliver the commencement address of 1959.

There were also offers from several television networks and from leading magazines for my life story. But I could not comply. It is a great temptation to rationalize a prison record, to excuse or sentimentalize the experience. And in its way, this is a good sign. It proves a man is ashamed. Because if you are not ashamed of having been in prison, you are hopeless and must forever consider yourself alienated from society. The second reason I declined is that I am a writer, and I do not want to impose upon my audience with sensationalism or a sob story. All that I want to "work" for me now and in the future is what I write as an essayist, and nothing else. I have no intention of ever exploiting this situation. If there are factors which lawyers call "mitigating circumstances," I shall discuss these with my sons and no one else. For the rest, the record must stand, based on the due process of law. There can be no deviation from this; otherwise all struggle for principle is a fake.

I will admit a silver lining in this incident. Over twenty-five years ago I disassociated myself from the commercial milieu. I did not want to make money nor endanger the well-being of my family by any ambitious venture (and maybe this hurt them, I don't know). Whenever I thought I was going too fast, I'd say to myself, "Pull back, fellow, relax." Instead of a participant, I became a spectator and the only thing that worried me now was that I shouldn't die laughing.

Watching the passing scene has also instructed me. And so have the many subscribers who have corresponded with me over the years. And so did the people who wrote me after *Only in America* appeared. And the people who wrote me after they saw me on Ed Murrow's *Person to Person*, and on the programs of Dave Garroway, Jack Paar, and Arthur Godfrey.

This is what I've learned: we were happier when mother emptied the drip pan under the icebox.

Our unhappiness, of course, cannot be blamed upon the refrigerator. It would have been nice if our mothers and grandmothers had had one. A refrigerator would have saved them work. The refrigerator is only an indirect contributor to unhappiness. What happened was that we made of the refrigerator a status symbol. It became not simply a convenience in which to store and freeze food, but a possession which helped measure and confer respect. A refrigerator cannot do this. All it can do is keep food fresh and make ice cubes for bourbon. A man who buys one is not a better man for the purchase.

"Comfort," said Kahlil Gibran, the Lebanese poet, "is a stealthy thing that enters the house as a guest, and then becomes a host, and then a master."

It was in thinking of the days before we let comfort corrupt us that I once wrote a story titled "For 2¢ Plain." The story was about the joys and wonders of the Lower East Side of New York where even a hot-dog pushcart was an adventure. I wrote about the "polly seed" nuts we used to buy, and of the boys and girls eating grapes as they walked together along the street. I remembered in this story how the entire East Side civilization was addicted to seltzer (carbonated water) and of the great variety of sweet drinks mixed with seltzer. You bought a drink from a man behind a marble counter at any of the hundreds of soda-water stands scattered through the sections. A small glass cost a penny— "Give me a small plain." No syrup. Syrup cost another penny. For a large glass, you said, "Give me for two cents plain." As the man filled the glass, you said casually, still holding tightly to your two pennies, "Put a little on the top." You wanted syrup, of course, but you didn't want to pay the third penny. The next time you tried it, though, the man insisted on your two pennies first before he started to fill the glass. "I know my customers," he'd say.

I told about all of the wonderful sights and people in my neighborhood. I told of Benny, one of these soda-water men, who wore a coat he had brought from Europe that reached to his ankles. He would clutch a handful of that coat, feel it a while, and tell you whether or not it would rain the next day.

I looked upon these delights of life in America from the top floor of a cold-water tenement on Eldridge Street, between Rivington and Delancey. But I know with all my heart that whether you look down a path leading from a farmhouse near Fountain Run, Kentucky, or out of one of the magnificent residences in the Myers Park section of Charlotte, or up along the cobbled hills of San Francisco, these pleasures and joys await you, too—"for 2¢ plain."

HARRY GOLDEN

*Charlotte, N. C.*
*May 1959*

PART 1

*Have Gray Flannel,*
*Slightly Rumpled*

# TV antennas on Tobacco Road

THERE was a movie not long ago which portrayed a tumbled-down ol' South. It was called *Baby Doll*, and, as far as life is concerned, it was a good movie. But, as far as the South is concerned, it was a scream.

And the best proof of this is that the movie played all over the South without a ripple. When you are poor you do not want your early beginnings paraded before you. But when you are rich you exaggerate those struggles and speak with pride of the times you got up at four o'clock in the morning to milk the cows and deliver the newspaper, and the South is rich today—fabulously rich—and getting richer every minute.

There is no ol' plantation house with a baby crib. Not on your life. The South today is a churning, whirling, sprawling, brawling area of huge hotels and Du Pont and Celanese and guided missiles and the hydrogen bomb, and of three quarters of a million people lining the streets for the retail merchants' Thanksgiving Day parades, and of a day-to-day industrialization without parallel in the history of our country. The Chambers of Commerce cannot even keep up with the advertising brochures; all they can do is advise you where you may possibly find a parking space for your car.

But there is an interesting story behind this. Many of my fellow liberals in the North love to hang onto the "Tobacco Road" idea of the South. And the white supremacists of the South cling to the idea of Uncle Remus rolling in laughter under the magnolia tree. Well, that's all gone. There's no Tobacco Road and there's no plantation and there's no Uncle Remus. Tobacco Road today is full of TV antennas, with an electric washing machine on every back porch, and Mrs. Jeeter Lester is not begging ol' Dude to bring her a turnip. She is getting dressed up for the Tuesday Afternoon Garden Club or the League of Women Voters.

Under that magnolia tree is the country club with a French chef who gets $8,000 a year; and the delicatessen stores are loaded with Presbyterian folk who are asking for "Jewish rye bread," and down in Dallas they have a Gourmet Club in which they serve matzo-ball soup, chicken à la Russe, tossed green salad, and baba au rhum with Chablis.

The Northerners who refuse to give up the Tobacco Road idea feel this legend helps emphasize the struggle to end racial segregation. But if the South were still Tobacco Road, there would be no problem about ending racial segregation at all! The Negro was satisfied with his status when he looked around and saw nothing but the poverty of the cotton-mill towns. He was satisfied to be out. Today the story all around him is, oh, so entirely different, and now he wants in. This has been the pattern of all social and economic change in history. Only when things are good do the people want them better. Only twenty-five years ago the Negro would tip his hat to you as you walked along the street. Well, he doesn't tip his hat today. And neither is he rolling in laughter under the magnolia tree. He doesn't have time. Today he is walking briskly along the street on his way to pick up his little girl at the dancing school; that is, if he's not arguing a new writ before a Federal judge. He is not in Egypt. He is standing squarely on top of Mount Nebo—and he wants the Promised Land because it is finally within his reach.

Now if Tennessee Williams and Elia Kazan are serious about producing a movie about the South as it really is today, I am willing to provide them with the following outline, free of charge:

I would have Eli Wallach play the role of a manufacturer of ladies' foundation garments, slips, and brassieres, with a factory on West Thirty-sixth Street and Seventh Avenue. The International Ladies' Garment Workers' Union is after him to sign a new contract, and Eli decides to clear out of New York. He makes arrangements for a new factory in the magnolia-scented town of Kenilworth, South Carolina, where the folks are raising a half-million dollars to provide him with the new factory building.

To throw the union off the track, Eli calls his new brassiere factory "Balance Agriculture with Industry, Incorporated," but he has made one big mistake. He has recently promoted Baby Doll, his former model, to a 50 per cent partnership in his business and she is now following him down to Kenilworth in her new Jaguar. And this is where old Karl Malden comes in. Karl plays David Dubinsky, who has been keeping an eye on Baby Doll all this time, and he catches up with her in Charlotte, North Carolina. They play hide-and-seek in an old plantation house which now houses *The Carolina Israelite*, and in the scuffle Dubinsky succeeds in getting Baby Doll to sign the new contract on behalf of Balance Agriculture with Industry, Incorporated.

The big scene, however, is where the mayor of Kenilworth is dedicating the new factory: "We are mighty proud of the new factory, Mr. Eli, and on behalf of all your good neighbors of Kenilworth I hereby hand you this certificate which makes your company rent-free, water-free, power-free, and tax-free for the first five years of your operations; and one thing more, Mr. Eli, and I'm certainly mighty proud to be able to say this to you-all, we are a very peaceful little town here with no trouble and you can be sure of one thing—you'll never be bothered by them union fellows down here. . . ."

Just then Baby Doll rushes onto the grandstand, followed by David Dubinsky, who waves the newly signed union contract and shouts into the loud-speaker, "We start picketing tomorrow."

## Cowboys and Indians

I STILL like Westerns and I understand I am no different from the other fifty-five million people who own television.

I think the majority of the American people still like those Indian chases. The Western has changed very little since I was young. There are more villains today with complexes and neuroses, but the little bit of Freud hasn't changed the Old West much, no siree, pardner. In the thirties, I remember, some of the Hollywood magnates thought the Westerns were losing popularity, so they made one of the first "adult" Westerns. The name of this picture was *Stagecoach* and it was directed by John Ford. It wasn't any more or less adult than the previous Westerns. The Indians chased the stagecoach, and there was a bank embezzler who waved a six gun at the hero, and a town girl who had worked in a gambling house and whose heart was as big as the stagecoach but who'd been around more often.

The one exception was that the hero kissed the girl in the end and presumably married her. Even with this love interest added, the Western still perseveres. And there are reasons for this. First is the fact that the Western is peculiarly American. The Greeks celebrated their hard view of life in tragedy where the hero was always defeated; the Germans in abstruse philosophy; the English in the five-act Elizabethan drama; and the Americans in the image of a couple of cowboys with lariats and five-gallon hats and six guns. There are formal proportions to the Western for it is always a story of good and evil. Most Westerns are like the old Toby plays that used to tour the sawdust circuit. Sometimes the Devil gets God down, but he never pins His shoulders to the mat. What makes the Western better than the Toby play, however, is the fact that there is a real West and there were real cowboys and maybe something like that which you see on the film did happen. F. Scott Fitzgerald said that the first settlers here found before them a jungle but within one hundred and fifty years had made that jungle into a playpen. The Western helps celebrate this accomplishment. Another reason for the continuing popularity of the Western is that it is inherently a good story. The granddaddy of all Westerns is really the novel *Don Quixote* by Cervantes. Dostoevski, who was no mean novelist himself, called *Don Quixote* the most impassioned utterance of the human tongue. *Don Quixote* is a simple story about an old man who wants to revive chivalry and decides to set out in the world on a sorry-looking nag named Rosinante. Don Quixote is accompanied by his page, a fat peasant named Sancho Panza. Everyone they meet thinks Quixote is crazy. Everyone except Cervantes. For the truth of this novel is that Don Quixote makes the world a better place for having toured it. Everyone who meets him is benefited by the encounter. What Cervantes is really saying is that Don Quixote is right and the rest of the world is mad. Don Quixote is the Platonist and Sancho Panza the Aristotelian. This relationship is repeated in many Westerns. The Lone Ranger and Tonto. Hopalong Cassidy and his guitar-strumming, tobacco-spitting side-kick. One is the Platonist, the idealist; the other the Aristotelian, the materialist. Together they make the West a better place by ridding it of the bad guys. In reality we know that both Don Quixote and Sancho Panza and the Lone Ranger and Tonto are the two different parts of the human personality.

Another reason for the success of the Western is in the type of sedentary life we all lead, a life without obvious heroism or exertion. Can I sell that term policy? Will the new fund drive give us that printing contract? Will the car hold up another winter? We think of these as prosaic worries, because they occupy us all of the time. But here is a man on the screen who has no such worries. He is not worrying about the next mortgage payment on the five-room ranch house or whether he can hustle up another candy store for the ice cream account. The Western hero has little money (he has some mysterious source of income that we never know), but he is never in financial trouble. All he has to worry about is something simple, like will he be ambushed at Dry Gulch Pass. All his worries are heroic and they are the easiest kind of worry. Once the hero has routed the rustlers and saved the girl he doesn't have to wade through miles of paper work in court—or even pay for the girl's dental work after they are married. He's free to ride off to the next town where the bank robbers have kidnaped the sheriff and sold firewater to the Indians. The Western is the great escape mechanism and it admits us to a more heroic world than the one we know.

# The tyranny of the telephone

THE New York Stock Exchange did business for nearly a full century before the telephone was invented; and you wonder how they built the railroads, stretched the country across a continent, got married, and raised families without the telephone. But they did. In fact, Shakespeare wrote *Hamlet*, and Mozart even composed *Don Giovanni* without the help of the phone.

There's something about it that only a trained psychologist could explain. You receive a letter and you either open it or leave it unopened, as you wish. You put it in your pocket, or in your apron, or in a bureau drawer. It awaits *your* pleasure. This is even true of a visitor. He rings the bell or knocks on the door and you still hold the initiative. You can open the door at your leisure, or under certain circumstances you don't even have to answer it. But let that phone ring and all hell breaks loose; in summer and winter, in bed or out of bed, in the bathtub or up on the roof, you make a beeline for that instrument, over hill and dale, in the darkness with the furniture falling to the left and the right; nothing matters except to reach that instrument; and then what? A wrong number perhaps, or some fellow says, "How are things?"

# Fluoridation

I WAS thinking about the resolution passed by the D.A.R. against the United Nations, foreign aid, the New Deal, the income tax, and fluoridation.

Why fluoridation?

Most of the ultraconservatives who are against the New Deal and foreign aid are also against fluoridation.

Yet we liberals are no better, are we? If you are for the New Deal, the United Nations, and Adlai Stevenson, you are supposed to be *for* fluoridation. Why?

I have no special opinion on fluoridation. I am always willing to leave these matters to the public health authorities. We went along with them when they arrived with their needles to vaccinate us (much against our will) and it has worked out fine, so why should I dispute them on this matter? I haven't looked into it carefully and even if I did, I wouldn't know what I was talking about. Perhaps it does help *only* the children of a certain age, and if that is the truth of the matter, perhaps they can arrange a faucet for fluoridated water for the children and a separate faucet for beer for the adults.

Meanwhile, I'll follow the guidance of the health authorities.

But I still go down the line for the United Nations, foreign aid, Adlai Stevenson, and the New Deal.

# The best conversation

I HAD a letter from an English lady recently. She was an intelligent correspondent and she told me she was now living in California. She writes that she is "appalled" by the "lack of culture" in America, and how Americans are not able to discuss anything important at all thoroughly. My English correspondent went on to say that she had been all over the world—Malaya, Paris, Singapore.

When she sat down to dinner in Caracas she said people talked about Rembrandt; and when she visited the home of a diamond dealer in Kimberley they discussed Shakespeare's sonnets; and in Calcutta they knew about Dylan Thomas and the political situation in Algiers.

Well, in a way, I agree with this English lady. I certainly admire the places she's been. But I also disagree. If I were in Kimberley, South Africa, I would ask my host where they found the Kohinoor diamond and I would want to see a diamond mine. He could talk quite intelligently about these subjects, I'm sure.

And if I were in Calcutta, I would ask: "What is Nehru going to do about Pakistan—never mind Algiers and Dylan Thomas—tell me about next door."

People talk best about their everyday concerns. But people are still people, and unless you're interested in them as people, they won't talk well about anything. It is very curious that ten years ago I thought the discussion of the baby's formula was absolutely needless.

If every baby in the world were fed Pablum and water, I thought, American conversation would be one hundred per cent improved. Then I became a grandfather. There are infinite gradations among the formulas for different babies—and it makes you wonder about birth and growth and life.

When you talk to people you have to let them decide what's important. I have a son, Richard, who is a stage manager, and he does not tell me about the architectural features we need in new theatres or about Arthur Miller's philosophy, but he tells me that Sir John Gielgud makes it a habit to say good night to every electrician, stagehand, and backstage policeman after the final curtain. In its way this is very important to know about Sir John. It explains why he is one of the world's greatest actors. Or listen to two poets talk. They don't talk about meter or rhyme or even editors. Usually they talk about planting and how their zinnias are doing.

One of our problems, I think, is that we don't discuss the

arts or politics naturally. We try to sound too intelligent and too sage instead of human. The best abstract discussion of Shakespeare I've ever had was not with another son of mine, William—who teaches Shakespeare—but with a booking agent who was arranging a Shakespeare lecture for me.

He had a profound and honest comment to make. He said, "What I most admire about Shakespeare is that he was a guy who said when he made enough he was going to quit, and when he made enough, he quit."

## Education of an immigrant's son

IT's hard to realize that only thirty-five years ago it was a scandal for ladies to smoke. I remember a crowd standing in front of Churchill's restaurant on Broadway at Forty-ninth Street and, when I stopped to see what was going on inside, I heard whispers all through the crowd, "There she is . . . there, right behind the post . . . see her?"

It was a woman smoking a cigarette.

One of the advantages of being born in the ghetto of the Lower East Side is that you are born an "adult." By this I do not mean that you were a precocious child necessarily, or smart beyond your years. I simply mean that at a very early age you were made a participant in the problems of the adult world around you.

I saw a friend of mine, also eight years old, standing beside his father's pushcart. I still remember the expression on that boy's face as he listened to his father discuss a proposed purchase with a customer. He watched his father's every move, and, oh, how sad that boy looked when the customer walked away without buying! The whole thing amounted to pennies, but the boy looked up at his father with deep sorrow, as if to say: "Don't worry, we'll sell the next one."

A peddler was through at 11 o'clock at night. He paid off his merchandise and the fee for his pushcart. When he came home he placed the $2.40 profit on the table. It was in silver and pennies, and the mother awakened the two smaller children so that they too could share in the joy of the moment. I saw that, and I thought of it many times, years later, especially when I saw a fellow throw a twenty-dollar bill on the bar to buy drinks for men whom he had never seen before in his life.

This early adulthood had other advantages. You remember more. Thus, a fifty-seven-year-old fellow like myself remembers a full half century.

I can think of only two other half centuries in history which were as important as ours. One is the fifty years following the conversion of Constantine to Christianity and the other, the period beginning in 1776 and ending with the Napoleonic Wars.

Our half century certainly belongs with these in view of the tremendous changes at every level of culture and our expansion into "one world."

About two years ago, the press made a big to-do about a prospective American ambassador who did not know the name of the prime minister of Ceylon, and this is the key to the upheaval we have seen. Fifty years ago, no one except a few fellows over at Rand McNally's were concerned with such places as Ceylon. A college student could perhaps tell you the names of a few Senators from other states, and there were few college students. Our political lives revolved around the Tammany Hall leader and the local aldermen, just as the folks in the agricultural areas of our country looked to the sheriff and the county commissioner. Britain was a great country off somewhere where King Arthur and his knights used to live, and where Henry VIII had a whole flock of wives. The monarchs of Europe—Hohenzollerns, Hapsburgs, Romanovs, Bourbons, and Savoys—were visiting each other every month or so for royal christenings. Occasionally the press would show a picture of Kaiser Wilhelm marching with his six or seven sons reviewing the troops.

The monarchs are gone, but there were other developments even more important. Lord Lothian was the ambassador from Britain in 1939, a handsome bachelor of fabulous wealth. At his first press conference the reporters asked him about the new war which had just opened in Europe, and Lord Lothian said, "Gentlemen, at the beginning of World War I, England took my estates in the general mobilization, and after the war, I got them back. The other day England again took my estates in the general mobilization, but this time I'll not get them back."

During these fifty years the Russian aristocrats were dispossessed by the Russian Revolution. The Prussian Junkers made the mistake that most of the ruling class has made through all history. "Make the agitator a member of the board of directors and we can control him." The French "Junkers" fell into the same trap. *"Better Hitler than Blum,"* they said, and one of their political leaders, Pierre Laval, stood at a railroad siding and counted off every third fellow Frenchman for slave labor in the German war camps. The French ruling class was willing to risk *all* with Hitler, rather than face up to another "old-age pension bill" with their own Léon Blum. No concessions; and this has always resulted in disaster and death! Twenty soup kitchens in Paris might have prevented the French Revolution.

England, too, was showing evidences of this corruption. But Churchill saved them; he was the man who was nearly killed in an automobile accident on Fifth Avenue in 1930. It's enough to send a shiver down your back thinking what would have happened to *us all*—without him.

The Russian government of landowners and clerics was sitting on top of a smoldering volcano, the ferment of revolution was steadily mounting. As a diversionary measure they unloosed a government-inspired program against the Jews. In April 1903, in Kishinev, the capital of the province of Bessarabia, a band of ruffians, encouraged by the violent anti-Semitic expression in official government circles, swept down upon the Jewish community on Easter Sunday. They killed, wounded, raped, plundered, and made thousands homeless. The events that crowded themselves one on top of the other were of great sorrow. The Triangle fire, the sinking of the *Titanic* with Isidor Straus, the Leo Frank case in

Georgia—and each time we placed a piece of black cloth on the window sill, and posters appeared in the store windows: WE MOURN OUR LOSS.

And then the Mendel Beilis case. In March 1911, a Russian boy was found murdered in Kiev. The anti-Semitic organizations began a campaign charging that the crime, having been committed on the eve of Passover, must be treated as nothing less than a ritual murder. The accusation fell upon Mendel Beilis, a Jew, the manager of a local brick factory, and by 1913 the case seethed throughout the world. The Catholic cardinal in Vienna denounced the folly as a vicious fable. But, where anti-Semitism is concerned, all logic is irrelevant, including the fact that this charge was first brought against the Christians and had sent hundreds of them into the Roman arena to face gladiators and beasts. (Through the centuries the Freemasons were also accused of ritual murder, once on the floor of the American Congress by Thaddeus Stevens, the fanatical enemy of the South.) The innocence of Beilis had no weight at all. But this time world opinion was very strong. The religious, political, and intellectual leaders of every civilized country sent protests. Eventually, a notorious woman criminal confessed that it was she and her gang who had murdered the boy as a suspected stool pigeon. Beilis was acquitted, and against the advice of his lawyers, went back to his little home in the country where, to his surprise, he was greeted with sympathy and congratulations by his Gentile fellow workers. There is a limit to everything, even the credulity of a peasant.

All these events seemed to come together so that today it is hard to tell in what order they happened. And it is immaterial. They were all a sort of prelude to the greater sorrow that was to come.

Where were you when the Archduke Francis Ferdinand was assassinated to set the spark for World War I? I was on Houston Street, outside the Little Hungary restaurant, with an armful of extras of the Yiddish press shouting, "Austrian Heir Assassinated in Serbia." We associate events in our own lives with the thundering events of the world. An "inquiring reporter" for a music column once asked me what was my favorite composition, and I answered at once: "Fritz Kreisler's 'The Old Refrain,'" much to her disgust with my lack of appreciation of great music. But what did she know of a moonlight night and a boat ride up the Hudson with my girl, and a three-piece string orchestra playing "The Old Refrain"?

Where were you when the Archduke was assassinated, ushering in the Age of Armageddon? The age in which it will become necessary for a manufacturer living in Ohio to know the name of the prime minister of Ceylon?

I made a good profit that day. We paid sixty cents for a hundred newspapers and sold them for a penny each. I must have sold at least four hundred newspapers that late afternoon of June 28, 1914.

From the newspaper profits I had spending money—and went to the movies. The movie house was called "The Gem" and the price of admission was "two for a nickel." The rich kid who had the three cents would pick the skinniest partner with two cents, because when the theatre got crowded the ushers made you double up in one seat. During the "intermission" a fellow would come along the aisle with a spray gun and squirt perfume over our heads, and the candy butchers would walk up and down the aisle yelling, "Candies, peanuts, and crackerjacks; a prize in every package." Once in a while a promoter would take the stage and offer special boxes for ten cents; and one of the boxes, he said, contained a five-dollar bill. One fellow, I remember, was outside the theatre offering a sealed envelope containing a "steel-engraved photograph of George Washington." When you got home you found that you had paid a nickel for a two-cent stamp. The movies were all silent of course, and the stars were John Bunny, Louise Fazenda, and Ford Sterling. Later came the serials with Pearl White, Arnold Daly, and a fellow by the name of Creighton Hale, whom I see to this very day. Amazing. In today's movies he's usually the fellow who hands the witness the Bible in the courtroom and says, "Raise your right hand." The guy must be indestructible. The weekly serial would end with the villain raising an ax over the head of the hero with everybody shouting, "Look out." You rushed back the following week to see what happened, but they had apparently forgotten all about the ax scene. The next chapter started off with an entirely different situation, and with the hero intact, of course.

It was a Galitzianer boy, a landsmann from Radowitz, who invented the art of playing the right kind of piano music to fit the action on the screen. He watched every movie, underscored the bit of music to fit the scene, and made a good living out of it. One movie theatre on Second Avenue tried "talking pictures" way back there in 1919. In opposite box seats a man and a woman talked through megaphones in an attempt to follow the action on the screen. Often they spoke in Yiddish to the lip movements of Mary Pickford and William S. Hart, and it was a scream! I'd give anything to see such a performance again.

The brothels were over on Allen Street and were full of young girls who were as innocent and naive as the customers they solicited.

After World War I, the brothel prostitute was plagued with the amateur competition which eventually destroyed her profession. The amateur began to call it "dating" and she was grossly insulted if you offered her cash. Instead, she accepted the equivalent in the form of a present. This helped her maintain the amateur standing and remove the stigma. The Puritan strain in our culture hounded the professional out of the brothel and forced her to move into an apartment next door, where she quickly became the best tenant. She gave the janitor a dollar every day. You gave him a dollar at Christmas time. But we all felt better when we closed up the red-light district and created for ourselves the illusion that the whole thing doesn't exist.

Fifty years ago, when folks would talk of rich men, they meant Morgan, Rockefeller, Astor, Vanderbilt, Mackay, Harriman, Schiff, and Warburg. And within those same fifty years, the singing waiter of the Bowery, Irving Berlin, would wind up lending money to Clarence Mackay, his father-in-law, of all things! And Al Smith, whom I once saw eating a "hot corn" on a street corner, would wind up wearing a high silk hat and having lunch with Du Pont.

Our debating clubs were concerned wholly with politics and the social sciences. We had heard the story of the young aristocrat, Franklin D. Roosevelt, who was out to smash Tammany. He had blocked the appointment of a Tammany man for United States Senator, and while it had happened a few years before, our debating coach was still very happy about the whole thing. Eventually another Tammany man was appointed and with the approval of Mr. Roosevelt, and I have often smiled about it all. What difference did it make to a flock of immigrant boys on the East Side whether the Senator was a Tammany man by the name of Sheehan, or a Tammany man by the name of O'Gorman? But such is the faith and the hope of the social worker. And, two years later, Mr. Roosevelt was photographed at Tammany Hall with the Boss himself, Charles F. Murphy, who had been fired from a job as a streetcar motorman, and who is supposed to have said, "If I can't drive horses, I'll drive men"—at any rate, that's what the social worker told us. Mr. Sheehan was just an innocent bystander, a casualty in the upward march of a politician. He was not the first one and he'll not be the last, either. There have been many such casualties. I remember speaking to a fellow in the Tombs who had been arrested the day before, for peddling dope. This time it was Thomas E. Dewey who was climbing upward, and the newspapers spoke of this poor addict as the "King of Dope Peddlers." The poor Italian had a running ear, and investigation at his home proved beyond shadow of doubt that in the preceding ten years he had never once had five dollars at one time that he could spend for a doctor. But there he sat holding his ear and reading about himself as the "King of Dope Peddlers."

The most wonderful developments in these fifty years have been in medicine, hygiene, and sanitation. How do you go about erecting a statue to the fellow who developed the chemicals that enable us to destroy garbage and filth? You look back upon it all and wonder how you survived. Every alley was knee-deep in filth.

And, in that fifty years have come the splitting of the atom and vehicles in space.

I remember as a boy being tremendously impressed with Winwood Reade's book, *The Martyrdom of Man*. He predicted the ultimate manufacture of food by chemical process in the laboratory and said, "Hunger and starvation will be unknown, and the best part of human life will no longer be wasted in the tedious process of cultivating the fields."

But there is another "invention" that philosophers and scientists have merely hinted at through the ages. I believe it will come to pass, and I believe it with all my heart and mind. I am confident that man will one day "invent" immortality—only in a limited form at first, perhaps. The life span will probably be two hundred and fifty or three hundred years to begin with. But the fact that science has been able to check so many of our contagious diseases and infections must lead one to the conclusion that it will find remedies for the degenerative diseases of the heart, blood, and the arteries. And after all, nothing else really matters but this—"to live, to live, and to live."

Because life is too short. Much too short. There is so much to learn and so much to do—and one day our descendants will look back upon us with very deep sympathy for all our unfinished works and for all our unfulfilled dreams.

# My uncle battled John D.

He really wasn't my uncle; more of a landsmann, but we always called him "Uncle Sholem." He had a small grocery store on Ludlow Street between Stanton and Rivington.

As a sideline, he also manufactured yahrzeit lamps. For the benefit of my non-Jewish readers, the yahrzeit lamp is an anniversary lamp—an ordinary water glass, filled up to within an inch of the top with wax and provided with a wick. A label in Hebrew is on the outside of the glass, and we burn them in our homes on the anniversary of a death in the family. After it serves its purpose, it is cleaned and used as a drinking glass.

My Uncle Sholem did a good business in these yahrzeit lamps. He sold them to other grocery stores; and, thus, he was a manufacturer and a wholesaler as well as a retailer. Then one day, along came John D. Rockefeller. I mean the original John D. Rockefeller; not Jr., or Nelson, or any of the present-day lesser ones. John D. Rockefeller began to make yahrzeit lamps.

My Uncle Sholem put up a heroic battle but, within a year, Rockefeller had won. Naturally, Uncle Sholem had bought his raw materials (glasses, wax, wicks, and labels) in very small quantities; his "factory" included himself and one part-time employee, a Polish woman who poured the wax; and, of course, it was impossible to compete with the powerful John D.

It is interesting to note that Rockefeller made no improvements in Uncle Sholem's lamp. Both competing lamps were identical—the same amount of wax, the same Hebrew lettering on the label. The only difference in Rockefeller's lamp was that, on the bottom of the glass, there was the circled inscription, "Standard Oil Company."

After losing to John D., Uncle Sholem continued to run his little grocery store, until his three sons became rich in the fur business, and moved the family up to Riverside Drive. He spent his last years as a man of leisure, sporting a heavy cane, taking a daily walk in Riverside Park, and telling anyone who would listen about the time John D. Rockefeller put the "squeeze" on him.

# Men and morning

PARADOXICALLY, a man is the acknowledged master of his house when he is *not* there. He is master of his house when he goes forth in the morning and comes home for dinner.

This is true even when a man is out of work. During the Depression, jobless men still roused themselves, shaved, put on the one neat suit, and left—to look for work. Somehow these men filled up the day. They followed up every want ad and waited in line with three hundred other fellows for a job which had been filled the night before. Or they sat in parks and watched the pigeons. Sometimes they simply tramped the streets. Toward late afternoon, they went home and reported no luck.

Perhaps it seemed aimless, but these men knew the simple truth. They knew that *a man must have a place to go in the morning.*


# How's Abe Greenberg?

INTERESTING—you deliver a talk before a non-Jewish audience, and invariably the folks coming up to the platform at the end of the lecture want to know whether you know "Mr. Cohen, who lived next door to us in New Orleans?" At first you are a bit disappointed. You've knocked your brains out discussing Shakespeare's *Macbeth,* or Clarence Streit's *Atlantic Union,* and the only comment you get is "Did you know the Goldstein family—they rented from us last year?" But after a while you get used to it. You realize that no disrespect is intended.

Which reminds me that when I get into a taxi (in Charlotte you can sit up front with the driver), the cabby takes a look at me and says, "How's my friend Abe Greenberg coming along?" I smile and say, "Do you ask all your fares how Abe Greenberg is getting along?" But I realize that the man means well, that basically he is merely trying to start a conversation in the only way he thinks he should start a conversation with a Jew, so I say, "Sure, Abe is doing well—I hope to see him in the synagogue tomorrow night."

# Who's on the dais?

SOME months ago I visited the offices of a famous comedian and I saw at least fifty steel cabinets full of three-by-five cards, and on each card a "joke" typed in triple space. A week later I read the *Saturday Review* article on "The Decline of American Humor" and this despite the fact that one fellow alone had some 35,000 jokes with punch lines carefully underlined. The time had come for me to laugh aloud.

Because what has really happened to American humor is that half the folks have been hanging onto those three-by-five cards, while the other half have been waiting for vaudeville to come back so they can tell racial, ethnic, and rural jokes. In the process we have missed one of the most wonderful of all changes in the social structure, the meeting of the second generation of "immigrants" from the farmhouses and mountain cabins of our country with the burgeoning, great American middle class.

You can no longer tell a dialect joke, for instance, when the fellow is actually sending his daughter to Wellesley, and neither can you tell a "hick" story when the man is now program chairman of the Lions Club. Thus it may be said that American humor has failed to take note of the development from "*Who's on first?*" to "*Who's sitting on the dais?*"

And when I write that the Jews of the South are forever looking for a tall, blue-eyed blond rabbi, I am not telling an ethnic or a racial joke. I receive overwhelming evidence when thousands of elders, stewards, and deacons of the other religious fellowships claim identity at once. Because at their own meetings one member always argues in favor of a new minister on the ground that the fellow looks especially good in a claw-hammer coat.

Things are coming rapidly to a head. The process is being accelerated. Now the mark of real status is *not* to sit on the dais, but to hide yourself way in the back, preferably behind a post. And so the folks can no longer diagnose each case on its merit, "What's he doing up there?" Instead they have to crane their necks around that post and say, "Why isn't Sam up there?"

## Suburban psychosis

A FELLOW came home from the office and noticed that his wife had been crying. "What's the matter, dear?" he asked.

And she gave him the terrible news: "Jim, one of *them* has moved into that vacant apartment upstairs."

And right then and there, on that evening about forty-five years ago, this fellow Jim started the mass exodus from America's cities when he suggested: "Let's move out into the country where there's lots of room for the kids." And so they went; and then each group that had chased out the previous group ran out to the suburbs; and each said exactly the same thing: "You know, if *one* moves in, a whole pack of *them* will come later." And so it went, in the manner of a cycle, and, in the end, as in a game of tag, the last man was "it." And thus did the Negro wind up with some of the most comfortable, steam-heated, elevator apartments in the big city, with a view of the Atlantic fleet lying at anchor, and the majestic Palisades, to say nothing of a drugstore, a grocery, and a theatre, each within a stone's throw.

And out yonder in the suburbs, our country boy began buying all sorts of gadgets, farm equipment, and rubber hose; and he learned all about plumbing and he traveled two hours each way, back and forth to his work every day; and, if he forgot to bring home the ice cream, the kids began to howl and he had to get into his car and drive eight miles to get it; and then he jumped for joy when his wife told him that the street will be paved out of the 1968 budget allocations if he signs the petition and pays the assessment, and that they will finally get sewers in 1971 if they agree to "annexation," which will make him a city boy again, but living in the country; and then, of course, the lights go out, and he can't find a new fuse.

And all of this wouldn't be so bad if the country boy could have remained "exclusive," but the folks he had run away from in the first place were now country boys, too, and new sets of people were coming in droves as a result of that damned new bus line which our original suburbanite had raised such Cain to get. He thought he'd have himself a nice bus to go back and forth in. He had no idea it would become a whole transportation system full of all kinds of strange people; but the poor guy had other worries—that lousy septic tank was backing up again.

And so he'll move back to the cities soon, sure as anything, and he'll try to sneak back, sort of looking over his shoulder to see if those folks are going to follow him again. And you can be sure of that, too; *they'll* be a-coming—all of which reminds me of that great gospel hymn: "There's no hiding place down there."

# Have gray flannel, slightly rumpled

SUCCESS is a relative term. I once saw a man jump out of the eleventh story of 74 Broadway because he lost a fortune in the stock market. After his widow paid off all his obligations, one hundred cents on the dollar, she had a little over fifty thousand dollars left—ten times more than 99 per cent of all humanity ever accumulates in a lifetime. Yet, for him, life was over. The widow had better sense. I saw her a month later with a handsome football player.

That fellow killed himself because he thought he had failed. On the other hand, many a man has reached the highest pinnacle of happiness with five dollars. At a critical moment in his life he has asked a friend for a five-dollar loan and has come away with the five-dollar bill. That's success.

I believe I went through the greatest humiliation possible.

One morning in the 1930's I stepped up to the ticket window at Red Bank, New Jersey, and I did not have the twelve dollars necessary to buy a commutation ticket for a month. I had to pay eighty-five cents for each trip, back and forth. When the conductor collected that eighty-five cents, it was humiliating. And after the third or fourth time I did not even try to act nonchalant with the explanation, "I forgot my commutation ticket, so give me a receipt for this cash so that I may get a refund." After three or four times I was no longer fooling the conductor or myself. But I went down like a man, and I gave the last quarter I had in this world to a waitress as a tip.

So what is success? At this writing I have about 110 books and 43 phonograph records more than I had when I came to Charlotte, North Carolina, years ago.

This is success.

## Arise, Sir Taxpayer

I NEVER met a man who thought he should pay no tax. What most people want apparently is some say in the matter of how they are taxed, not how much they should pay. In truth, I think many a man slyly enjoys paying his taxes.

In reality none of it is his tax money. Out of his $100 a week, his business firm deducts $21.20 which it sends off to the Internal Revenue. Our man never had that $21.20 to spend. Paying it involves no sacrifice or budgeting on his part. When he got the job, the personnel director told him it paid $100 a week and right away he knew, if he wasn't an imbecile, that he made $78.80.

Why continue the pretense? Well, it isn't all pretense. Our man has a say in government spending; he helps produce the goods and profits which contribute to the economy. And out of his $78.80 he does pay property and sales and luxury taxes. These taxes make him an integral part of the democratic system. The real reason for letting him think that the $21.20 is his is that this delusion cannot help but make him a better citizen.

This is where the real joy of paying taxes comes in. You're footing your share of the bill. More than that. If you've got it in America, you pay. In Italy this may or may not be so. I understand that an Italian movie star whose share of the profits from one movie alone could buy and sell *The Carolina Israelite* and a couple of printings of *Only in America* several times over declared her income for tax purposes as $23,811. Blinking at the tax assessment in France is so endemic that in the new constitution De Gaulle empowered revenue agents to add so many thousands of francs to a family's income if they have a maid, so many more if they drive two cars, so many more if they own a race horse. Liberté. Fraternité. Egalité.

In America, of course, property owners have always known what taxes are. And here, if anywhere, appear the inequities. The sixty-five-year-old widow, whose taxes on a two-bedroom house have quadrupled because out in suburbia all those young-marrieds want the most expensive terrazzo floor in the new school, is victimized.

It ought to be up to the builder who makes a big profit on those four hundred split-level shacks to support or provide the new school, just as many intelligent townships say it's up to him to provide the sidewalks. He passes along such costs, of course, to the people who use the facilities—those who buy the homes.

Still, all in all, the American and British systems of taxation are the best. The British system is, I believe, slightly better, since they reward you for paying big taxes. The reward is knighthood. Laurence Olivier and John Gielgud, two of the greatest actors in the world, pay their bills for trial by jury, constitutional government, and free education. And the Queen rewards them with knighthood. The United States ought to try something like that. Either give the man a knighthood, or let him throw out the first ball at the World Series.

# The schnorrers

THE word is out at the dog tracks and night clubs of Miami:

Schnorrers—stay clear of Columbia, South Carolina, on your way back to New York next season.

In Columbia they have decided to give each schnorrer, regardless of his story or gimmick, the sum of one dollar—no questions asked.

Literally, *schnorrer* means "beggar." But, historically, the schnorrer was a beloved wanderer among Jewish communities.

He was the medieval news reporter—and, for his food and lodging, he often performed services other than bearing gossip from place to place.

Frequently, he was a musician, a sort of wandering minstrel, or a *badkhan*—the jester at weddings. The schnorrer told jokes, and sometimes he danced and sang for the children of the village.

The American schnorrer is another story, of course.

Our American schnorrers begin to work their way down to Florida about the end of October, when it starts to get cold in New York. They hit most of the towns and use various angles and stories to get money from individual merchants, or from the organized fund in the community.

The modern schnorrer often calls the local rabbi and tells him that he is stranded. The question arises—how could you suddenly be stranded in a little town in eastern Virginia? The answer—he was recommended for a job in the vicinity which did not pan out. The schnorrers always spend the first few hours in town studying the terrain—the names of the streets and business houses.

I have studied three actual case histories in recent weeks; the technique was the same. Two of the schnorrers said that they had been given a bum steer about a job in the local plant, and the third schnorrer said that he had been advised that there was a job on the local newspaper. Of course he had already been to the office of the newspaper and was told very politely that there were no openings—so that when the rabbi called the newspaper, the editor said, "Oh, yes, Rabbi, Mr. So-and-So was here and we are sorry there are no openings." This of course gave the rabbi the impression that there had been long negotiations about the job, which of course was what the schnorrer wanted to establish. Now, says the schnorrer, he's stuck, and the first thing the rabbi does is give the schnorrer a dollar for lunch. Then the rabbi calls together three or four of his communal leaders to lunch privately with him. After lunch the rabbi is all set. He has fifteen dollars in cash for the schnorrer, plus an appropriation for lodging for the night. In my study of these schnorrer case histories, I spent a whole day with one of them, from his first interview with the rabbi to his disappearance. In one case we went to the hotel to check him in and the rabbi told the clerk, "Give this gentleman a room," and the clerk said, "With tub or shower?"; and the schnorrer spoke up, "With shower, please." In another case which I studied firsthand, the rabbi and I wound up carrying the guy's bags into the hotel.

In one of these cases a merchant told the schnorrer that it just so happened that he was rearranging the stock in his store and that he could use the schnorrer for about a week at a fairly good salary. But, in the morning, the schnorrer was gone with the customary fifteen bucks.

It is precisely because of such experiences that safeguards have been set up in some communities.

Columbia, as I have mentioned, now gives them one dollar. In Roanoke, Virginia, they give the schnorrer a bus ticket to the next city. The ticket has a stamp, "Not redeemable for cash." These two systems, of course, apply only to the average schnorrer who comes through town for a handout.

Other and adequate provision is made by the Jewish communities when illness or an obvious legitimate need are involved.

In fact, Jews of many cities have set up a fund for such a
purpose. They appoint a chairman—one whose business is
easily accessible to both schnorrers and traveling Jews in real
distress. They rely on the chairman's judgment in handling
donations.

And these chairmen become remarkably adept at recogniz-
ing the schnorrer. The chairman is usually a busy man. Often
there's a schnorrer or two waiting in the store while he's busy
with a customer. So some chairmen have worked out a pretty
fair system. They tell the schnorrer to get out of town, that
there will be no further handouts, and without any discussion
they give the donation, across the board—if the schnorrer has
a beard, he gets ten dollars, if he's clean-shaven he gets five
dollars.

The schnorrer, of course, is not completely lacking in
awareness and sensitivity. Next year the schnorrers from the
North who followed the Seaboard Air Line down to Florida
in 1958 will switch over and follow the Southern Railway,
and the schnorrers who followed the Southern will alternate
and give the folks on the Seaboard line a break.


## Son of Dixie, and some daughters

FOR all his huge bulk, his diabetes, and his addiction to
twelve black cigars a day, Judah P. Benjamin certainly got
around. Born in the Virgin Islands, he emigrated to South
Carolina, received his primary education in Fayetteville,
North Carolina, and later attended Yale University. He practiced law in Louisiana, served two terms as Senator for that
state, declined President Pierce's offer of a seat on the
Supreme Court, and, on the day Abraham Lincoln was inaugurated, strode out of the Senate arm in arm with Senator
Jefferson Davis. He served in the Confederate cabinet as
attorney general, secretary of war, and secretary of state.
After Lee's surrender, he bade his chief farewell at Danville,

Virginia, disguised himself as a Negro "mammy," slipped through the Union lines in the Carolinas, Georgia, and Florida, and escaped to British Honduras in an open boat.

If ever there was a "wandering Jew," it was old Judah P. Benjamin. Born a British subject, he achieved distinction in America, won new fame and honor in England, and died in France. In 1948, we dedicated a granite marker to his memory in Charlotte, North Carolina.

Why 1948? And why in Charlotte?

The North Carolina chapter of the United Daughters of the Confederacy had picked Charlotte for its convention city in 1948. The organization usually includes in this annual event the dedication of a historical marker. One year it marked "the spot where Jefferson Davis stood when he heard of Lee's surrender"; another year, "the site of the last meeting of the Confederate cabinet"; and so forth.

For the 1948 convention, the historian, Mrs. J. A. Yarbrough, recommended that a marker be dedicated to the memory of Judah P. Benjamin. For background she offered photostats of letters written by Mrs. Jefferson Davis indicating that Judah P. Benjamin had been an overnight guest at the home of Abram Weil, a Jewish merchant of Charlotte, who had given sanctuary to most of the Confederate leaders and their families.

Mrs. Yarbrough's resolution was passed unanimously; the chapter would gladly "accept a gift of a granite marker, in memory of Judah P. Benjamin, and sponsor its dedication."

Mrs. Yarbrough mailed us a copy of the resolution at the office of *The Carolina Israelite*, and we assured her there would be no difficulty in securing the marker for her organization. We brought the matter to the attention of the two Charlotte temples, the Conservative Temple Israel and the Reform Temple Beth El, and the trustees voted the necessary funds without hesitation. Mrs. Yarbrough and I then applied to the City Council for permission to place the marker on city property. Permission was granted without debate, and we ordered a stone with the following inscription:

## JUDAH P. BENJAMIN

Attorney-General, Secretary of War,
and Secretary of State of the
Confederate Government,
was the Guest, April 26, 1865,
of Abram Weil, whose home stood
on this site.

This monument in his honor
was placed by
Temple Israel and Temple Beth El,
the Jewish Congregations
of Charlotte, N. C., as a gift to the
Stonewall Jackson Chapter
United Daughters of the Confederacy
October 1, 1948

Dr. Hunter B. Blakely, president of the local women's college, agreed to deliver the dedicatory address; and the story was released to the press.

At this point, however, a banker in New York sent a letter to his mother-in-law in Charlotte. The mother-in-law, a member of the Stonewall Jackson Chapter, had portions of the letter mimeographed and a copy sent to every member:

. . . My pleasure in scanning the pages of my home-town [Charlotte] newspaper was interrupted this morning when I saw and read the enclosed article relative to a memorial to Judah P. Benjamin. This leaves no doubt in my mind that the United Daughters of the Confederacy have been completely "taken in" by the editor of this "Jewish [*sic*] Carolina Israelite" and, unless they withdraw their support of this project, will be made an unwitting tool in another scheme which is nothing else but propaganda for the Jewish race. . . . The U.D.C. might also find food for thought in the fact that nearly all Communists in America are Jews, and that most of the funds and agitators used in stirring up your Southern Negroes are Jewish in origin.

The argument may be used by some of your members that "our local Jews" are "good Jews". . . . But be not deceived—the so-called "good Jews" are "good" only because they are as yet unrevealed, and even the "good" ones work hand in hand with the most objectionable of their race. The effrontery of this propaganda attempt will become more apparent if one examines the role which this Judah P. Benjamin played in Confederate history. He was nothing more than a communistic Jewish politician from the North. . . . In fact, the "visit" in Charlotte, which has been made the flimsy excuse for these proceedings, probably was made while Benjamin was in flight while your fighting men of the South from whom you "Daughters" descend, stayed on and faced the consequences of defeat. . . .

Two days after the distribution the Stonewall Jackson Chapter held a special meeting. Mrs. Yarbrough presented her case well. Aside from the morality involved, she pointed out that the two Jewish temples did not initiate the project, but had responded to solicitation for a "gift" to the Confederate Daughters. It was all to no avail. The chapter voted to rescind its sponsorship, and the secretary was instructed to notify us officially that the name of their organization "must not appear on any Benjamin marker." The vote fell two short of being unanimous, Mrs. Yarbrough and the lone Jewish member being the only dissenters.

The trustees of the two temples, of course, were upset. Innocent bystanders, they now found themselves with a major controversy and an unwanted slab of stone. Many were all for dropping the granite into the Catawba River and forgetting the whole thing as quickly as possible. One of the rabbis called on Mrs. Yarbrough and urged her to drop the matter, arguing: "We will have to go on living in this town with these people." Mrs. Yarbrough replied: "Rabbi, have you considered that you will have to go on living in this town with me, too?"

That same night Mrs. Yarbrough made a trip to Little Rock, Arkansas, to the home of Mrs. John Wineman, president-general of the U.D.C. Mrs. Wineman, in turn, telephoned Mrs. A. L. Thompson, president of the North Carolina division of the organization, who immediately called a meeting of her board in Greensboro; they voted unanimously to accept the gift of the marker on behalf of the state organization. We then ordered the stonecutter to shave off two inches of the granite and replace the words "Stonewall Jackson Chapter" with "North Carolina Division."

The Stonewall Jackson Chapter decided to resist to the bitter end. A group of their most prominent members appeared before the City Council to demand that the permit to erect the marker on city property be withdrawn. They were armed with affidavits to the effect that the marker would impede the movements of people getting on and off the city buses. After a long and heated discussion, the Council voted to let the permit stand.

The next day another crisis loomed. Dr. Blakely, the college president scheduled to deliver the dedicatory address, pulled out.

With only two days left before the dedication, we called on Dr. Warner L. Hall, minister of the Covenant Church, which is probably the largest Presbyterian congregation in America, bringing an official invitation signed by our two rabbis. Dr. Hall readily accepted. We sent his photograph to the morning paper with the story of his acceptance. The paper is delivered at 7:30 A.M.; at 8:00 A.M. a delegation from the Stonewall Jackson Chapter appeared at Dr. Hall's home. He told the group, "My Jewish colleagues have invited me to speak at one of their functions, I have accepted, and you have told me nothing that would justify my withdrawing."

The hour finally came, but when the rabbi opened the ceremony with the invocation there were very few Daughters of the Confederacy in sight. The Stonewall Jackson Chapter, as "host lodge" of the convention, controlled the program, and their leaders had called for a "special memorial prayer service" at the exact hour of the Benjamin dedication, thus keeping most of the delegates glued to their seats in the convention hall. But Mayor H. H. Baxter was there, and so was Mrs. Wineman, the president-general, and Mrs. Thompson, the state president, and Mrs. Yarbrough, and of course Dr. Hall, who delivered a prayer for brotherhood just as the memorial was being firmly set into the concrete of a Charlotte sidewalk.

# Ginger Rogers and Napoleon

ONE of the great series of newspaper stories of all time is the manner in which the Paris press handled the escape of Napoleon Bonaparte from Elba. I have capsuled the time into a few days, but the headlines are substantially true.

First day: The monster has escaped.

Second day: The criminal is laying waste to the countryside.

Third day: The dictator is on his way to Paris.

Fourth day: Bonaparte is at the gates of the city.

Fifth day: All France rejoices as our glorious Emperor Napoleon makes a triumphant entry into Paris.

Now we come to Ginger Rogers.

The merchants of Charlotte spend a lot of money and effort on an annual Thanksgiving Day parade. It is a worthy event, a sort of R. H. Macy parade in miniature, and great fun for the children. Each year a famous personality is engaged to attract the thousands of people of the surrounding rural and textile mill communities. One year it was Hopalong Cassidy, another year it was Fulton Lewis, Jr., and this year it was Ginger Rogers.

But, at the last moment, Miss Rogers canceled the date and left the managers of the parade without the name attraction (it was a success anyway).

Here is how the Charlotte press handled the Ginger Rogers project (I have again capsuled the time into a few days, but as in the case of Emperor Napoleon, the Ginger Rogers head-lines are substantially accurate).

First day: Ginger Rogers, gorgeous star of stage and screen, will be our guest this year.

Second day: The delightful Ginger Rogers, dancing partner of Fred Astaire, tells the secrets of her beauty.

Third day: Ginger Rogers, Oscar-winning screen star, will also lead the parade.

Fourth day: Ginger Rogers, stage, screen, and TV star, has agreed to sign all autographs.

Fifth day: Ginger Rogers, 54-year-old former motion-picture actress, has canceled her appearance in Charlotte.

# A pulpit in the South

IT HAD been an ordeal for both the rabbi and for Morris Witcoff, president of Temple Emanu-El.

Rabbi Geller had occupied this Southern pulpit for two years, coming directly from the Hebrew Union College at Cincinnati. Now his two-year contract was drawing to a close, and it had been Mr. Witcoff's painful duty to notify him officially that the trustees would not renew. The rabbi decided to take a long walk before going home.

Mr. Witcoff had spoken for the board: "Rabbi, you're a good scholar, a good teacher, and your work with the children and the adult study group has been very good, but Rabbi, to be perfectly frank with you, what we really need here is a pastor and not a scholar."

Trustee Bleckman had said: "Rabbi, here it is: we just cannot seem to get close to you. You do not mix enough. How many visits have you made to the members? We urged you last year to visit them regularly. But you never got around to it. You never made the rounds."

Trustee Rosenbaum had interrupted: "Rabbi, out of twenty-two newcomers to Elizabeth since you have been the rabbi, the Conservatives got nineteen and we got three.

There's something definitely wrong. You never seem to get a new member. You just do not mix enough."

The president of the Sisterhood, June Greenberg, had summed it up: "Rabbi, you just don't mix enough."

And so now Rabbi Geller was taking a long walk toward the square. The square was on the crest of a hill, where the buildings fell back and shrank away from a grove of elms and brick walls. In the center of the square was the statue of the Confederate general. From the temple office two miles away he could see the tip of the general's sword poised skyward. He had measured that walk several times. Usually by the time he reached the base of the monument he had been able to work out an entire sermon. On this walk, however, he was free to take his time and think his own thoughts.

Sarah would take care of the details of moving. He suppressed a grin when he thought of what his friend Herman Gordon had said when he first met Sarah.

Gordon, a local newspaperman, considerably older than the rabbi, had been the Gellers' first social visitor in Elizabeth. And he minced no words when he opened the door: "I hear a new rabbi has come to town who has a thousand books; I wonder if I may please see the books." Rabbi Geller and Mr. Gordon had then spent that entire first Sunday in Elizabeth uncrating the books, after which he had stayed for dinner and remained a close friend ever after. Not that his friendship had counted on the positive side of the ledger with the board. At the final meeting, Trustee Bergstreet had said, "Rabbi, you've spent more time with Herman Gordon than with any other five members of the congregation, and what does Gordon give—the minimum, seventy-five dollars a year."

What was it that Gordon had said when he met Sarah that first Sunday? Oh yes: "Rabbi, now that I've seen your wife, I advise you to resign and enter law school. A beautiful rebbitzen is suicide with the girls of the congregation. There's nothing the Sisterhood likes better than to work with a plain-looking rebbitzen, and if she's very plain, ah, she's wonderful.

What a charming person, and so very, very accommodating. Rabbi, this will never do."

The rabbi was halfway up the hill. He could see the forage cap in the left hand of the Confederate general dangling above the stirrup.

What of his future? Anticipating the decision of the trustees, his application for a new pulpit was already in the hands of the Placement Committee in Cincinnati.

Hadn't old Rabbi Toback warned him? Rabbi Julius Toback was sixty-three years old and the spiritual head of Temple Beth El in the neighboring town of Kenilworth, South Carolina. Rabbi Geller had discussed his problem with his senior as far back as a year ago, and the elderly rabbi had said: "Geller, you have to make up your mind to one thing. Elizabeth or elsewhere in the South, the pulpits are all the same. There was a time when I had your ideas on what we called at college 'Classical Reform,' and that's why I am holding down the pulpit at Kenilworth, South Carolina, with a congregation of twenty-four families." Rabbi Toback continued with a smile: "And even at that, I'm not so sure of myself. I hear rumblings among my families. Some of them want me to take my cap off during services."

Rabbi Toback had speculated that both their problems were part of the bigger problem—that half of each Reform congregation wants no more and no less than a Unitarian service, while the other half, from the "newer element," wants to cling to rituals and practices with which they became familiar in their youth.

Once Gordon had said, "Rabbi Geller, if I am to keep you as a friend here, you'll have to sell those thousand books and learn how to be a good master of ceremonies at the Sisterhood Brisket Supper."

Rabbi Geller read the inscription under the Rebel general: "Dedicated to the men of Elizabeth who answered the call of duty, and valiantly laid down their lives for God and their beloved South."

He stopped to refresh himself at the water fountain. Dusk was beginning to settle and the general looked more majestic than ever hovering above the church spires of the Southern town.

Rabbi Geller reviewed in his mind the never-ending effort of Jewish middle-class life in the South to become one with the population mass surrounding it. He recalled the recent discussion he had had with Rabbi Toback and Herman Gordon on the subject. Toback, with his nine Southern pulpits over a thirty-year period, had paradoxical footnotes to contribute. For one thing, he pointed out that the few Jewish "non-conformists" in the South such as the union organizer, the public welfare worker, or the member of the Urban League, were sources of great anxiety to the Jewish community at large, who feared the "Gentile reaction." Yet somehow these very same Jewish odd-fish seem to have more contacts and friends within the white Protestant society than do the main body of Jews, for all their desperate effort to reflect the habits and the prejudices of the majority. Rabbi Geller had noted that the main Jewish community's desire to mix seems to express itself chiefly in a man's ambition to join the Gentile country club, or his wife's to join the Gentile book or garden club. When these attempts fail, he gives up, aggrieved, and seeks consolation in a more intensified "Jewish work."

He had once told his fellow rabbi, "One thing shocked me when I came South, the almost unbelievably intense fear of anti-Semitism."

"Of course, you are not wrong," said Rabbi Toback. "And how strange that this terrible fear of anti-Semitism exists at a moment when anti-Semitism as a political weapon is at its weakest."

And Gordon had agreed, "They jump at shadows, and at every chalk mark on the sidewalk; and they also keep themselves informed of the hour-by-hour itinerary of Gerald L. K. Smith."

Then, Rabbi Toback had observed, "It is all quite understandable. The Jew in the South is, so to speak, among the unemployed and unemployable, as far as the general community is concerned. There are no clerks, salesgirls, mechanics, civil servants, or white-collar workers among us. Even in a comparatively large city like Elizabeth, you, Gordon, and Rabbi Geller here, are the only two Jews in town who are not self-employed. We form a self-enclosed proprietary class, in short—a middle class. And you know, of course, that fear is the great middle-class disease, and in this respect the Jews are no different from the Gentiles. The Gentile middle class, too, experiences constant, gnawing fear: 'government controls,' 'labor unions,' 'Negroes,' 'taxes,' 'Roosevelt,' 'Truman,' and others, which they substitute from time to time. The Jew experiences a fear that is more pronounced, since as a member of the middle class *and* a Jew, he feels himself thus doubly exposed."

It was getting dark and Rabbi Geller roused himself from his thoughts. Sarah would be waiting. He decided to walk down the hill to Liggett's to phone her. On his way, he thought of the note he had received only a few days before from Rabbi Toback.

Rabbi Toback had sent him a few excerpts from a sermon he had delivered the previous Friday evening at Kenilworth: "I told my congregation that the Gentile is neither fascinated by, nor interested in, what Horace Kallen had called 'the amateur Gentile'; that basically the Gentile feels more at ease when confronted with a definite asserted value, whether it be 'rabbi,' 'CIO,' 'Roman Catholic,' or anything else. Even though he may be hostile, he would rather have ten recognizable values than one ambiguity. To him an ambiguity is an enigma which he has neither the time nor the inclination to examine thoroughly. I summed up the sermon with my favorite statement: 'For us, there is only one possible road to complete relaxation as happy members of this society; either you become a self-respecting Jew, standing unafraid for what you are and what you stand for—or you become a Christian.'"

Sarah wanted the rabbi to wait in front of Liggett's, she would pick him up. She said that a telegram had come for him and perhaps he might want to answer it while they were downtown. Rabbi Geller instructed her to open the telegram immediately.

It was from the Placement Committee in Cincinnati. They wanted to know whether the rabbi would be interested—the pulpit at Kenilworth, South Carolina, had opened up.

# Life in the American middle class

IN PREVIOUS years the fund-raiser had always relied on local talent for his publicity work. But this time he comes to town with his own press assistant. Oo ha, something big is brewing.

Fund-raising has made extroverts out of thousands of quiet and shy fellows throughout the land. This of course is true at all levels of the American culture—Protestant, Catholic, and Jew—except that with the Jew, as usual, it is more so.

Take the fellow who has led a very quiet life. Once the fund-raiser takes him under his wing, this man becomes highly articulate, often a veritable whirlwind when it comes to communal "leadership," and "saying a few words" at committee meetings and banquets.

The professional, of course, merely guides the fellow along without his knowing it, and during the process the fund-raiser becomes the most self-effacing guy in the world. He leaves everything to "the leaders." With a face on him as serious as that of an Under Secretary of State, the fund-raiser first appoints his committee—chairman, co-chairman, vice chairman, assistant chairman, and associate chairman—which takes care of five "leaders."

But nursing along the leaders is not the only job of the fund-raiser. He is ever on the alert for the "sleeper." He knows that there is always the fellow who sits far in the back behind a post who can be made into a "big giver" with kindness and wisdom.

The idea is what the fund-raiser calls the "crackerjack technique" which translated, means, "Get the fellow started."

Maybe the guy buys only a one-hundred dollar bond; this does not fool the fund-raiser.

He begins to work slowly, and let's face it—Bonds for Israel have done as much for the Jewish middle class in America as they have done for Israel itself. Within a short time the Bonds for Israel fellows have molded the rawest of the raw material into men of prestige and status; in short, *leaders*.

The sleeper is usually gun-shy, and he will try to stay away from all the small gatherings, like committees, for instance, or what they call "parlor meetings." He'll take his chances only at the big meeting, the banquet; and for two very good reasons: (a) the banquet provides him with some degree of anonymity, for every banquet hall has at least four posts to hide behind; and (b) the pressure of the personal touch is absent at the banquet, and he can get away with what the fund-raiser calls "the minimum."

But the fund-raiser is not disappointed. He only wants to get the sleeper started, knowing full well that a bit of gentle prodding will make the sleeper dream of someday sitting up there on the dais himself.

The first order of business is for the fund-raiser and his press assistant to call an initial meeting of the leaders, the fellows who are already tagged. What's the potential? How much can be raised? The next thing on the agenda is whom to get for the big meeting. The ladies meet separately and with them the order of business is reversed: (a) Whom to get for the big meeting? (b) What's the potential? At both meetings it is suggested that the fund-raiser call the national office and see whom they can send.

Of course the whole thing had been all arranged a month before the fund-raiser arrived in town. The instructions are in his pocket: "Try to get the people of Kenilworth to hold their annual banquet for Bonds on the ninth. George Jessel will be in Miami for the big meeting on the eighth. May be a good idea to get him to drop off at Kenilworth on his way to Cleveland where he's due on the tenth; but you must do a big job on the potential if we can swing it." (It should be noted here that Mr. Jessel volunteers his services often. Few men make a greater contribution to this cause than the famous trouper.)

(There is no more interesting man in America today than the fund-raiser. I literally love the ground he walks on—in gratitude for the thousands of words I shall yet write about him.)

The inevitable Jessel denouement, however, must bide its time while the fund-raiser greets every directive and suggestion from the leaders as though he were hearing the stuff for the very first time in his life. "Call the national office to see whom we can get," says the top leader. "A very brilliant idea," says the fund-raiser. "I'll do it right away; but please, fellows, help me out; the talent we can get depends on the potential—whom we can get depends on how many bonds we can sell."

The women at their own meeting begin to discuss the banquet personality to the exclusion of everything else. "Wouldn't it be wonderful if they could arrange for a debate right here in Kenilworth, South Carolina, between Nasser and David Ben-Gurion?" This is said in sort of a half-jesting way, but a few ladies are actually chuckling with their heads. "Now, girls, this is nonsense, let's get down to business—I think we should ask them for Milton Berle or Marlene Dietrich." Another lady says that Dagmar "did a marvelous job for Bonds" last year in Chantilly, North Carolina, and the discussion continues until the fund-raiser comes in with a few light touches, innocentlike: "Listen, folks, I mean no offense, but Kenilworth is strictly a Jan Barth or Molly Picon town, and I do not mean anything against these great artists, and it is silly to talk about Milton Berle or Dagmar; but I'll tell you this, off the record; I have just heard from the national office; for a $100,000 potential I believe they will agree to a number-one attraction; it is all a matter of timing," continues the fund-raiser, "like the big stars for the annual Chanukah Festival or for the Night of Stars itself."

It is at the third "parlor meeting," this time a joint meeting of the leaders and the ladies, that the fund-raiser finally breaks the news. (Breathlessly): "Folks, I just found out something big! I think I can get you—George Jessel, but this is entirely up to you. With a $100,000 potential, I think I can swing it with the national office."

Two women jump up, both talking at once: "Don't worry about the potential, grab Jessel, don't worry, we'll do the rest."

One of the leaders, a bit more sophisticated, says quietly, "You better call national and tell them to hold Jessel for us, I think we'll make it all right. Speak to Max Cohen himself." Max Cohen is an officer at the national office and this leader knows him personally. At the mention of Max Cohen the fund-raiser looks tremendously impressed. "A good fellow, Max," repeats the leader. The fund-raiser, who is America's greatest authority on *noblesse oblige,* does not use the name "Max." With great humility, he says, "I'll call Mr. Cohen right away at his home," and the leader beams as he repeats, "Yes, call Max right away and give him our decision."

But the fund-raiser knows exactly how to drop a bombshell, "Please, folks, don't put me on the spot, you know what it means if I ask national to send Jessel?" By this time the press assistant has also burst into tears at the plight of his buddy, the fund-raiser, who is now what he calls "on the spot." The phone rings and wearily the fund-raiser begins his conversation with Mr. Max Cohen at national.

"Don't take no for an answer," shouts the wife of the very top leader.

Now everything is all set for the real tsores (troubles) to begin.

At this stage of the game the fund-raiser holds the reins very loosely; he lets the leaders take over completely. They now hold regular weekly meetings to "complete the arrangements," and at each meeting, the fund-raiser is asked, "Are you sure Jessel is coming?"

He says yes, but he makes it sound like a rather weak yes for good and sufficient reasons.

Now the dinner itself has to be arranged. What to serve? And what about the method of admission? This is a headache. The leaders have already made their bond pledges, of course, and some of them suggest that admission should be by participation. You've got to buy a bond to get in. Another leader says, "Why should we give every Chaim Yonkel George Jessel? Is it coming to him? Let him buy a bond if he wants to come." Another leader agrees: "Let him stay home and look at television if he doesn't want to buy a bond."

Eventually an agreement is reached. The entire community will be invited and admission will be the purchase of one bond, any denomination, even a hundred-dollar one. And now comes the big argument. The top leader speaks, "I am glad we got this admission-by-the-bond through, because we can now make sure of something I've been arguing about every year—NO SOLICITATIONS AT THE DINNER. Let's enjoy it for once. Let's be dignified. Now that we are asking for admission-by-bond, I shall insist, no solicitations at the dinner."

They are all agreed and this time they are taking no chances.

They ask the fund-raiser to please stand up; an indignity which catches even him by surprise. The top leader says, "No solicitations at the dinner, is that agreed?" The fund-raiser looks hurt—his virtue is being questioned, and he stretches out his hand: "I want to shake hands with each of you so there'll be no question."

It is the most solemn moment of the project.

The champagne party will take place at 6:30 P.M., the main dinner at 8:00 P.M. At this point even the rabbis say it is a bargain. The rabbinical reaction to these fund-raising projects is usually a slight tilt of the head, and the remark, "ehe." And this is not out of unkindness or lack of devotion to the cause. But at no other moment in our culture is it as clear that the American rabbi has lost his classical function. It brings him the confirmation of what he has long suspected, that basically the laymen have taken over, following the pattern of the surrounding Protestant middle class.

During the final stages of the arrangements the chairman tells the two rabbis that they will be on the program, one for the invocation and the other, the benediction, and he leaves this decision up to them. The rabbis are worried about something else, too. Fund-raising takes the "top dollar" usually, and that means another delay for the addition to the Sunday School. The Protestants have the same trouble. In some of the smaller towns of the South a ten-day revival by a dynamic tent evangelist has often set the church building fund back six months.

A few more important details are ironed out. Should we announce the individual big gifts from the dais? The real "big giver" says, no, it's not necessary; but the fund-raiser comes to his rescue: "I know how you feel, Dinty, but it will help the enthusiasm all around and do a good job for Bonds. You must let us announce your name."

The next thing, of course, is, Who shall sit on the dais? But at this stage the matter falls into proper place of itself. The leaders, the three other big givers, Mr. Jessel, the Mayor, the two rabbis, and the fund-raiser. Now the question: What about the wives of the men on the dais? In the large cities of the North this is not a problem. Some of the tradition of the Hebraic patrism still remains; but, in the South, which is a matriarchy, the wives normally sit with the husbands. Eventually a compromise is worked out. The wives will sit together, right below the dais at a table which will be raised two inches above the regular tables—a sort of little dais.

And now for some real trouble. There are rumblings by the lesser lights, all over the city. They always leave out at least one authentic leader somehow; and in addition there are a dozen others who honestly believe themselves to be leaders. The acceptances to the formal invitations are coming in oh, so very slowly, a mere trickle. The affair has been widely advertised, including three follow-up letters. The daily press of the South goes all out for Jewish fund-raising affairs, for two basic reasons: (a) the Anglo-Calvinist civilization is really a sort of detribalized or "Aryan Judaism"; and (b) they regard any "Jewish" project in the community as a religious event. Thus the Bonds for Israel dinner is handled quite normally by the church editor. (The events at the Jewish country clubs of the South are also treated as religious news.)

So far there have been five separate stories in each of the local newspapers, including the one with a two-column cut of George Jessel under the caption, "COMING TO KENILWORTH."

And there is a bonus story for the fund-raiser when the drama critic and movie editor of the daily press writes a special piece on Jessel, minus the religious angle.

It has been covered thoroughly but now when one of the Hadassies talks to a prospect, the prospect says, "Where is the dinner going to be held?" and "Who did you say was coming—Jessel?" This is what is known as "the needles," part of the same rumblings of the lower echelon in town. The folks know that there have been big doings going on during the past three weeks, and all they get out of it is the formal invitation—to come. Two women meet on the street; one is the wife of a leader, and the other is the wife of a member of the lower echelon, and Mrs. Leader says, "Sandra, I'll see you at the affair," and Sandra says nonchalantly, "What affair?" And Mrs. Leader replies: "The affair for George Jessel next Sunday night, my Joe is on the committee"—which of course is the point of the whole thing. You lose considerable status if you acknowledge the printed invitation as official. Sandra will come and she will say, "Dinty Witcoff [a very big giver] called us up last night, he insisted we come as a favor to him." (This statement always serves to restore the status that may have been lost in not being in on all the preliminaries.)

No one comes without a face-saving statement of some kind.

Then the folks ask each other, "Will it be kosher?" and the answer is always the same, "Not for me, mind you, Joe and I do not care for ourselves, but the rabbis will be there and anyway for an affair like that it's nice if it's kosher; instead of a shrimp cocktail we're having that fruit cup au Barringer."

But still only a trickle of acceptances, and the leaders are worried. But the fund-raiser knows that everything will turn out fine. Somewhere along the line, civic pride enters the picture. How will it look if the hall is half empty? It would be a shame for George Jessel. They now begin to cut the corners a little. They let it be known, unofficially of course, that it's all right if you bought a bond last year; all right, so he didn't buy a bond; it's a community affair after all, isn't it? In short, the leaders do not want a flop on their hands, in addition to which they are also fighting the "communal calendar." Things move fast in the community. A week later there is the Hadassah Donor Dinner, and then that book review, and before you know it—it's Brotherhood Week again.

The telephone committee is in full swing. But at this stage in the proceedings the fund-raiser would like to be the owner of a travel agency. The pre-fund-raising exodus is on—in full swing.

"I've got to be in New York on a buying trip that night—arranged long ago." "We are going to see our daughter at the college up in Virginia." "We always leave for Miami this week." If the fund-raising project is in the winter, they are going to Miami; if it's summer, they have reservations at the seashore; and for the retailers it's bad because it's getting close to the Christmas season, and this means any time after Labor Day.

The final press conference is held. The leaders are asking everybody to calm down, be prepared; and the local newspapermen, radio and TV fellows crowd into the last press conference—primarily because they love Jewish pickles. There's something about Southern newspapermen and Jewish pickles that's amazing.

Everything is all set. Jessel's plane is due to arrive at 4:30. He will go to the hotel to rest and change clothes. The champagne party begins at 6:30, and the dinner at 8:00. One by one, each of the leaders has whispered confidentially to the fund-raiser, "How about bringing Jessel up to the house right after the affair? I'll have just a few top leaders and we can have hors d'oeuvres on our patio." The real big giver tells the fund-raiser that for himself it doesn't matter, "But my two little daughters said they won't go to sleep until I bring him home, so you can see what I'm up against."

Then the radio man wants Mr. Jessel in his studio at

exactly 5:15 for his "Interview with the Personality of the Day," a daily feature.

To all of this the fund-raiser smiles enigmatically. He's stalling. Actually he hasn't the faintest idea about Mr. Jessel's plans for the evening; all he knows for sure is that the national office has routed Mr. Jessel from Miami to Cleveland with a stopover at Kenilworth. That very morning he received a telegram from the Miami fund-raiser, "Not sure about Jessel being on 4:30 plane, may not arrive till 7:20. Meet both and be sure he catches 11:15 for Cleveland."

The thing is now snowballing. When Mr. Jessel doesn't arrive on the 4:30 the press assistant calls the radio, press, and TV to tell them of the change in plans and that Jessel will not be able to appear for the various interviews, but please come to the dinner. There will be a press table and you'll enjoy Mr. Jessel's message. (The fund-raisers never use the terms "speech," "address," or "entertainment"; it is always "message.")

Mr. Jessel's plane gets in at 7:31, a few minutes late, but he says he is prepared to go directly to the banquet hall. It's a long drive and the program is in full swing.

The whole audience rises as Mr. Jessel enters with the fund-raiser and the press assistant; the dinner is served; Mr. Jessel delivers his highly entertaining speech, full of humorous anecdotes, with the required bit of pathos at the finish.

He sits down to a thunderous ovation. The dais and the little dais are aglow, but there's one strange thing about it— I should say, one strange individual. No one saw him come in and no one has introduced him. He is a distinguished-looking man and he is sitting in the chair reserved for the fund-raiser, who is now walking up and down behind the dais whispering to the various leaders and big givers.

And the program continues. The top gifts are announced; the women's gifts; everybody is thanked; and, finally, the fund-raiser asks the chairman to introduce the stranger.

The stranger, it turns out, is a leader in his own right, up 'n Lansing, Michigan. While on the plane, he says, he "ac-

cidentally" heard of this great event in Kenilworth and decided to stop off to pay his respects; he says. Actually this
fellow is what is known in sports as a ringer; a fund-raiser
kept under wraps and disguised as a leader for very special
jobs. It is he who now takes care of that no-solicitation-at-
the-dinner proposition: "In Lansing the drive brought in
$122,000. Please let me go back to my home town and tell
them that here in Kenilworth, a smaller city, you good people
were able to top our own Lansing mark." He now goes into
a pitch for new pledges with the subtlety of a sand-blaster.

The leaders look at the fund-raiser with fire in their eyes,
but the fund-raiser, who now looks like butter wouldn't melt
in his mouth, tells them that he shares their chagrin: "Can I
help it if the fellow lets his enthusiasm run away with him?"
The ringer has come out of the West like Lochinvar and adds
$11,000 in smaller pledges to the total.

And, as the folks are making pledges in response to the
ringer's brilliant solicitation, Mr. Jessel, the fund-raiser, and
the press assistant quietly slip out to the car for the long
drive to the airport and that 11:15 plane for Cleveland.

## The clock raffle

IN A MIDWEST city, two or three sisterhoods combined to
finance a summer camp for poor children.

They used a clock raffle for this fund-raising project, and
this is how it works. A raffle ticket costs one dollar. You write
your name and address and pick the "time," for instance, one
minute after three. After all the tickets are sold, the committee winds up the clock and puts it in the vault under the
supervision of an officer of the bank, like the quiz show used
to do.

Everything was all set for the big kickoff meeting and tea
at a downtown hotel. A total of four thousand, eight hundred
tickets had been sold and the prize was a beautiful color television set. The committee went to the bank, the officer opened

the vault, and officially recorded the "winning moment," the moment at which the clock had stopped. The winner was twelve minutes after five. Now one of the ladies on the committee screamed, "That's Shirley's ticket, my friend Shirley wins!" And with that she ran to the phone and joyously notified Shirley.

The bank official replaced the clock in a box, sealed it according to protocol and the whole party set out for the kickoff meeting and tea. On the way downtown the car hit a big bump. No one thought this was important at the time.

The news that the clock had stopped at twelve after five had spread like a prairie fire, and there was much bantering humor as the committee and bank official took their places on the dais. There was silence as the clock was unveiled, then a gasp as the face of the clock was held toward the six hundred ladies. Instead of twelve after five, the hands of the clock stood at eight minutes to six, and it was ticking away like mad.

Shirley fainted, the committee resigned in a body, and as I left I saw thirty angry women gathering around the bank official.

# The writers were in Boston

NORTH CAROLINA has been referred to as "the valley of humility between two mountains of conceit" (Virginia and South Carolina).

The Southern generals and colonels all come from Virginia, South Carolina, Alabama, Tennessee, Georgia, and Mississippi. North Carolina produced the privates, the foot soldiers. It mustered the most men in the Civil War and suffered the most casualties. Yet on top of all of that the sentiment had been very strong against secession. The story is that Zebulon Vance, then governor, was ready to declare for the Union when news came that Lincoln had called for mobilization, and the governor thus lost the initiative. But this "humility" goes way back to the earliest beginnings of the country.

It was right here, between Kings Mountain and Guilford Court House (Greensboro) that these North Carolinians cut Lord Cornwallis to ribbons. By the time he got to Yorktown he was ready to hand his sword over to the first kind man he met.

But the boys up in Boston were writing the early histories of our country, and so they made a big deal out of Bunker Hill, where the Americans were on top of the hill, and lost—and they forgot about Kings Mountain, where the Americans were on the bottom of the hill, and won.

# The town's lone Jew

WHEN he opens the store in the morning he may not know it, but the folks automatically identify him with Jeremiah, Isaiah, Amos, and the Second Coming, and all of this imposes a tremendous obligation on our "lone Jew" in a small Southern town.

When the Baptist Sunday School teacher is puzzled by some involved Biblical problem he immediately runs over to Goldstein's to get the information, right from the original source, as it were, and usually poor Goldstein hasn't the faintest idea what the fellow is talking about.

Recently I came into a small town to address a Lions Club, and as usual my gracious hosts remembered not to serve me the ham which was on the menu for the day. Instead they brought me a chicken platter, which in their extreme generosity, they had prepared in pure country butter.

During the dinner, my host, the leading citizen of the town, told me that he had been anxiously awaiting my coming: "I asked Mr. Goldstein, a f-i-n-e Jewish citizen in our town, what happened to the Ark of the Covenant, and he told me to ask you when you came here to speak."

As I discussed the Ark with my host, I thought of poor Goldstein; with the bottom falling out of the textile machinery market, this fellow keeps worrying him about the Ark of the Covenant. But such matters are part of the daily life of the lone Jew in a small Southern town.

# Jefferson and Komotow

I HAD the honor of making a speech at Colonial Williamsburg, and the Charleston (South Carolina) *News and Courier* wrote a lengthy editorial wanting to know why I was invited to this shrine of our American civilization. Why was I invited? I was no Southerner, they said. They said that all I was was an "immigrant from New York's garment district."

Wasn't this a fine argument to come from a Southern gentleman?

But the Charleston *News and Courier* did hit the nail on the head when they referred to the New York City garment district.

Thomas Jefferson put political freedom into the Declaration of Independence. And Nathan Komotow, a Jewish immigrant from Eastern Europe, helped put democracy into practice. Komotow invented a knife that cut through forty thicknesses of cloth at once. Editors can now wear the same suit as bank presidents. Before Komotow, it was homemade breeches for everybody except the bank presidents. The mail-order catalogue for 1908 indicates that the big sellers for men were overalls and pants. But Komotow's invention meant that a tailor could cut forty vests in five minutes and no longer could you distinguish at sight a taxi driver from the owner of the cotton mill.

Komotow gave democracy new energy, and this was, I think, one of the ideas behind Williamsburg, Virginia; and it is precisely this *persisting* new energy in democracy that will make Colonial Williamsburg survive another few centuries.

# This was some Cadillac

"KING SOLOMON made himself a chariot of the wood of Lebanon. He made the pillars thereof of silver, the bottom thereof of gold, the covering of it of purple, the midst thereof being paved with love, for the daughters of Jerusalem."

—From THE SONG OF SOLOMON

# Come and see us

IT TOOK me a long time to understand this old Southern custom—"Come and see us."

It was puzzling at first. I would meet a newspaper colleague with his wife in a restaurant or on the street; we'd chat for a few moments; and at the end of the conversation they would say, "Come and see us." I immediately answered, "When?" which threw them into utter confusion. But I am no longer cynical about this. Their amazement, I have since learned, was not really horror, not even ordinary chagrin. "Come and see us" is merely the Southern way of saying "goodbye," which carries with it its own charm, of course.

Now I do not ask "When?" In fact, I beat them to the punch. It is I who say "Come and see us," which is a sort of guarantee to each of us of our individual privacy, and everybody is happy.

# Hudson seal to mink

THE Hollander family of Newark, New Jersey, had developed a secret formula to dye the pelt of the muskrat and they called it Hudson seal. The Hudson seal made a magnificent coat, and it looked better and wore longer than real sealskin. After World War I millions of American girls and women hoped that one day they would own a Hudson seal coat, or even a jacket. But now the women turn their noses up at Hudson seal. They'll consider nothing less than mink. What's happening to all the Hudson sealskins? There is a great demand for them in Europe. The middle class of Europe is now in its Hudson seal stage. When Europe begins to wear mink, our stenographers will wear ermine, like King Henry VIII. Is there anything between mink and ermine?

## Sam, you made the nose too big

BECAUSE the overwhelming desire of the upper-middle-class American is for a Greek profile, the orthodontists have a thriving profession. Day and night the orthodontist toils, straightening teeth, measuring braces, correcting small oral irregularities. But after the mouth and jaw are sufficiently Greek, it becomes patent that now the nose is too big. Another industry flourishes. It is all a mess.

## What happened to free enterprise?

WHAT'S happened to Free Enterprise and Moral Fiber? Some of the Southern states are going all out in their handouts along the lines of the welfare state, creeping socialism, and all that stuff. The result will be that we will raise a whole new generation of Southern manufacturers without moral fiber. Some of these states are spending fortunes to bring in new industry; they are handing out free land sites, new roads, sewers, free wiring, and no taxes. I can see these manufacturers shivering for the lack of moral fiber every time they go out to make a bank deposit. O, where are the men who chopped down the trees and carved a civilization out of a wilderness? O, where are the snows of yesteryear? What happened to free enterprise?

# What are pickled pig skins?

FROM the *Columbia* (S. C.) *Record*, reporting the trial of one William R. Kittrell, Jr., charged with operating a public nuisance "because of prostitution and loud noises":

Geraldine Davis, one of the witnesses today, testified that she had sexual relations with men she met at the Shady Grove cafe, charging them seven to ten dollars each time. She said that she and her "date" would go into the woods where the acts took place. She said she collected the money before she took the men out, and that she would turn the money over to Kittrell, who would give her back half of it at the end of the day.

She filled one such "date" on the night of the raid, she said. Norma Rucker, third of the three girls arrested, was declared a "hostile witness" to the prosecution by Judge G. Duncan Bellinger when she tried to repudiate a sworn statement that she had previously made to law-enforcement officers. Under cross-examination by Solicitor Hubert E. Long, she admitted one sex act on the night of the raid. She had previously denied doing anything but serving "beer, cokes, pickled pig's feet, pickled pig skins, and potato chips."

The Rucker woman said that the prostitution was on her own time. She testified that Kittrell paid her eight dollars a week, plus ten per cent of the proceeds of the juke box in the place. "My biggest job was to get people to play the 'piccolo,'" she said.

What interested me in this news item was that business about the pickled pig skins. What the Sam Hill are pickled pig skins?

PART 2

*Enjoy, Enjoy*

# The East Side revisited

I STOOD in the doorway of the tenement on the Lower East Side of New York and looked at the flights of stairs my mother had climbed so often with her black leather market bag.

I felt sad for a moment. I'd been back before a few times, but I hadn't really explored the neighborhood for nearly forty years. There have been many changes, of course. The elevated structures of the Bowery and First Avenue are gone and there are a few new housing developments. But what is amazing is that so much of it is exactly as I knew it as a boy down there before World War I.

We lived at 171 Eldridge Street, a cold-water tenement house which must have been thirty years old in 1905. It is still full of tenants. Originally the toilets were in the yard in back. Later on came the inside toilets, one to a floor, serving four families. And I want you to understand that I am talking about substantial families—father, mother, approximately five children, and three boarders.

I examined the names in the mailboxes of the tenement of today, and where once there had been Rabinowitz and Cohen, there were now Perez and Amici. And as I stood in that hallway which had been my own for my first fifteen years, the Negro and Puerto Rican kids looked at me as if I had just dropped down from the planet Mars.

You can write a social history of our country by walking through a neighborhood. First were the Germans, then the Irish, the Jews, the Italians, and now the Negroes and the

*For 2¢ Plain*

Puerto Ricans, and each group leaves its deposits for the future and stores away its memories. What manner of children, of what nationality and history, will be staring at the "stranger" when the Puerto Rican actor or Negro vice-president of the United States comes back fifty years from now? I am certain that this scene will be acted over . . . "and in accents yet unborn."

I visited the University Settlement, of course, at 184 Eldridge Street. This is where Eleanor Roosevelt once taught dancing to the immigrant children. A few blocks farther west was the Christadora House, with Harry Hopkins, and helping Lillian Wald from time to time at the Henry Street Settlement were Herbert H. Lehman, Henry Morgenthau, Jr., Frances Perkins, Gerard Swope, A. A. Berle, Jr., and Charles A. Beard. And so the secret is out! Now you, too, know where Franklin D. Roosevelt got the New Deal. Right out of the settlement houses of the teeming slums. Bury the dead, take care of the widows and orphans, teach the young mother how to take care of her baby, and make sure the fellow has a doctor when he gets sick. . . .

I went to Katz's Delicatessen store on East Houston Street, and surprisingly Mr. Katz knew me. I had delivered some packages for him many years ago. I remember when the place opened. Two newly arrived immigrants established it and they called it Iceland and Katz. Mr. Katz's nephew is the present owner. I never knew what happened to Mr. Iceland. It is a huge establishment today. I had a hot pastrami sandwich, pickle, and beer.

I looked up to the third floor of 173 Eldrige Street where lived my friend Morris Kaplan of whom I once wrote—the boy who went fishing every Sunday and created such a rumpus about it. But I stole a furtive glance down Rivington Street toward the corner of Forsyth to a low red building where Bertha Katzmann lived. Bertha was probably the most blue-eyed, blonde Jewish girl in the entire world, and every single one of us black-haired, brown-eyed boys felt his heart pumping away like mad every time we saw Bertha walking home from school. Her father was a violinist for the Philharmonic Symphony Orchestra, which gave her tremendous social status in addition to her rare beauty. During a scholastic event at the 71st Regiment Armory, I looked up in the balcony where the girls were singing, and I watched Bertha waving that little American flag and singing "The Stars and Stripes Forever," and I have thought of that scene a million times during these past forty-three years. I wonder where she is today.

Then I walked down to Seward Park and I experienced a feeling of great warmth as I saw, still standing at the far end of the square, *The Jewish Daily Forward*, with the sign underneath, Arbeiter Ring (Workman's Circle). We used to pick up our papers right on the sidewalk, two for a penny, and sell them for one cent in those days, and I learned how to dispose of the first batch quickly. I found out about the meeting halls. There were always a few hundred meetings going on all over the East Side.

I thought of the khazar (pig) market in Seward Park. Here the immigrants stood around with symbols of their trades, waiting for a casual employer to come along. One man held up his saw or hammer to indicate that he was a carpenter, one fellow carried panes of window glass, and others stood around with sewing machines strapped to their backs.

At the other end of Seward Park once stood P.S. 62. We were all jealous of P.S. 62, which had tremendous prestige in athletics. Her pupils were the first Jewish boys out of the East Side to travel around the country playing in championship basketball tournaments. It becomes a tradition. Notre Dame for football, Holy Cross for baseball, and C.C.N.Y. for basketball, fed by P.S. 62, where Nat Holman himself had been a student. The game of basketball was invented by Dr. Naismith and the Y.M.C.A., but the East Side boys made it a national pastime. It was the only game you could play in the settlement houses and schoolyards; and on every roof and basement you would see the barrel hoop with a flock of kids practicing baskets by the hour. There was the inevitable soul-searching up at Columbia University when it was necessary, according to leadership protocol, to appoint a Jewish boy as the captain of a varsity team. His name was Sam Strom. A year later, Dartmouth had the same "problem" and it was settled with far more grace. There was a player down there by the name of Moscowitz whom everyone called "Mosco." He played in an exhibition game up at the New York Athletic Club, which would not suffer a Jew to cross its threshold, and there they were, all the N.Y.A.C.-niks standing on seats and yelling themselves hoarse—"Mosco," "Mosco."

It was right there in Seward Park that William Jennings Bryan spoke before my day, and where I heard Charles Evans Hughes deliver a campaign speech in his contest with President Wilson in 1916. It was in this district that a friend of my family was the assemblyman, Judge Leon Sanders, a fine gentleman. The alderman was an Irishman by the name of Peter M. Poole. When he ran for re-election, he plastered the district with Yiddish posters and called himself Pincus Meyer Poole. The Jews got the point all right and laughingly voted for the guy. Later John Ahearn became the leader. I'll tell you about these Ahearns someday and we'll all die laughing.

Seward Park is now a city playground with a full-time director, a young fellow recently out of Brooklyn College who looks after the kids and supervises their play. Today the majority group is a tossup between Negroes and Puerto Ricans, with smaller groups of Jews, Poles, Ukrainians, Italians, and a fair sprinkling of Chinese. I spotted the few Jewish boys in the park, who were undoubtedly Orthodox and probably going to a Yeshiva (religious school). While the little Puerto Ricans and Negroes had stomachs as flat as a board, these Jewish kids were literally bursting the seams of their trousers. I made a prediction to myself. I said that the mothers of those Jewish kids were watching them at that very moment and soon they would be coming along with some snack. Sure enough, along came a mother toward one of these boys with a large paper cup full of a chocolate drink. Ah, "Ess, ess, mein kindt" (Eat, eat, my child). The old tradition never dies. I remember when young women practiced sitting postures to simulate a double chin, the mark of good health and good fortune and "She's so good-natured."

You were fifteen years old and you already weighed about one hundred and forty-five pounds, and if perchance you weren't hungry one evening and dawdled over your supper, your mother raised a terrible fuss: "Look at him, nothing but skin and bones." Food. Eat, eat. The tradition was born in the ghettos of Eastern Europe as both the symbol and the means of survival.

And I went toward the Williamsburg Bridge at the foot of Delancey Street, and I thought of the story of the first anti-Semitic disturbance in that homogeneous enclave of Jewish immigrants. It had happened a few years before I began to read, but it was still the talk of the neighborhood. The Chief Orthodox Rabbi Yankef Joseph had passed away and the funeral procession was proceeding to the Grand Street Ferry while the Williamsburg Bridge was still under construction. As the procession passed the R. Hoe Company (printing machinery), some of the employees threw discarded type metal down upon the heads of the mourners, and, at one of the windows, there was a hose pouring out scalding water. Dozens of people were hospitalized. A riot squad of police ran into the building but they could not properly identify the criminals. Before that day was over every single window of the huge R. Hoe Company was shattered and some of the Irish cops helped smash out the entrance of the building. In addition, the company suffered great loss through many lawsuits. There was no evidence to indicate the owners and managers of this establishment were involved in this thing, but we all know that hate always brings on more hate and everyone suffers, including the innocent bystanders.

As my afternoon of memories wore on, it was time to enjoy a "for two cents plain," only now it is for five cents plain. I stood at the stand with its marble top, and when I asked the fellow to "put a little on the top" (syrup), he waved his hand at me in disgust, "I knew that trick before I was born." He didn't believe that I had made the request out of nostalgia. I was just another "wise guy."

The next stop was the establishment of the late Yonah Schimmel who invented the knish (a kind of pastry of either potatoes or buckwheat groats—kasha—tenderly spiced and lovingly encased in a baked crust). I ate one of each—potato and kasha. Mr. Schimmel's large photograph with his beautiful black beard is still in the window, and I wondered how he would have felt if he had known that someday Yonah Schimmel's would be advertising "cocktail knishes." How do you like that? little bitty things. As we go up and up in this world, the knishes go down and down. I was glad to see, however, that they still make potatonik, a potato pudding full of fine spices in a carefully baked brown crust. My mother made wonderful potatonik, although her real specialty was mammaliga, a soft corn bread. She cut it with a thread and you packed it full of sharp cheese, or you could also use it with meat dishes to sop up the gravy.

And then I visited a clothing store—the kind where you could "Buy a Suit for Hymie," and I had a hilarious time. I explained to the storekeeper in Yiddish, telling him everything I had written about this operation. The fellow had a delightful sense of humor, patted me on the back and kept saying: "You remember, you remember."

I stood in front of the old P.S. 20, which is now the Manhattan Trades School. I went into that building every day for eleven long years, eight years to public school and three years to the East Side Evening High School, and a few doors away had been the Rivington Street Library, where I read whole shelves of Verne, Hazard, Bulwer-Lytton, Dumas, Hugo, and later Emerson and Henry George. A few years ago I read in *The New York Times* that the Rivington Street Library was being closed. I wrote a letter of warmth and appreciation to the librarian in charge of the closing, but I never received a reply.

And I looked up to the top of P.S. 20. Ah, the old Roof Garden where Mr. Brown supervised the dances during the summertime. In those days the roof was brilliantly lighted and the entire neighborhood waited for the signal, the playing of "The Star-Spangled Banner." Our mothers sat at the windows just looking toward that Roof Garden. The immigrant milieu in America would never tolerate the changing of our anthem to "America the Beautiful." We know. We are connoisseurs of America. We know that it is not the place, but the *idea* of America that is important. The most beautiful "amber waves of grain" are in the Ukraine and in the Wallachian wheat fields of Romania; and I suspect that "from sea to shining sea" would be an appropriate description of the Mediterranean and the Baltic; but "Oh! say can you see, by the dawn's early light . . ." Now that means something—"that our flag was still there . . ." There's the symbol of a great political experiment in human dignity.

And finally the day's events were coming to a close with a dinner on Second Avenue in the establishment of Moskowitz and Lupowitz. In my day this was known as plain Moskowitz's and I remember how we sat outside at the curb listening to Mr. Moskowitz play the Romanian zither.

The steaks and roast beef covered wooden planks about twenty-four inches square, but, after all, steak and roast beef could be had anywhere. No, this was no steak-and-roast-beef night for me. I started off with chopped chicken liver and a great big piece of radish. The chicken liver of course was well steeped in pure chicken fat. The waiter brought the ubiquitous bottles of seltzer. Then I had noodle soup with kreplach (the joy of which the late Senator McCarran did not fully understand), then I ordered a beautiful piece of boiled beef with a side platter of delightful stuffed cabbage—holishkas—which I worked on with a fork in one hand and a slab of rye bread in the other. For dessert I had compote—and a snifter of Three Star Hennessy brandy. All this time, of course, the three-piece orchestra was playing the delightful tunes of the East Side, like "Leben Zul Columbus" (Long Live Columbus) and "A Breevele der Mamen" (A Letter to Mother).

I inquired about the original Mr. Moskowitz and I was amazed to hear that he is still living and actually playing his famous zither somewhere in Washington. How old could he be today? Of course he could still be under eighty, but he was close to middle age then, or maybe it was merely the usual child's age-distortion of the adult world. Anyway Mr. Moskowitz was quite an institution. During the summer, whole crowds gathered outside to listen to him play. His music was both soulful and wild. After each piece, everyone used to cheer and pour more wine, while Moskowitz, with his glistening bald head, bowed and bowed as though it were his debut, instead of the regular ten performances a night.

And so this was a day on the Lower East Side, and, with a bit of imagination, I could "see" my parents and my friends, and I could smell the smells, and I could talk with the parents and relatives of the thousands of people, all over America, who have been writing me all these years. . . .

"We must have passed each other on the street."


## The miracle of Goerick Street

CONSIDERING the poverty of the family, it wasn't such a big miracle, which is precisely what made it so fascinating, so utterly defiant of reasonable explanation.

It happened about 1910 and it involved a family of five living in a tenement flat on Goerick Street on the Lower East Side. The father was Reb Sholom, the cantor of a small congregation of immigrants from the big city of Odessa on the Black Sea. The cantor himself had come to America about five years before with his wife Clara and their three children —Jacob, who was now ten; Philip, nine; and Esther, six.

The cantor's earnings were dependent upon the pledges of the members of the small congregation, who were mostly peddlers and garment workers. To these wages he was able to add a few small fees every Sunday at the Washington Cemetery in Brooklyn, where people sought him out to chant the prayers at the gravesides of departed loved ones.

Despite poverty, it was a happy family, and this was because the cantor was a man of dignity, kindness, and piety. Years later his children would look back on it all and say that their father was what we would call a "morale-builder." He kept his family together with honor, good humor, and wisdom. He often told his children that he would never interfere with their hopes for their future, but they would be much happier as Americans, in whatever station they chose, if they continued to follow the rules and rituals of the Jewish faith. Let it be said, too, that the family's devotion was shared by neighbors and members of his congregation. The poor cantor achieved the respect reserved for a learned rabbi.

It was about this time that the miracle first occurred.

It was a Wednesday night and the two boys had asked the mother if they could afford to have their shoes repaired, and she said that she would see about it on the following Monday. But the shoes were not repaired on the following Monday; they were repaired that very night. And no one knew how. They all remembered the same details. The cantor and the boys had recited the evening prayers; they had supper; the older boy did some homework; the little girl helped her mother with the dishes; they sat around the table and talked for a while; then everyone went to bed. Everything was the same as on every other weekday night. The boys had put their stockings into their shoes, placed them under the bed, the lights were turned out, the door was bolted. In the morning, the boys pulled their shoes from under the bed and they had been thoroughly repaired—with new soles and heels and a high polish. They did not know what to make of it, and when they asked the cantor for a possible explanation, he shook his head: "Well, let's get on with our morning prayers."

But the matter did not end there. Not at all. Three months later the shoes were repaired again, under similar circumstances, and this time little Esther's shoes also were rebuilt. *But why the shoes?* If it was really a miracle, why repair just shoes for a family that needed so many other important things? They asked themselves this question over and over again. They wondered about this each time a pair of shoes was repaired during the night, and it happened every few months over a period of six or seven years—and no one could explain it.

Of course, the children did not let it rest at that. When a

pair of shoes needed repair, they watched, and they watched. They took turns and watched all night, time after time. Nothing. It was only on a night when they finally gave in to sleep that the miracle happened. They never saw or heard anything during all those years that their shoes were periodically repaired.

The story was told to me by a lawyer in one of our large Eastern cities. He is Jacob, the eldest son of the cantor Reb Sholom (the cantor died in the late 1920's). I was an overnight guest of this lawyer, who enjoys great prestige. The oldest families in his city make him the administrator of their estates, and, while he did not say so, he was actually relating everything that he had achieved to what his father had meant to him, and what his father had taught him. His brother Philip is a manufacturer, and the sister Esther, just as the cantor had hoped, had married a "learned man."

The miracle of Goerick Street?

Reb Sholom had made his decision as he walked off the gangplank into America. He was not a cantor in Russia. He was a shoemaker; and he did not come from the big seaport Odessa (which is like saying you're from Chicago or Philadelphia); he came from the small village of Glotsk. He yearned for status, not for himself, but for what it would do for his children. They would not be the children of the poor shoemaker.

He was wise enough to know, too, that in America, the social classes did not have the meaning that they had in the old country, but he also knew that these distinctions were too deeply rooted not to survive for at least one generation.

No, Reb Sholom thought, even if he were to remain poor, he would make a new life—one in which he would attain status without money, so as to bring to his home conversation and fellowship and the kind of environment that helps a son to become a lawyer, and helps a daughter marry a learned man.

He then tackled the most difficult part of his goal with determination and optimism. Study! He read far into the night, every night. He practically memorized the Scriptures; he studied the Talmud and the Commentaries; he read the books of the learned men of the past; and he went to the shul every day and listened; he remembered everything he heard at the weekly discussion the rabbi conducted with his elders. And all of this took him about four years, while his wife earned enough to keep the family by taking in the sewing of a garment contractor.

About this time the old cantor of the shul died and Reb Sholom applied for the position. He had had no cantorial training at all; in fact, he did not even have much of a voice; but there was something about the manner in which he chanted the prayers. His deep affection for every word he was uttering convinced even those highly critical Orthodox Jews that all this man had to do was *recite* the prayers to hold them in the spell of his own piety.

And now his son, my lawyer-host, was filling his pipe, and I took advantage of the moment to ask the obvious question.

He shook his head in answer. "No, not even my mother could tell us where he kept his shoemaker tools. I am convinced she never knew.

"But, since none of us ever heard the tap of a hammer, we suspect that on these occasions he got out of bed in the middle of night and repaired our shoes in the cellar of that tenement house on Goerick Street."

# A passport to heaven

WE HAD a cousin of my mother whom we called Aunt Maryim who spent her entire life seeking out good deeds to perform.

I recall clearly this tremendous drive to perform a good deed among pious Jews. This was not the Boy Scout type of good deed, which one might come across accidentally, like finding an elderly lady who needed help across the street. This drive to do a good deed was entirely different. You went out specifically to find the deed, and it assumed tremendous importance. Each day brought new opportunities, and the belief was strong that these deeds were entered in a heavenly ledger where they were carefully studied, with the credits awaiting the individual when the time came for him to be judged.

Aunt Maryim went to bar mitzvahs, births, engagements, weddings—but mostly to funerals. At funerals the "good deeds" multiply quicker; they are more dramatic; because at funerals one good deed, like crying over the deceased, brings on a multitude of other good deeds, like taking some of the deceased's clothing to a poverty-stricken household. She made the clothing fit, and was always carrying around old shoes, hats, pants, and skirts. She collected for all the charitable institutions and she wouldn't leave a man's place of business until he gave her a donation. Aunt Maryim became sort of an institution on the East Side and she was a fixture at all the functions and affairs of orphan asylums and other institutions.

Maryim's husband was a sexton in a shul on Rivington Street and as a sideline he repaired umbrellas. After a windstorm, Aunt Maryim would go out on the streets picking up discarded umbrellas for her husband to repair and sell. She collected thousands of dollars for institutions, poor individuals, war victims; she accumulated dowry money for girls she had never seen. She never took a cent for herself, but she prided herself on one virtue, that she could cuss out her umbrella-fixing husband for two hours and not repeat a single klula (cuss word) twice. Her husband was very proud of her, and, being a pious man, felt that living with her was worth all the heartache since it assured him of a passport to heaven. One day Aunt Maryim fell and broke her hip, and she prayed for many weeks in the synagogue after that and redoubled her efforts to find good deeds. She was convinced that the accident was a punishment visited upon her because "bad thoughts" had entered her mind while she was dancing with Judge Gustave Hartman at one of the orphan asylum functions.

# The "Bintel Brief"

THE "Bintel Brief"—literally, a package or a bundle of letters—was the open forum section of the great *Jewish Daily Forward,* the largest foreign-language daily newspaper in America. During the days of unrestricted immigration *The Forward* was a sort of classroom for the immigrants.

Reprinted here are letters from the "Bintel Brief." They were written between 1906 and 1908, and I am indebted for the translation from the original Yiddish to George M. D. Wolfe, who presented it in the form of a study to the Training School for Jewish Social Work in 1929.

I selected these few at random:

My little girl wants to pierce her ears for earrings. She says all the girls here have pierced ears, but my husband says no, that in America you do not pierce ears any more, but the girl is crying and tell my husband in the letter what is the best to do.

My husband reads *The Forward,* but where does he read it? In the barbershop where he goes all the time with those other card players. Let him see this letter.

Is it a sin to use face powder? Shouldn't a girl look beautiful? My father does not want me to use face powder. Is it a sin?

My son is already twenty-six years old and he doesn't want to get married. He says he is a Socialist and he is too busy. Socialism is Socialism and getting married is important too.

I am a Socialist and my boss is a fine man. I know he's a capitalist, but I cannot hate him. Am I doing the wrong thing?

*The Forward* had no right to publish that story. A story

like that will only make more atheists and we have enough too many of them already.

We live on the top floor on Allen Street and the rent is eleven dollars. We have one room and a bedroom and it is dark and filthy. Some of my friends have nice four rooms, clean and nice, because they take in boarders and the rent is paid that way. But my husband says no, he will not take in boarders. I ask him and he says that if it's a girl boarder I'll become jealous and if it's a man that he'll become jealous. He doesn't care how we live. He is in the shop all day and comes home to eat and then he goes again to the lodge. I beg him to take in boarders and he is like steel against it. Let him see this letter and what you should tell him.

If we had fifty space platforms revolving around this planet, the human story would still be told in terms of a man and a woman and the love of a home, and whether a little girl should pierce her ears for earrings. "All else is commentary."

# Yossele Rosenblatt

I GREW up in an "anti-Yossele Rosenblatt" home. My father and older brother were 75 per cent Kwartin men, and 25 per cent Seidel Rovner worshipers. If someone should favorably mention the talents of Yossele Rosenblatt, my father would start a long lecture.

Yossele (Little Joseph) Rosenblatt was one of the most famous cantors of American Jewry. He was of short build with a full black beard. He had a fine tenor voice, with a remarkable falsetto. His son, a rabbi, Dr. Samuel Rosenblatt, has written a heartwarming biography of his father. I remember when the cantor died. Most of New York was very sad, including my father.

When I say that I grew up in an "anti-Yossele Rosenblatt" home, I am merely emphasizing the ebb and flow of life on the East Side. The intellectual Jews fought over their heroes with great violence and many a rolled-up newspaper came into play as men fought over the relative merits of a poet, a cantor, or an editor. One of Cantor Rosenblatt's contemporaries, a kindly old man with a flowing white beard, Seidel Rovner, was a frequent visitor to our home. I remember how thrilled I was to hear my father hum a liturgical melody with him and then my father would turn and say, "That's Seidel's." It seems to me that this elderly Seidel Rovner composed the most tuneful synagogue chants, melodies that could be whistled. But in my house it was all-out KWARTIN. According to my father he possessed a certain skill which was not understood by the average layman. But coming back to Yossele Rosenblatt. This delightful singer of Israel was offered all sorts of money to perform in the opera, but refused on the ground that it was against his religious scruples. However he did go on the concert stage. The cantor more or less surrounded himself with the synagogue even on the concert stage; but I believe that he was not really a concert singer, and it was fortunate that his religious scruples kept him from opera, because it would have been disastrous. When he stuck to the liturgical music of the synagogue he was tops, but when he went over to grand opera it was another story. He was fooled by the American audiences who came out of curiosity to hear a "rabbi" with a beard sing "Mother Machree," but when he tried operatic arias before a highly critical musical audience, as in Buenos Aires and San Francisco, the results were far from satisfactory.

In those days the cantors filled the synagogues from one end of the country to the other and Jews traveled many miles to "hear a chazan." Those were the days when a Kwartin and a Sirota could fill Hunts Point Palace in the Bronx with a seating capacity of four thousand. The decline of the cantors set in with the advent of the English-speaking rabbis. They kept cutting out parts of the liturgy—"Most people can't understand Hebrew"—and gradually the rabbi replaced the cantor, who had held a very high status in the traditional synagogue. It was not unusual for the cantors to be applauded because of the emotion they aroused. Kwartin used to get an ovation when he entered the temple. In some synagogues they had to post watchmen at the door to keep the people from leaving after the cantor was through.

I remember those days very well—the days of the cantor, the High Holy Days, the crowds and the excitement, and the two or three young Communists who were always haranguing the crowds near the entrance to the temple, telling the people they'd do better to go to some hall to hear a lecture. They should live so long.

## Enjoy, enjoy

THE system in all those homes in those days was that the children spoke English to their parents, and the parents answered them in Yiddish.

My mother, may she rest in peace, did not speak English. I hesitate to say that she *couldn't* speak English. I am still not sure. But in our home on New York's Lower East Side she did not speak English.

I remember that we had a telephone installed along about 1920 and the conversation was nearly always the same when one of us called home to say that we'd be late or something. My mother picked up the receiver and I'd say, "Hello, Mom, this is Harry." My mother always answered in Yiddish, "Harry's not home."

"But Mom, THIS is Harry."

Came the one reply, "Harry's not home," and then you heard the fumbling with the hook, the receiver, and usually a crash.

You smiled a bit and decided the only thing to do was to get home when you were expected. As I say, maybe she knew more English than we gave her credit for.

My mother spent her entire life cooking and sewing. On

the Day of Atonement she went to the synagogue. On that day she dressed up in a black dress that made a loud noise as she walked. She wore a gold watch on her breast with a fleur-de-lis mounting. The rest of the time she was in the kitchen at the stove or in the bedroom at the sewing machine. She died in 1924 never having seen a movie nor heard a radio broadcast; and a few weeks before her fatal illness she had taken her first automobile ride. She sat on the edge of the back seat, pleading with the driver to stop so she could get out.

Her English vocabulary consisted in the main of two words —"enjoy" and the old East Side reliable "likewise." Both these words, particularly "likewise" were of tremendous importance to the immigrant people. They poured all their love for America into those two words—"enjoy" and "likewise." When my mother served our meals and placed before us a dish which may have turned out particularly well, she would always say, "Enjoy, enjoy." This word covered hundreds of other situations. When the school had an outing and we all went off with our teachers, the last thing we heard as we went out of the door was "Enjoy, enjoy." But of all English words there was nothing to compare with "likewise." It took care of a multitude of situations. When your mother was called to school and the Gentile teacher started off by saying, "How do you do? You have a smart boy," your mother smiled and at each pause in the conversation she said, "likewise, likewise." It also took care of all introductions. If you introduced anyone to your family, the exchange of pleasantries included at least a dozen "likewises," on both sides. The more assimilated folks also used an entire phrase to good advantage. This phrase was "by the way." How it got started, I don't know, but when the folks were out walking and met someone whom only one of them knew, the introductions were very important, and they invariably started off with, "By the way, meet my friend so-and-so." The phrase "by the way" was also used to good advantage by storytellers and public speakers. Of these three important usages of the English language, the word "enjoy" was seldom used by itself. It was always repeated and "by the way," was of tremendous help to the new Americans. But "likewise" somehow remains a veritable symbol of the New World.

# No opium in the elevator

AFTER the first few weeks behind the desk of the Hotel Markwell, I wouldn't have changed jobs with the editor of *The New York Times*. Managing that hundred-room house on Forty-ninth Street, thirty yards west of Broadway, was like reading the *1001 Nights* with such narrators as Stendhal, Zola, Boccaccio, Dopey Benny, Samuel Leibowitz, Broadway Rose, Rabelais, Jenny-the-Factory, and Damon Runyon.

My brother Jack had operated two small European-plan hotels in Manhattan, and in 1932 he had acquired the Markwell. There were few newspaper jobs open at that critical moment of my life, and Jack had tactfully suggested that I take the job of manager and day clerk.

I managed the hotel until the spring of 1938 and for over five years was able to observe the Broadway scene from the "inside."

Across the street was Jacobs' Beach, where the men of the fight game congregated. I set aside a conference room for managers, promoters, and matchmakers; a typewriter was always available for a young sports writer by the name of Jimmy Cannon and for an older sports writer by the name of Hype Igoe—a breed of men that has made New York the true Seventh Wonder of the World.

To my right was the Paradise night club, with Paul Whiteman, Johnny Hauser, Goldie, Jack Teagarden, and Ramona. Some of them lived in fancier hotels, but they stored their instruments in my basement, and changed their clothes in my rooms. And many a musician gave me his money for safekeeping when he was going on a drunk.

To my left was the Forrest Theatre, where one of my former guests, Maude O'Dell, was playing Sister Bessie in the original *Tobacco Road*. Miss O'Dell died in her dressing room one night, and Vinnie Phillips took her place and continued in the role for another two years. The world doth move. I had no idea that my own place one day would be in the North Carolina that Maude O'Dell had spoken pridefully of as her home.

I gave away hundreds of tickets to *Tobacco Road*. This was common procedure when a new show was not going well. They'd give passes to hotel clerks to hand out to tourists on the theory that the tourists would go home and tell friends not to miss it. Then *Tobacco Road* was "banned in Boston," as the saying goes, and it went on to the longest run in theatrical history.

I never thought much of the play. It bored me to tears. It was nothing more than a surface caricature of a few stock characters out of vaudeville, the Southern counterpart of the stage-Jew with the derby pulled over his ears, the stage-Irishman with a red nose and a can of beer, the stage-Negro with a knife and a pair of dice.

Of the groups thus stereotyped, only the Irish knew what to do. As soon as the Knights of Columbus acquired some strength, they decided to take care of the stage-Irishman, and they settled the entire matter one Saturday night simultaneously in New York and in Boston—with eggs and tomatoes. The stage-Irishman disappeared from vaudeville, and to this day no one accuses the Irishman of being oversensitive, and few Irishmen have heard the label "chauvinist."

I was clerking at the Markwell at about the time when Jack Amron (a *Mr. Broadway* whose name rarely got into the papers) put up the money for Jack Dempsey's first restaurant. Mr. Amron also owned the Hollywood night club. Dempsey's was a first-class eating place on Eighth Avenue diagonally across from Madison Square Garden, but it was a failure (do not confuse it with the Dempsey establishment now on Broadway, a successful tourist restaurant). I met Mr. Amron one day and asked him how things were going. Pointing to the original Dempsey's, he said, "There, I give them a wonderful steak dinner for two-fifty and business is lousy." Then point-

ing in the direction of the Hollywood night club, Mr. Amron
continued, "Up there I give them food which is not fit to eat
for five dollars, but they also get three naked dancing girls,
and the place is filled to capacity every night. To hell with
good food."

I remember giving a room to Jack Johnson, the ex-heavy-
weight champion. He was working in a flea circus on West
Forty-second Street and he needed a night's lodging. I took
him in, beret and all. And the next morning, five or six non-
paying guests raised hell about my having a Negro guest in
the hotel. How do you like that?

Many small hotels become headquarters for specific trades
and occupations; the burlesque girls go to one place, the
carnival men to another, and so forth. The Markwell had in-
herited a fraternity all its own—the ocean-liner card sharks.
I knew them all and listened to a thousand interesting stories.
Occasionally two of them would be off with their beautiful
luggage only to return two hours later with the announcement: "The purser tipped us off—no one with real dough on
this trip."

When the card sharks returned from an ocean voyage, they
went straight to the typewriter in the lobby, even before
shedding their overcoats. They wrote a letter and sent it over
to the post office marked "registered mail, return receipt requested." The letter was to the American Express Company
as follows:

Gentlemen: On an ocean voyage on the S. S. so-and-so
on such and such dates, the undersigned won the following money orders in a series of poker games from the
following people . . .

This was for the card shark's protection. Usually the first
thing the "score" (sucker) did when he hit dry land was to
send a telegram to the American Express Company that he
had lost his book of money orders and would they please stop
payment on same and send him duplicates.

But like most gamblers, prostitutes, and touts, the seagoing card sharks were excellent hotel guests—no noise, no drinking, and no practice of their profession on the premises.

The big heartache came from the tourists. Some of them would steal everything they could lay their hands on—towels, sheets, pillowcases, blankets, Gideon Bibles, and electric bulbs. The Markwell is probably the only hotel in the world where a guest once stole a medicine cabinet off the bathroom wall. How the guy got it out of the hotel is still a mystery to me.

I leaned backward to keep the hotel straight. I established a direct line of communication with Lieutenant Coy of the Forty-seventh Street police station (this is the headquarters you saw in the movie with Kirk Douglas, *Detective Story*). I recalled that when Wilson Mizner managed a Broadway hotel he had notified his guests that there would be no smoking of opium in the elevator. I put this same order into effect from the first day. And I had trouble with only one guest. I shall call this fellow who had been a vaudeville hoofer in his early days Frank Jones. Now he was about forty and still slim and handsome. He earned a hundred dollars a week dancing with the mistress of a very fat and very rich construction tycoon. Many of these old, fat tycoons hired an "escort" when they took a mistress out on the town. Thus, if the tycoon's wife or his wife's lawyer spotted them, the tycoon could pretend he had just happened by while two handsome young people were having a good time. Jones went along on these night club trips in his evening clothes once a week and got paid off his hundred dollars in the hallway of the gal's apartment before she and the tycoon went upstairs. Jones smoked opium. I was sure of it. The opium smokers do not consider themselves addicts. They call it a "pleasure smoke." What stopped me from throwing this Jones out of the hotel was the fact that we had no evidence. One day when Jones had gone to the race track I had a friendly narcotics expert examine his room. There was no doubt that opium was being smoked there, but where was the evidence? Smoking opium involves elaborate preparation. You cannot hide the evidence in your pocket. First of all you have the pipes—with their yard-long stems; and then the burner, a sort of Bunsen burner that roasts the opium pellet, and the tongs with which you lift the roasting opium pellet into the pipe. All of this the opium smokers call a "layout," and it is bulky. But where was it? We never found a trace of it. Years later, in the 1940's, I learned about Jones' hiding place. He told me.

The hotel had a perpendicular sign running down the entire length of the ten-story building, H O T E L  M A R K-W E L L. The broad bottom of this heavy neon sign was directly opposite Jones' room. Somehow he had had a tinsmith cut a panel in the side of the sign and all he had to do was lean out the window for his equipment. He told me this and he walked away with his lopsided walk and I thought, "You put one over on us, but brother, you can have it."

The hotel, of course, did not earn its operating costs and interest. My brother had bought it for the price of the mortgage, and, with a low rate of interest, he was willing to wait for the return of prosperity, which, of course, was just around the corner.

I had not been manager long, however, when I discovered that several people connected with the place were indeed making it pay. I came upon this intelligence when an employee of another hotel offered three hundred dollars cash if I put him on as a bellhop at the Markwell. Why should a man offer a three-hundred-dollar bonus for a twelve-dollar-a-week job? I took the necessary steps to eliminate this source of revenue for the night shift, by putting into effect three new rules: (a) no room was to be rented to a "single" woman, (b) no female was to be allowed to visit a male guest, except in the lobby; and (c) no couple could get a room unless they had baggage.

Of course I made some exceptions to my single-women rule. I had, for instance, Pauline Boyle, a famous theatrical agent who had helped launch the careers of such performers as Spencer Tracy, Pat O'Brien, and Ralph Bellamy. There was Mamie McBride, a seventy-five-year-old stalwart for whom the late Henry Chesterfield paid the rent out of some

fund of the National Vaudeville Artists. Another guest I shall
call Ann Clarke because of her present eminence, a charming
Southern girl with two remarkable talents, playing the piano
and consuming whisky. There was also Florence Walker. Miss
Walker operated a sight-seeing bus which was the only commercial vehicle permitted to pass through the gates of all the
major race tracks, from Aqueduct to Havre de Grace. This
exclusive privilege had been given her for life many years
before by one whom *Time* magazine would call her "great
and good friend," the famous private detective, Captain
Pinkerton. Miss Walker knew every owner, trainer, breeder,
jockey, and bookmaker in the East.

But, during the last three weeks of her life, her Italian bus
driver and I were her only visitors at Bellevue. She wrote a
note leaving me a set of ivory poker chips that had once belonged to America's greatest gambler, Mr. Canfield; but,
since I do not play cards, I passed them on to a friend.

# The ghetto and the plantation

IN TIMES of stress our minds go back to a happier time.
We recall the days of childhood, or the days of an earlier
period in history. The idea that we can never again be as
happy as we were then adds charms to our memories.

The middle-class Jews of America think back upon the
cold-water flats of the Lower East Side and the Southerner
thinks back upon the plantation society, and both are thinking of the past because of the same fears—mobility of the
urban middle class, the uncertainties surrounding their status,
and the social changes involved in industrialization of an agricultural society.

I believe Southern dramatists and novelists have gone a bit
overboard in debunking the Old South. Their revelation that
only a small percentage of the folks owned slaves and that
the great majority were poor tenant farmers is irrelevant.

What difference does it make whether his great-grandfather had a plantation or not? He is hanging onto an idea; that is the important thing.

And Tara, the Old Plantation, the Old Plank Road, the Old Homestead have the symbolic validity of the settlement houses on East Broadway.

I'm a settlement-house man myself, of course, and I think back fondly, too, to Anschel Chvawk, the lemonade man. He drove a wagon with a huge glass vat, full of lemons and chunks of ice, and sold his product all over the East Side at one penny a glass. On hot days I always thought how good it would be to take my shoes and stockings off and jump into that big lemonade vat, like the French girls making champagne.

On Grand and Cannon Streets was the Manhattan Pie Baking Company and kids could get six cuts of day-old pies, six different kinds, for a nickel. They were "seconds." You could also buy a lot of seconds at the big bakery on Willett Street, where crackers were three pounds for a dime. In Katz's and in Knabe's you got a big veal cutlet with French-fried potatoes for a dime.

The Socialists, of course, were important then. Morris Hillquit was a brilliant speaker, and so were Louis Waldman and Congressman Meyer London; but my own favorites were Scott Nearing, Algernon Lee, Norman Thomas, and August Claessens. Claessens was a Roman Catholic and of course the Jews were pleased and flattered when he threw a few Yiddish words into his speeches.

Tammany Hall did everything to harass the Socialist spellbinders. Occasionally a few Tammany henchmen would set up a soapbox on the corner opposite the Socialist speaker. When the Socialist began to speak, the Tammany Hallniks would begin to sing: "Tammany, Tammany; swampum, swampum, get the wampum, Tammanieee." Tammany had the help of the police, and the big thing was to demand a license from the Socialist and thereby upset his meeting. "Where is your license to speak here?" demanded a policeman of Claessens one evening. Claessens stalled as the cop made a path in the crowd around the stand. With perfect timing Claessens then shouted: "My license to speak here was given to me on July 4, 1776, in the City of Philadelphia." The cop scratched his head and ran back to the call box to ask the desk sergeant what to do next—and the crowd roared.

The soapbox Socialists were advocating social security, unemployment insurance, and public housing, and they were harassed and arrested. Now Richard Nixon is for social security, unemployment insurance, and public housing, and this could happen only in America.

How many thousands of Jews fondly remember the intellectual vitality of the East Side—an intellectual vitality without parallel in our country's history.

It was the desire to learn and it began early. It began with the young Orthodox boy when his father wrapped him in the talith (prayer cloth) and opened the book to teach him his first aleph (the letter A), and occasionally the folks went far back into the folklore and dropped a coin on the page as the boy was concentrating, and they told him that an angel had dropped the coin as a reward for passing his first lesson. And you remember the quiet of the holidays, and on every second block a sign, "Lecture Tonight," and technical schools, the kind that our educational experts are now demanding for all America. The clubs and debating societies became so numerous that authorities found it necessary to permit use of classrooms, and kept the public schools open at night.

And how they voted. You heard the word "vote" for days before and after an election. Children boasted to one another, "My father can vote," and factory workers and peddlers always carried their "second papers" (final citizenship) in their pockets.

My district, "The Ate" (Eighth Congressional), was the largest Jewish district in New York, which meant, of course, the largest in the Western world.

Such are the memories cherished by so many thousands of the middle-class Jews of America.

It is more than nostalgia and memory of a family and a home. It is remembering earliest beginnings. Earliest begin-

nings may not always be pleasant, but when they turn out to
be successful you honor them all the days of your life.


# Poison ivy terrified Tammany

It was probably our section's teeming mass of humanity
that gave the elementary school· teachers the idea when it
came to writing compositions. The subject nearly always was,
"Would You Rather Live in the Country or in the City?" Or,
if it was "The City Versus the Country," you were expected
to give an argument for each side.

When it was time to write about "the city," we were experts; but, in stating the case for "the country," I must admit
we floundered a bit. Of course most of us had had some experience in growing grass between the cracks in the sidewalk.

In the summer months, especially during a dry spell, we
would get up early, and, armed with a cup of water, we
would rush out into the street to water our patches, and
we would count the blades to make sure we were progressing.

To this day you can tell an old East Sider by the way he
walks, whether he lives in Charlotte, Detroit, or San Francisco, because a boy who grew up on the East Side will never
step on the cracks between the blocks of sidewalk cement.

We had still other contacts with rural life.

Twice a year our teachers would take us to the Bronx Zoo.
Most of us carried pencil and paper on these trips to record
notes on such phenomena as trees, birds' nests, wild animals,
and snakes.

We could also draw heavily on our experience on the "Big
Semiannual Tammany Hall Outing." This was a boat excursion to Bear Mountain up the Hudson River, and it was
sponsored by the local Tammany Hall boss, whose slogan
was: "A sound body makes a sound citizen."

The Tammany Hall leader was terribly afraid of poison ivy.
We were briefed for an hour before each trip on how not

to catch poison ivy. Tammany Hall had reason to fear it. A case of poison ivy could not only reduce the chances of the boy's becoming a good Tammany voter eight or ten years hence, but there was a great danger of actually losing current votes.

The parting words we heard from the hundred open windows as we marched off to the boat were: "Don't let me hear that you got poison ivy."

By the time we reached our destination we were so terrified of catching poison ivy that we could not enjoy the country.

We were very careful not to brush up against branches or clumps of bushes and many of us literally tiptoed along the grassy slopes of the beautiful Hudson palisades.

But the Tammany outing was counted a success if we were able to report truthfully: "No, Mama, I swear I didn't catch poison ivy."

# A klug zu Columbus'n

A FAMILIAR expression among the immigrants of the East Side was, "A klug zu Columbus'n," which, freely translated, meant that Columbus should have broken his head before he discovered it (America). The expression was always used in good humor and often with sincere fondness.

The Jewish immigrants associated America with Columbus, which seems logical enough. Perhaps it was a sort of mass inspiration to right an injustice inflicted upon the Genoese explorer by the interloper Amerigo Vespucci. Even the Italians, who had a big parade on Columbus Day, did not have the same feeling about the matter. They thought of the famous explorer wholly in terms of a national hero of Italy. They did not make the words "America" and "Columbus" interchangeable as did the Jewish immigrants.

To the Jews Columbus was a contemporary. And why not? What's 1492 to a people who have been contemporaneous with all of recorded history? Yesterday—that's what it is. Thus

when we came to America in 1899, or thereabouts, we had
one fact established in our minds—that we had been preceded
by Columbus, that's all.

And, of course, everybody said, "A klug zu Columbus'n."
If the kid got into a fight and came home with a bloody nose,
his mother said, "A klug zu Columbus'n," or if the steam
wasn't hot enough in the Turkish baths the old gents were
sure to say, "A klug zu Columbus'n."

My mother would be walking home with her basket from
the market and she would tell of the promises made to her
by Jehovah about everybody living under his vine and fig
tree in the land of Canaan, and then she would look up to
our top-floor tenement flat opposite the Wallers' horse stables,
and she would say, "A klug zu Columbus'n."

But, of course, it was a term of endearment all along.
When the first child was born on American soil, the immigrant mother referred to her new child as "Mein Columbus'l"
(My little Columbus). This child was special. And, interest-
ingly enough, the young brothers and sisters who had been
born in Europe felt no resentment. It was *their* Columbus'l,
too. And so complete was this Columbus identification that
the entire East Side sang a popular song from one of the
successful Yiddish musicals, and it was called "Leben Zul
Columbus" (Long Live Columbus).

## Enoch Arden and the clothing industry

WE ALWAYS did some kind of work after school. For a few
years I sold Yiddish newspapers and during the Passover
season I delivered matzos. Once I worked as errand boy and
sweeper in a hat store. The manager was a fellow by the
name of Kokush. The little fellow could sell hats in every
language and he had four or five signs posted in the window
which proclaimed that, "Here is spoken Polish, Russian,
Italian, German, and Yiddish." Up on the corner was a

restaurant operated by a Mr. and Mrs. Garfein. Well, Mrs. Garfein was a very huge woman with a shining pleasant face who was the cashier in the restaurant. Kokush fell desperately in love with Mrs. Garfein, but it was entirely one-sided. Mrs. Garfein knew nothing about it, and I am sure Mr. Garfein, who was twice the size of Kokush, was also ignorant of his silent rival. Mr. Kokush's only demonstration of his deep devotion was to sit in the restaurant and look at Mrs. Garfein. The moment I came into the store after school, Kokush would say, "I am going for a coffee." Between three and six o'clock Kokush went for a coffee at least four times. He would drink the coffee slowly, and look at Mrs. Garfein.

But what changed all this was the day the "Eldridge Streeters" came. On the Lower East Side the boys divided into "Streeters." If you lived on Rivington Street you were ready to die for Rivington Street and fight to the death against the Allen Streeters.

Well, on this day, while Kokush was out for a coffee, about ten Eldridge Streeters swooped down upon the hat store. Holding a "sword" up against my belly, the hoodlums fitted themselves out with brand-new caps—all ten of them, and each boy took along an extra cap for "my little brudder." They warned me not to tell Kokush until they had rounded the corner, which instructions I followed to the letter. When I finally arrived at the restaurant, there was Kokush looking at Mrs. Garfein, and I was very sad when I had to tell him what had happened. Mr. Kokush told me to get a policeman, while he ran back to the store. Poor Kokush never again went out for a coffee during store hours. I remember him standing at the curb, hour after hour, just looking toward the restaurant where Mrs. Garfein was the cashier.

Later, while going to the East Side Evening High School, I worked for a manufacturer of ladies' straw hats, Arnold Rosenbaum & Company. I was fifteen years old, but fat and strong, and I was a sizer. Let me explain the duties of a sizer. The machine operators, all girls, sat in two long rows facing each other, about thirty on each side. These girls took the raw hemp or straw and sewed it into a hat according to specifications. But it was still a more or less shapeless mass when the hat came to me. I worked beside a huge vat of boiling glue into which I dipped the hats, about three or four at a time. I made sure that I also immersed the spot where my fingers held the straw.

Every time I dipped the hats I thought of Thetis, the mother of Achilles. She attempted to make him immortal by bathing him in the River Styx, but the water did not touch the heel by which she held him. He killed Hector, but was himself killed when Paris wounded him in his only vulnerable spot—the heel. There was no Achilles' heel in any of my straw hats, but to this day I can hold my right hand under scalding water without pain or damage. After I took the straw hat out of the glue I put it on a wooden block approximately the shape the headgear would eventually assume and hammered it out with the palms of my hands.

The following morning the dried hats went to the blocker who put them in a hydraulic press which worked by steam. He had to keep a hat in the press just long enough for it to assume its permanent shape but not a single moment too long, or it would burn. The hat blocker was a fellow by the name of Yonkel, a recent immigrant from Russia who did not understand a word of English. Apparently he had carefully worked out his own timing system. He sang two lines of a Yiddish song he had brought from Russia:

> Es vet kommen a zeit
> Ven se vet nisht zein vos tzu essen.
> (There'll come a time
> When there'll be nothing to eat.)

He put the hat in the press and pulled the lever and sang out, "Es vet kommen a zeit," and then he raised the lever on the second line, "Ven se vet nisht zein vos tzu essen," and if you added that *krechtz* Yonkel gave at the end, it represented the exact length of time the hat was supposed to be in the press. With those two lines of his song as his guide, the man never spoiled a single hat. I heard the two lines of that song five hundred times a day, every day for over a year. I never did hear the rest of it.

During one summer vacation I delivered pants for a Mr. Wasserman, a pants contractor. I delivered the pants to the best tailors on Fifth Avenue, as well as to a few on lower Broadway who served the Wall Street tycoons. I learned that a suit made to order involved only the coat as far as the exclusive tailor was concerned. The pants were made outside by a pants contractor. The exclusive tailor supplied the material and the measurements. The pants contractor cut the cloth and his operators sewed the pieces together. Then each pair of pants was rolled into a bundle and delivered to Italian women in the tenement district. These home workers were "findishers." The women referred to themselves, "Ima da findish" (finisher). These women sewed in the pockets and fixed the buttons. There were no zippers in those days. When I picked up the finished pants, I gave the woman a little ticket, and, at the end of the week, I took all her tickets, gave her a receipt, and brought back her money, based on piecework. I never remember paying out any more at one time than it costs now for a pint of Early Times bourbon. The pants contractor put the final touches on the garment, and pressing was the last operation. Then about ten pairs of pants were slung across my shoulder, each with a label pinned to the cuff, and I delivered them on a mapped-out route. The pay was seven dollars a week.

I was supposed to work from nine in the morning to six in the evening. On a very hot day when everything had been delivered, Mr. Wasserman left at two o'clock and said to me, "I'll be back at half past five." But he never came back, and at six o'clock I locked up and went home. Later I found out that Mr. Wasserman went to Coney Island for a good time and just wanted me to hang around the full time. After I got on to him, however, he would leave at two, and I left at five minutes after two, even with his I'll-be-back-at-half-past-five business. It wasn't such a bad job. I took the streetcar on my deliveries and I always had a book in my pocket. I memorized "Enoch Arden" and Gray's "Elegy" on that job.

# I was a $300 angel

LESTER was a handsome actor who was also a theatrical manager, a promoter, and a super-salesman. It was while he was a guest in the hotel I managed just off Broadway that Lester got his great idea.

Lester's idea was to establish a repertory company in Manhattan and produce such melodramas as *Nellie the Beautiful Cloak Model, No Mother to Guide Her,* and *Over the Hill to the Poor House*—the type of show in which you hiss the villain and drink beer during the performance. But that was only part of Lester's idea. Instead of using "regulation" actors, Lester planned to produce his shows with a cast composed exclusively of "little people"—midgets.

It did not take me long to close the deal. For three hundred dollars, payable in six weekly installments, I was to own a 10 per cent interest in the production, including road companies, motion-picture rights, and a share of the profits from the sale of beer and pretzels. Lester closed a deal with William, a "little people" entrepreneur, and soon rehearsals began with a company of eight midgets, including William, in *No Mother to Guide Her*. Lester arranged for the use of the President Theatre on West Forty-eighth Street. His contract contained a clause for the right to change the name of the theatre to the Midget Theatre "after the first one-hundred-days run of the play."

Ann Clarke, the talented pianist, joined the company as arranger of the musical score and director. In lieu of salary, she agreed to accept 5 per cent of the profits.

*No Mother to Guide Her* opened on December 25, 1933. At 8:30 P.M. there were exactly seventy-four people in the audience and at least forty of them were guests of my hotel.

Ann Clarke was in the pit playing the opening music and, as the curtain rose, all the midgets seemed to be talking at the same time.

The top of Ann's piano was slightly below the line of vision from the orchestra seats. The audience saw only her hand raising the glass to the top of the piano. When the hand would reach back, and while she was drinking, they heard one-handed piano music.

After a while the audience was in hysterics watching the hand and the glass. Then the midgets got to fighting among themselves on the stage and everyone walked out and went home about halfway through the third act.

That was the shortest run in the history of Broadway—a one-night run of two-and-a-half acts of a three-act play.

Calm settled over the hotel the next day. Lester left for upstate New York to see about a managerial job. A close examination of the daily press revealed that only the *New York Post* had reviewed *No Mother to Guide Her*.

It was early in the morning of the second day after the events at the President Theatre that I heard the voices. I looked around but saw no one. I pulled the plugs out of the switchboard and listened for a moment, but there had been no mistake. I leaned over the marble top of the hotel desk, and, sure enough, the voices were those of midgets— about four or five of them. The spokesman quickly told me the purpose of their visit. They wanted the balance of their rehearsal pay. They had been given to understand that the show had the backing of a "big hotel man," and for that reason they had played along with Lester. The next two weeks were rough ones for me. Wherever I went, I saw midgets. They called me on the telephone and every morning a midget was waiting for me in the lobby. Finally I sat down with Mr. William himself, gave him a complete history of my relatively remote connection with the production, proved to him that I was merely a glorified hotel clerk, and he took it with surprisingly good grace.

For two weeks I did not see Ann Clarke, the pianist. Soon, however, Franklin D. Roosevelt changed everything.

Miss Clarke and the rest of my guests got jobs with the Federal Theatre Project of the WPA, and most of them began to pay room rent with those green government checks for $23.80 each; and right then and there I coined the phrase: "This could happen only in America."

Where else can people on work relief live in a hotel just off Broadway?

## The Sweet Sixteen party

I DO NOT hear anything about those old Sweet Sixteen parties any more.

On the East Side the poorest family gave a daughter a Sweet Sixteen party. It was a big event—undoubtedly springing from the same tradition which, in higher economic brackets, produced the coming-out party or the debutantes' ball. All cultures and peoples have had some sort of ceremony for the maiden when she became eligible for marriage.

How the old folks scrimped and saved, and how nervous the young girl and the parents were when the guests arrived—especially the young boys. The byword at these parties, if you could hear anything above the giggling, was "Sweet sixteen and never been kissed," and in those days it was literally true.

And the Sweet Sixteen party was no green light either. Not by any means. The parents had to see the boy and give him a thorough going-over before any courting was in order. The mother would make discreet inquiries in the meat market about the boy's mother, and the father would be doing the same thing with respect to the male parent. Of course, the boy's parents would be doing it, too, only more thoroughly. It was very important to have nice relatives by marriage. Each family took into serious account the character, standing, appearance of members of the "opposing" family, down to second cousins.

In a boy, learning was the first qualification—how much

learning does he have? Serious consideration was also given to how much learning the father had. A learned father shuddered at the thought of his child's marrying into a family where the opposite father was not a learned man.

But after World War I a change came to the Lower East Side and to the rest of America, and the question now was "How much does he earn?" or, "What kind of a car does he drive?"

However, I see a renaissance coming! The tremendous energy directed to technology and money-making will soon seek an outlet in books and culture.

I see a renaissance of learning. So take heed; set your children toward the sun; put them on the right course, because, when this comes to pass, even the wonderful Sweet Sixteen party will come back.

## The Verein doctor

IN THE Jewish culture, we always avoided revealing the full extent of our sorrow in order to keep going (and also confuse the evil eye). Nothing was ever discussed in precise terms. Either we talked around it or used a euphemism.

Thus, you would never say a relative had tuberculosis. You always referred to tuberculosis as "a touch." The immigrants pounced upon this linguistic convenience. "He has a touch of bronchitis," they heard the doctors say, and so now tuberculosis became "a touch." "He has a touch." This was not so devastating and it sustained the illusion that the workingman could continue going to the shop every day. This happened in the days of the sweatshop and the Jewish cemeteries in Brooklyn and Maspeth filled up with workers who died of "a touch." In those days we joked about tuberculosis: we called it "Jewish asthma," just as we called some people "Jewish millionaires" because they had $3,000 in the savings bank.

The "Verein" doctor understood all of this very well. The immigrant Jews formed fraternities here, usually based on the places of origin in the old country. We called them "societies" or "Vereins" and one of the benefits of membership was that you had the services of a doctor. All of this has been erroneously propagandized as "socialized medicine" (which all of us will come to anyway in another twenty years with our growing maturity). The Verein doctor had nothing to do with "socialization." He had to do with health and survival. He was not only a doctor but usually also a philosopher.

The Verein doctor worked in the days before specialized medicine and of course lacked the wonderful remedies and specialized skills doctors have at their command today. Actually, his main weapon was psychological. Your father was sick. There was sorrow in the house. Suddenly the door opened and Dr. Frankel came in—and everybody felt better. His very presence was a comfort. In the Verein you paid fifty cents every three months and that entitled you to a doctor and you'd be surprised how many doctors competed for the appointment. They had no way of knowing that many of these immigrants and their children would rise up in the world and keep them on as personal physicians for life. They were Verein doctors who healed the sick, inspired confidence, and then went into the kitchen and had a glass of hot tea with your mother. A confinement case was "extra" —fifteen dollars was the Verein assessment—and if you were a member of the Verein, you received a discount on your medicines. I remember the huge apothecary where we bought the prescriptions. It was right next to Mandell's bank and it was owned by a man named Lindemann who always gave me a piece of kondel-zucer (rock candy) when I came in.

These wonderful men, the Verein doctors, climbed four or five flights of tenement stairs countless times a day. When they discovered Jewish asthma in the chest of a sweatshop worker, they knew they could not advise him to go to a warmer and drier climate. This man had a wife and four children in the house and couldn't afford to lose one day's wages. What could the doctor do for him? Often only prescribe cough medicine and tell the workingman to rest as much as possible after work and once in a while the Verein doctor would write on the prescription slip, "Join the cloak-makers' union."

# She waited thirty-two years

WE OWE a great debt to Dr. Samuel Buchler, legal scholar and humanitarian. Dr. Buchler was one of the founders of the New York Jewish Court of Arbitration, an organization which saved the state of New York millions of dollars in court costs. In addition, the litigants could secure immediate settlement and satisfaction, with each represented by counsel. Before each session three judges were appointed, a rabbi, a businessman, and a jurist. The decision was announced as soon as the arguments were presented, as was the custom in ancient Judea. At each session, a jurist of the New York courts was present to attend to the compatibility of the rulings with the laws of the state.

A record of the cases would offer a writer the ideas for a few thousand wonderful short stories as well as the history and the psychology of our people.

Here's a sample:

The woman was sixty-one and her husband a year older. She was suing for divorce. She spoke without passion but with deep conviction. She said that her husband had never been a good man. He was unkind, stingy, and selfish. One of the judges asked her the obvious question: "You have been married thirty-two years and now when you are both past middle age you want a divorce; if your husband is all you say he is, why haven't you asked for a divorce before?"

The woman persisted: "My husband was never a good man; I never had a happy day with him, but I could not ask for a divorce until now; first there were the children, then measles, then school, and bar mitzvahs, illnesses, report cards, engagement parties, preparations for everything, and finally weddings; and now that the children are married and settled, I want to be alone and away from a man who never had a kind word for me in thirty-two years."

Two other witnesses gave testimony. The divorce was granted.

## Soup greens and Caruso

Two weeks before the High Holy Days, the teeming tenements of the Lower East Side took on an atmosphere of high expectation. There were no longer factory workers or scholars, peddlers or teachers. There were only Jews preparing for the annual period of rededication.

Then on the first night of the High Holy Days, the streets became silent, dark, and deserted. The men who experienced this can never forget it. I say men because the girls were kept in the house. All year there had been the unceasing din of voices, haggling over purchases, shouting from the windows, the thousands of horse-drawn vehicles and pushcarts clattering over the cobblestones, and a million other sounds in two or three different languages and in ten different dialects and accents. But now the street stands were boarded up and the stores were shuttered. Everybody was home around the table, and the heavy aroma of the mouth-watering dishes followed you into the darkness and the amazing silence of the street.

We lived on Eldridge, between Rivington and Delancey. I was always interested in the names of the streets. This was the exclusive residential section before the Revolutionary War and many of the streets were named for members of the nobility and colonial governors.

The immigrants had their own private pronunciations for the streets: Assick (Essex); Eldrich (Eldridge); Riv-INK-ton (Rivington); Stentin (Stanton); Ritt (Ridge); and Orchard, with an initial *h* and a final double *t*. And so for the first time in its history the telephone company had to change the name of an exchange, because when the folks called an Orchard number they had the telephone operators in hysterics. They changed it to Drydock, and precious little the folks could do with that one.

We had our share of bad boys who wound up in Sing Sing, but the vast majority worked from the day they were able to count change. We sold newspapers, handkerchiefs (two for a nickel), "five o'clock teas" (a cracker which we bought by the box of fifty for a nickel and sold five for a penny).

We referred only to our American schoolteachers as "Christians." We did not use this designation for our non-Jewish neighbors, whom we called Italians, "Polacks," Russians, Ukrainians and "Irishers."

The first Negro I remember was a big happy fellow whom we kids followed for two or three blocks. We were not disrespectful or abusive, but only curious, and the big fellow kept turning back to us roaring with laughter, and I remember his gold teeth as though it all had happened yesterday. We were familiar with the Chinese, of course. Chinatown was ten blocks away.

Another outsider was the alcoholic unfortunate, usually a woman, who waited outside the "family entrance" of the beer saloons for a handout and slept on straw provided her by the generous manager of a pushcart stable. This woman had undoubtedly been discarded by her uptown civilization and sought refuge in a district where no one knew her and where the barrier of language would provide her with some insulation against the rejection and her terrible torment. Usually, she was a prostitute, but not in the truest sense of the word. She practiced it only when she had to, as a means to an end—whisky—and as fast as one was found dead in some alley, another would soon be making her rounds. We called these women "Mary, Mary, Sugar Bum," with the cruelty for which all children are infamous.

The tenement houses were built close together and families

occupied an average of five rooms for approximately thirty dollars a month rent. But, of course, all the rooms, including the kitchen, were sleeping rooms, depending on the size of the family and the number of boarders. On those terribly humid nights for which New York is famous, we slept on the roof, or on the fire escape. Then came the rains and the scurrying inside, dragging the wet sheets and pillows behind. The window sills were used for cooling food and that made it risky to walk on the sidewalk. Nearly every day you heard the loud explosion of a bottle of seltzer crashing upon the sidewalk below. In the early days the garbage would also be thrown out of the window, and Friday night was particularly dangerous.

There was poverty and distress, but there was always food. In 1910 you couldn't carry the groceries you could buy for four dollars. On market days my mother always took one of us along to help her carry the basket and the side packages. She usually spent all of three dollars and thirty cents. And the butcher always gave you a big piece of liver, free, "for the cat." One day each week I would gather up the accumulated newspapers and take them down to the vegetable man who used them for wrapping paper, and in exchange he gave me a big package of soup greens, an assortment of soup-stock vegetables. Very good, too. You can't get a plate of soup like that today. They are not ashamed today to charge you thirty-five cents for a plate of turkey broth. My mother used that stuff to rinse out the pot.

My mother made potato soup with those greens and browned onions. You could eat half a loaf of bread with a huge bowl of that soup and it was quite a meal. This was topped off with a penny. You could buy many things with a penny. I traded with "Cheap Haber" on Rivington Street. The owners of all these penny stores used the prefix "Cheap"— "Cheap Abe's," "Cheap Max's." Often we waited for the second penny and went to the movies. I remember when the news leaked out that our movie idol, Bronco Billy Anderson, was a Jewish boy whose real name was Sam Aaronsohn. The elderly Jews spat three times to show that they were not impressed. A Jewish cowboy yet? What else will happen to us in America? As yet there was no cultural pride in cowboys, prize fighters, or basketball players. The East Side heroes in my day were still the cantors in the synagogues, the famous violinists, the journalists and poets, and above everyone else the Yiddish actors on the legitimate stage. To all of these was added the special dispensation for a Christian, Enrico Caruso, whom the Jews on the East Side loved with great passion. (Two of the most beloved Christians in the history of the American-Jewish community were Enrico Caruso and Theodore Roosevelt. I doubt whether anyone else, before or since, has ever enjoyed the same degree of reverence and devotion.)

I believe the memories of the East Side linger for many Jews because, there, for a moment in history, we were the "majority." Wherever you looked, you saw a member of the clan. It was a huge clubhouse, poverty and all.

This is what made the East Side—a ghetto with all the advantages of living within a homogeneous community, and yet in freedom. You could enter the "open society" whenever you felt like it. No one stopped you. The entire American civilization was waiting.

I have written a great deal about the Lower East Side of New York. I may have inadvertently repeated myself a few times, of course, but, on the other hand, I haven't really begun.

The quarter of a million words I have written to date are only by way of introduction.

# The pencil was a prop

In the old days everybody had his picture taken. The immigrant shed his Old World clothes and the first thing he wanted to do was have his picture taken "as an American." The portrait studios made lots of money. I remember we had six or seven pictures of various relatives hanging on the wall and each of the subjects wore eyeglasses and a few of them also held a pencil in the right hand. This is very funny, and yet it is so downright sad that it catches you in the throat just thinking about it; because you realize how desperate was the drive for education, status, making something of oneself. They had seen doctors, lawyers, and teachers with eyeglasses. And therefore every picture gallery had a box of assorted styles of eyeglasses. When the fellow posed you he said, "How about a pair of eyeglasses?" knowing you would be too shy to suggest it yourself. You acted a bit coy, but you were very grateful to the man, especially when he also put a pencil in your hand.

## Pumpernickel and Scott's Emulsion

THE general health on the East Side was good—plenty of pumpernickel bread, butter, and sour cream. Sweet cream was for those who had tuberculosis. When a woman asked for sweet cream in the grocery, all the other women would step aside respectfully and let her be served first, because she had sickness in the family; everybody was very sad.

Did you ever rub garlic on the crust of a piece of pumpernickel top-heavy with chicken fat? Good slabs of whitefish and onion, pumpernickel bread, a pint of beer for the adults or coffee with lots of chicory for the young folks—and you were all set for the winter. Overcoats? Who needed overcoats? We had Scott's Emulsion. The immigrant women just loved that Scott's Emulsion—with the advertisement of the fellow in a slicker and rain hat hauling a big fish—and with all of that you went out to conquer the world. The point of the whole matter is that so many really *did* go out and conquer the world. Surgeons, scientists, artists, manufacturers, tycoons, lawyers, judges. It is probably the most amazing immigrant story in all history.

# From door to door

THE pack peddler worked from door to door throughout the district. His pack was heavy with merchandise—oilcloth, thread, needles. The fellow would put his pack in front of him and knock on an apartment door. The woman came and he said, "Missus, you light the Sabbath candles this Friday at twelve minutes after six, and I wish you a good Sabbath— perhaps you need a few candles? No? Thread? A bread knife?" And he went through the entire list of merchandise. Finally, when the woman indicated she did not need anything, he strapped the pack on his back, extending his palm, and said, "You maybe can give a Jew something for the Sabbath?"

On Thursday and Friday you also saw the "khrane man." Khrane is horseradish. The fellow rode around on a little wagon with a grinding machine. You bought horseradish and the fellow ground it up for you right on the spot. Another fellow sharpened knives. He rode a bicycle-type conveyance with a grindstone between his knees in front of him; the foot pedals provided transportation and power for the grindstone. Both the khrane man and the knife sharpener dealt in services which brought two and three pennies at a time, but I dare say many of them eventually sent sons through college.

# When skirts covered ankles

ON A RECENT trip to New York, I found myself in front of Number 64, The Bowery, where one of my school chums lived, an Italian boy by the name of Paresi. Paresi's father owned a shoeshine stand up on Madison Square near the Flatiron Building. In those days, shoe shining was big business. On Sundays thousands of people would promenade down the street patronizing the shoeshine parlors, and the

free-lance shine boys on the street. The prices were three
cents for a standing-up shine and five cents if you were provided a seat. Paresi's father had one of those "sitting down"
places, with three chairs perched high above street level.
Opposite his shine stand was the trolley car stop, which
crossed Fifth Avenue over to Broadway. It was a pretty
high step up to board the trolley, and the ladies had to
lift their skirts to get on. Paresi's father used to tell how,
when the wind was blowing hard, many a sport would keep
sitting on his high perch saying, "Give me another shine."

## To drive a hack—$20,000

IN THE old days a taxi driver went to a poor man's bank
to borrow $200 and he needed two co-makers. Today the
bank will give him as much as a $15,000 loan on his medal-
lion.

There are about 13,000 cabs in New York and some years
ago the City Council closed the books on taxicab licenses.
These licenses cost $60 a year. For this $60 you got a medallion—the tin badge which you see on the hood of each taxi.
Now when the City Council froze the number of taxicabs,
this medallion rose in value. It was likely the sharpest rise
in the history of bull markets. The $60 medallion now sells
for anywhere between $17,000 and $20,000, not counting the
taxicab itself. Many individual cab owners and certainly the
companies who owned fleets of taxicabs became rich overnight, with an asset which only the accident of time and
numbers created for them.

In discussing this matter with a dozen taxi drivers, I found
that this $20,000 investment is gilt-edged. It is better than
buying an apartment house, although owning a cab entails
harder work. Two fellows get together and they have about
$3,000 each. They buy a medallion for $20,000, borrowing
most of the money from the bank. They run their cab around
the clock, each of them driving twelve hours in succession,

and they succeed in paying their notes to the bank while averaging a net income each of about $6,000 a year.

I have often wondered what would happen if some fellow came along with the $60 for a taxi license and took his case to the Supreme Court.

## The block party

ONE of the first successful experiments in community activity was the block party. Originally Tammany district leaders had arranged these open-air gatherings to promote enthusiasm for political candidates. But later, welfare workers and interested parents arranged these affairs on their own, in the interest of good will in the community. The block was lighted up and the police co-operated by posting no-traffic signs on the opposite corners. There was always plenty of local talent—singers, dancers, musicians, and comedians. This was not unusual when we realize that most of burlesque, musical comedy, and Tin Pan Alley came from the tenement districts. There were street dancing, contests of all sorts, and some comedian usually gave a German dialect impression of "If You Knew What the Milkman Sees," and, of course, everyone sang "The Sidewalks of New York."

I remember going to an Italian block party and watching twenty or thirty little Italian girls dance the tarantella to the singing and clapping of some five thousand people of the neighborhood. In forty years I doubt whether a month has gone by that I haven't thought of those Italian children and the melody of that Sicilian tarantella.

## The evil eye and baseball

THE basic superstition of the East Side centered around the fear that something would break the spell when everything was going all right. Too much praise was the greatest danger, because it would call attention to the evil spirits, who, out of jealousy, would harm a handsome child, a prosperous business, or a happy home. No one really knows the origin of this. We do know that the superstition is universal, including, of course, the habit of knocking on wood when you hear good news. Take an example in America where the same superstition exists. It is almost a crime to call attention to the baseball game while a pitcher is heading toward a no-hit performance. No member of the team will utter a word, or even look at the pitcher. They must talk of other matters. This is all to distract the attention of the evil spirits. Inning after inning the pitcher will go back to the players' dugout and no one will say a word. So here we have Anglo-Saxon ballplayers from Texas, Georgia, and the Carolinas steeped in the folklore which we thought was singularly an Eastern European tradition. It is interesting to note that the fear of the evil eye is automatically transferred to the spectators in the stands. No one yells while a man is pitching a no-hit game. Instinctively they try not to look at the pitcher. They talk nervously about things completely unrelated to the ball game.

## Chicken soup was the cure-all

ON THE East Side no matter what happened in a household—if the kid was run over, or if someone had an accident, a cold, or pneumonia, the neighbors would rush into the house with chicken soup. This was the cure-all, the greatest remedy ever invented. "Let me get you some nice chicken soup," the women would say to anyone who was sick, disappointed in love, or out of a job. I believe this chicken soup remedy has roots in most of the cultures of our civilization. Where the Jewish women, at the first sign of illness, said, "I'll make some nice chicken soup," the women of the entire Gentile world have said, "I'll make you some nice broth." This suggests the possibility that chicken soup and broth really did do wonders for the sick, the tired and the hungry.

This may be the reason we have made some progress despite war, terror, and tyranny. What better symbol of human kindness than the one created by the women of this world—"I'll make you some nice chicken soup"—"Let me get you some nice broth." It must have sounded like a prayer to many of the sick and distressed.

PART 3

*We're on a Single
Ball of Twine*

# A Yiddishe mama

FIVE dollars was a matter of tremendous importance in our household on the Lower East Side of New York. There weren't many five-dollar bills for use at any one time. I was a kid of about ten or eleven and I lost a five-dollar bill. My mother gave it to me to buy something and I lost it. I don't know how, but I lost it and that's all. I sat in the park most of the day afraid to go home. I walked the streets. Wherever I went I kept looking for that five-dollar bill. I knew that this was foolish, but I was frantic. I kept thinking that maybe I'd find another five-dollar bill to replace the one I lost. Finally it was dark, and I just had to go home. I hardly knew where or how to begin. What could I say? But I had to say it. I told my mother that I had lost the money.

She grabbed me tight and seemed to be as happy as could be, and kept repeating in Yiddish over and over again, "It's better than giving it to a doctor."

# May it be a boy

MANY of my non-Jewish friends want to know all about this business of the Jews' always praying, "May it be a boy." The religious Jew wanted his first-born to be a boy, of course. A boy says kaddish, the prayer of mourning for the parents after they are dead. It was merely a question of substituting terms. What they really meant and often said was, "Thank God for one-who'll-say-kaddish." Once a boy was born into the family the deep concern for proper mourning after the parents' death was over. Three times a day, during the year after a parent dies, a dutiful son goes to shul to say kaddish, thus insuring the heavenly well-being of the deceased. Actually the basic struggle of Jewry was to survive and the intensity of this belief was as much social as religious. Through the kaddish the deceased parent remained part of the community for a long time even after death. When you live in ghettos under restrictions and oppression, you cannot afford to lose anyone, not even the deceased, as long as you can possibly help it. There was great rejoicing at the birth of a boy, and sometimes the whole family danced around the bed of the mother and child.

I remember when my younger brother's wife, Annie, was in the hospital for her first baby. It was a girl. My brother Max immediately put through a call to my father and it was a delightful conversation:

Max: Hello, Pop, well, Annie had the baby and Annie is in fine shape.

Pop: All right, let's thank God everything is all right.

Max: Oh yes, everything is fine, Annie is fine.

Pop: This is very good news, my son.

Max: Oh yes, Annie is fine.

Finally my father busted loose: What's the matter with you? It's not so bad! Suppose *it is* a little girl, so what? It's not so terrible. . . .

Max: Annie is fine. . . .


## Crime and barbaric punishment

THE British House of Commons has voted to abolish capital punishment. Up in Massachusetts, that noble lady, Mrs. Herbert Ehrmann (head of the Society for the Abolition of Capital Punishment) has victory within her grasp. She has worked unceasingly over the years with what is practically a one-woman organization.

North Carolina, which has shown itself capable of true greatness on many occasions, has all but followed the Mother Country in the final elimination of the act of legal barbarism. By two amendments in the Legislature, mandatory death sentences have been removed for conviction in crimes of burglary, arson, murder, and rape. A defendant who pleads guilty to first-degree murder is automatically subject to a life sentence. *For a Southern state this is a remarkable development, and the manner in which it was handled is worthy of careful study throughout the country.*

The abolition of capital punishment is not a "public opinion" project. Contrary to the fairy tale of the wisdom of the taxi driver and the man-in-the-street, let us face the fact that the taxi driver and the man-in-the-street are hanging jurors. In every capital case from Socrates to Vanzetti, they have said the same thing: "I say, let's hang 'em." This requires tactful handling—the constant attempt to "communicate" through a few key people, the few people who really mold public opinion.

But, while progress is being made here in North Carolina, things are not so hopeful everywhere.

Up in New York, for instance, John O'Donnell of the *Daily News* (he who peddled the story of the Wacs and contraceptives during the war) wrote a column in which he recommended a system of prolonged torture for convicted kidnapers and murderers. He writes, ". . . [let us] inflict unusual punishment . . . [as] prolonged as medical science can accomplish . . . as merciless . . . as ancient torture . . . [all this] . . . to be imposed publicly in the Yankee Stadium before television cameras. . . ."

If Mr. O'Donnell's system of prolonged torture is calculated to *punish* the criminal, he is wrong. No matter how "prolonged" the torture may be, we now know that it has no punitive effect beyond the first serious blow. Almost at once there is a complete paralysis of the nerve centers which renders the subject insensible to pain. Often this paralysis sets in even before the first blow is actually struck. In nine cases out of ten the mere opening of the cell door is enough to destroy all contact with reality. The march to the electric chair and the sitting down are purely mechanical. Even the outcry of the one being tortured is psychological, merely an association of ideas between the raising of the bludgeon or whip and his memory of pain. In one area of this highly enlightened O'Donnell thesis, he apears to be on solid ground. The public torture of a criminal would be a wonderful therapy for many of those who viewed it, but not in the way Mr. O'Donnell thinks. The folks used to bring their picnic baskets to all public hangings. But for public torture they really went to town. The emperor of Rome came out with thousands of cheering onlookers, who felt quite *spent* when the fun was over. For the sexually impotent particularly, public torture is a joy beyond words.

If Mr. O'Donnell's public torture idea was calculated to serve as a warning to others, we enter into a highly controversial area in the history of human behavior. The findings would seem to indicate that *punishment is not a deterrent to crime*. A murder was once committed outside the death house at Sing Sing, and the murderer was the trusty who polished the electric chair before each execution. William E. H. Lecky, in his *History of European Morals*, writes that in old England when they hanged pickpockets, all the pickpockets of the country would come to ply their trade among the folks whose attention was diverted.

Where we have fallen down in our handling of kidnapers, sex criminals, and murderers of children is in our lack of scientific preventive measures. The great criminologist, Dr. Fredric Wertham, knows what he is talking about when he says that over half the criminals charged with such offenses had already given society ample warning—they had previously been in the toils of the law, or in mental institutions, or in clinics under observation, time and time again. It is here that our law and criminal procedure have been wholly inadequate to keep these people isolated, and in other ways protect society from them.

Yet, the legalized murder continues.

In North Carolina we use gas to carry out the sentence of death. New York and many other states use the electric chair; others continue the old-fashioned method of hanging, and one state (Utah) gives the doomed man or woman a choice between hanging and shooting. Which is the most humane?

In the gas chamber a man sits in a chair with mighty leather tentacles hugging him close. Beneath the chair there is a jar containing acid. Above the jar there is a tiny chute in which, behind a little gate, are several lumps of egg-shaped pellets. There is a stethoscope fastened with tape over the doomed man's heart, connected to a long tube which comes through the wall. A cord is pulled, the little gate opens, and a pellet flops into the acid. There is a little bubbling, the doctor listens to the stethoscope. It's like a game. The man in the chair in the sealed room trembles. His face flushes, then turns purple. His eyes roll —he coughs and coughs, then a gasp, and it's the end. They say that sometimes there are convulsions for at least two minutes while he is choking to death. Seldom does the heart stop pounding before five minutes.

In the electric chair the convicted felon is strapped tightly, with a hood over his head containing an electrode. There's a small sponge placed between his head and the electrode to carry the power. The spot on the head where the wet electrode rests has been shaved. Another electrode is attached with a small wet sponge to the right leg below the knee. The warden gives the signal and the switch is thrown. The man in the chair lurches forward violently. The smell of burning flesh fills the room. As the current is reduced the doomed man relaxes a bit as the air is expelled from his lungs. Sometimes a second shock is necessary. Once in New York three shocks were required to put a man to death. Even at that, the rumor persists that it is the autopsy which follows that really finishes him. That, I wouldn't know. Electrical engineers would know more about that.

The states which hang their murderers say that their method is the most humane. If the hangman knows his business and puts the knot in the proper place the trap will break the man's neck quickly—say in about one minute.

The elimination of capital punishment will someday mark the end of a criminal code which was once the most ferocious in the world. Two centuries ago England executed little children. After hanging, the body was cut in quarters, salted down (they called it "atomizing"), and delivered to the relatives; all except the head. In the history of Dr. Ford, England's famous hangman, we find that in the year 1807 a crowd of eighty thousand gathered to witness the hanging of two murderers. Twenty-eight people were trampled to death in the crowd. For well over a century the position of official hangman really was a "concession." He received no pay, but he made a good living by selling pieces of the rope for a shilling. Often a few chiselers would be selling bootleg rope, and on one occasion one such chiseler was beaten to death when the people discovered that they had been *cheated* and had bought pieces of *unused* rope.

Many more legislative steps still remain to be taken in affirming the sanctity of human life and the futility of killing by the state.


# We're on a single ball of twine

I WAS thinking about the individual's tie with history as I read the wonderful reviews of the Ketti Frings play, based on the novel, *Look Homeward, Angel,* by North Carolina's Tom Wolfe.

Thirteen years ago, one of my sons received his first paycheck as a member of the news staff of *The Charlotte Observer,* and he said to me, "I think I'll go to Asheville this weekend to look at Tom Wolfe's house."

"A four-hour bus ride each way just to look at his house?"

He looked surprised at my question. "I just want to look at his house, that's all." And off he went.

And one man in the great mass of humanity is insignificant, but at the same time he is the very essence of it all. We are like the eye of the hurricane. The whole of civilization really revolves around *us*—each of us *individually*.

My son had attended Belmont Abbey College and Father Cuthbert Allen had asked him to write the press releases for the college, and Harry delivered them in person to Mr. Ernest B. Hunter, the recently retired assistant publisher, then managing editor of *The Charlotte Observer*. Mr. Hunter looked them over for a year or so, and finally said, "Son, would you like to be a newspaperman?"

And my son's grandfather, my father that is, was a bearded immigrant from a small town in eastern Galicia, where he had once seen the Emperor Franz Josef of the Austro-Hungarian Empire; and Franz Josef had been to conferences with Disraeli and Bismarck and he had known Metternich, who had, in his time sent a letter or two to Thomas Jefferson, the Secretary of State in the Cabinet of our first President, George Washington, and this brings us to one beginning; and all of us have similar histories—connecting links that bind us together.

Father Cuthbert Allen of Belmont Abbey goes back to the Benedictine monks in the monasteries of Europe who helped keep civilization alive in the age of darkness, and Ernest B. Hunter belongs to the Anglo-Calvinist Cavaliers and the Roundheads who came to the South to carve a civilization out of the forest, and all of this had something to do with my son, who goes back to another beginning, back there when our ancestors stood before the wall of the inner Temple of Jerusalem and defended it against the armies of Hadrian. All of it is tied together. All of us are on a single ball of twine, and every few yards or so we meet, like, for instance, in a common cause, or in a common undertaking, or just to look at a house, the house of a North Carolina genius

who became a wanderer and who poured out his heart's
yearning for a home—a home to which he could never return.


# They left the women with the 4-F's

IF ALEXANDER THE GREAT had not conquered the world
the Greeks might very well have discovered America at least
one thousand years before Columbus set out on his expedition. Colonialism, like revolution, "eats its own child." Alexander took with him the flower of Grecian manhood and
stretched his garrisons from Tyre and Gaza to Syria, throughout the Persian Empire, to the River Oxus. So instead of
producing millions of Greek babies at home to preserve the
Greek civilization, the young men of Athens, Macedonia,
and the Grecian isles literally scattered the seeds of their
own destruction in every foreign land of the known world.

And thus the handsome Grecian maidens remained at
home listening to the middle-aged fellows recite poetry and
play the lute; and that is why the wonderful Greek civilization disappeared from the earth.

The mighty Caesar made the same mistake, and so did
the emperors who followed him. For generations the flower
of Roman manhood was all over the place, up there in
Britain, Gaul, on the Rhine, in Africa, Asia, the Middle East,
and Spain; while the Roman women were left with a few
middle-aged senators and all the other 4-F's.

Their men were physically creating the civilizations in the
northern forests and in Gaul which would destroy the
Roman Empire.

Actually all of this contributed greatly to the founding of
Christianity. In its earliest beginnings, Christianity was a
women's religion. With her husband and sons always marching off to some distant point, the Roman woman needed
something to give meaning to her life. The Roman lady of
some sensibilities began to listen to the Jewish perfume
woman who manufactured her products on the banks of the

Tiber. These women were among the first converts to the new religion. What they were really preaching, of course, was the strict sex and food laws of Judaism, and it came at the right time for the Roman lady.

The Roman men, off in distant military outposts, had a religion of their own. They worshiped Mithras, a soldier's god; but Mithraism lacked substance necessary to the growth of a religious faith—FAMILY and the HOME. The Roman lady had the children; and because she had the children, Christianity won a decisive victory over Mithraism and went on to conquer the world.

This is also the key to Jewish survival. The historians have wondered when and how the Jews came to the Rhine and to Spain; and Herr Graetz in his great *History of the Jews* limits himself to the statement: "The first settlement of Jews in beautiful Hesperia is buried in dim obscurity," but then Herr Graetz gets closer to the only logical conclusion, ". . . According to a chronicle, the most ancient Jews in the Rhine district are said to have been the descendants of the legionaries who took part in the destruction of the Temple (70 A.D.). From the vast horde of Jewish prisoners, the Vangioni had chosen the most beautiful women, had brought them back to their stations on the shores of the Rhine and the Main." The children of these unions were not Roman citizens, and so the legionaries showed no interest in them. Thus the mother was left unmolested in the upbringing and naturally fell back upon the faith, customs, and attitudes of her own people.

Thus, while the Roman legionaries were helping "preserve" the Jewish people, their wives and daughters at home were being converted to these same Jewish customs out of a need for spiritual uplift. For centuries thereafter the Jews were forced to live in ghettos, and a succession of church fathers passed laws prohibiting Jews from marrying Gentiles. All of this was supposed to be "punishment." It was exactly the opposite. It was an important factor in preservation.

Sex, more than any other single factor, has shaped the destiny of peoples and of entire civilizations. If "life" is the

opposite of "death," then sex is the epitome of that "life."
It is the "affirmation" of life itself, and that is why it has
had such a hold on the mind of man. It is easily accessible;
and therein lies the tremendous power that was able to
destroy the civilizations of Greece and Rome; preserve the
Jewish people; and lay the foundations of Christianity.

## "Mother is your best friend"

PHILIP WYLIE has called this American tradition of ideal-
izing mother "momism." There can be very little argument
with the facts of the matter. No one would object if an
American regimental slogan were changed from "Don't tread
on me" to "All that I am, I owe to my mother."

The question in my mind is: is this necessarily bad? Who
is being hurt?

If the day ever came that Americans stopped worshiping
their mothers, I would become fearful of our security. We
have learned from bitter experience that we must have symbols, and if the symbol is not *mother*, it is usually *Hitler*.
No mass movement, revolution, tyranny, or dictatorship was
possible until the symbol of the family—the mother—was un-
dermined or destroyed.

Mussolini built his Fascism on a new Italian anthem,
"Giovinezza" (Youth). He put them in uniform at the age
of five and permitted them to go home only to sleep. Hitler
of course did it more thoroughly. He exposed his youth to
sex experiences as early in their lives as possible in his
"Strength Through Joy" camps. The Communists established
their Children's Clinics early in the game—the place where
mothers left their children all day while they worked.

It is when the FAMILY tie is successfully broken that you
must prepare to sit in darkness for a while. Thus I snap
my fingers at my friend Philip Wylie and his "momism,"
and say that as long as the American boy continues to be

dreamy-eyed every time he thinks of mother, just so long will our American freedom be safe.

# On drinking whisky

A NATIONAL magazine, commenting on a serious study of alcoholism, alluded to that old ghetto observation: "Shikker iz a goy" (the Gentile is a drunk).

There was an immediate hurricane of protest. "What a disservice to the cause of interfaith unity!" the letters began.

On the contrary, I think it had precisely the opposite effect. Significantly, no Gentiles complained.

Personally I do not know of a single facet of Jewish life and its folklore that could not be properly explored in an honest press toward the end of so-called "better relations."

This "shikker iz a goy" legend was born in the small towns of Eastern Europe where the Jews watched Gentile peasants gather around a barrel of whisky of a Saturday night. But this myth had about as much validity as the stereotype the Gentiles created about the "shrewd" Jews. Let us not overlook the possibility that this shrewd stereotype may have gained acceptance precisely because of the Jew's sobriety.

I believe there are two basic reasons why Jews stay sober. One is metabolism and the other is sociology. Since the Jews have been drinking alcohol in some form or other for a much longer period of time than the Celts and Anglo-Saxons, they can resist its effects better. It's like snakebite.

It has been suggested that the tradition of saying a prayer before taking a drink has been an aid to Jewish sobriety. My father drank one or two shots of brandy a day for about sixty years and every drink was a ceremony. Every time he took his drink you'd think it was the first time he had ever seen the stuff. The drink was poured; he lifted the glass to the light; he smiled, Ah!—he'd gently roll the glass in his fingers, looking at the amber fluid like a biochemist examining a formula. He would drink it down, and such satisfaction and joy you've never seen! "Ah—that was a wonderful bit of liquor."

The other major reason that a Jewish drunkard is relatively rare is that the Jew finds it very dangerous to let himself go, for his own welfare and because he is ever conscious of the fact that his actions, to some extent, reflect upon his fellow Jews in the community.

Perhaps in all this we may find a clue to why old-time New York's Irish poor had such strong feelings against Jews. It was worth half your life to go into an Irish neighborhood in those days. (That is why the Jewish boys did not learn to swim. The Irish controlled the waterfront, and we were landlocked.) The Irish boy saw his father drink at the corner saloon, while the Jewish boys watched their fathers arguing politics and poetry in coffee cellars. In the next generation the Irish boy was able to put the matter into proper focus. And this new generation of Irish was able to resume its long and honorable history of philo-Semitism.

By this time, too, the Jews achieved a greater degree of tolerance, which put an end to the "shikker iz a goy" stereotype. In America they soon met another level of the "Gentile culture." These were the Protestant social workers in the settlement houses, who not only were abstainers themselves, but who were advocating prohibition. Now the shoe was on the other foot. Some of these Gentiles were climbing up five flights of tenement stairs to plead with a Jewish boy to stop going into the saloon.

By this time we had acquired enough education to feel kinder toward those Gentile peasants in Europe who drank whisky and beat their wives. Because on a broad basis it may be said that the Gentiles drank to excess for the same reason that the Jews ate to excess: poverty and frustration, and perhaps a bit of fear, too.

This drinking-too-much as against the eating-too-much culture survived into the second generation. The young Jews began to envy their Gentile associates who could run into a cafe for "a cup of coffee." To this day only the completely assimilated Jew can do this with any degree of authenticity.

If you suggest "a cup of coffee" to a Jew, the first thing he says is, "With what?" Who ever heard of drinking anything without eating, even if it is only a nothing, like a piece of strawberry shortcake, for instance? We learned how to relate language to help rationalize or minimize our excesses. We did this by the use of diminutives in talking about food and drink, "small," "a bit": "Give me a *small* bagel with a *bit* of lox." Out of the corner of her eye the Jewish housewife watches the baker slice off a huge part of the cheesecake and says, "It's too big, I wanted a very small piece —but all right, you've already cut it, so I'll take it." (The American culture took this wonderful gambit to its heart, always protesting at the offer of a second helping, "Just give me a sliver, that's all.")

This wonderful semantic idea of easing the conscience was used to good advantage in the drinking of whisky. The Jews rarely said, "Pour me a drink." It was always—"a drop." The old gents would say, "a trupp'n bronfon"—just put a little on the bottom of the glass; a drop. And after a while the whole bottle would be finished. (This whole idea carried over to the market place. A woman buying live fish to prepare for the Sabbath would say to the merchant, "Mister, how much for this very little fish?" or, "How much for this little bit of carp?")

When the second generation of Jews in America began to drink, the elderly folks said, "A klug zu Columbus'n." (The immigrant Jews never blamed the Anglo-Saxons for anything. For everything good in America they blessed George Washington; for everything bad they cursed Columbus.) They had reasons for their fear. I am using the authentic statistics for the year 1910. Out of 570 unclaimed bodies (non-Jews) in New York, they reported that 381 had died of alcoholism. (Out of a total of 51 unclaimed bodies of Jews, the Society Chesed Shel Emeth (burial society) reported only one died of drink.

I am convinced that the drinking of whisky is involved with some secret desire for self-mutilation. It robs the brain of its talent, and a full week of possible productivity is cap-

suled into an hour or two of stupidity and waste. T. S. Eliot
says that drinking is a conscious attempt to seek the unconscious.

William Shakespeare was the first man to use the term
"brain-washed" and he used it in a reference to use of alcohol.
Octavius Caesar tells of the first time he drank too much:

> It's monstrous labor, when I wash my brain,
> And it grows fouler.
> . . . I had rather fast from all, four days,
> Than drink so much in one.

Octavius almost lost his empire because of that one drinking bout; but he took the lesson to heart. He never did it
again.

## Don't look

I HAVE tried to weigh myself at least twice during the past
two years, but each time I just listened to the clicking of the
weights and measures but did not look at the results. I think
it's better that way. This system works at other times of
crisis. Once I dropped my glasses on the tile floor of the
bathroom, but I did not look. I merely felt around with
my hand, slowly trying to find the glasses, with my head
turned away. When I found them, I moved the fingers slowly
around the rims first, then touched one lens and finally the
second—with great relief. They were intact. If I had looked
at once, they probably would have been shattered to smithereens.

I learned this many years ago, when I was more or less
interested in precinct Tammany politics. My friend John
Duff (later a famous criminal lawyer in New York) and I
were watching the presidential election returns up at the
Joe McCormick Tammany Club, and the returns were beginning to come in on Al Smith and Herbert Hoover. Cheers

after cheer went up as the announcer called out, "Eighth District, Smith, 231, Hoover, 29; Eleventh District, first returns, Al Smith, 99, Herbert Hoover, four." And so it went for an hour or more, and finally John and I took the subway downtown to be on Times Square for the big celebration. As we piled out of the subway, *The New York Times* was flashing the news that Herbert Hoover had been elected—by a landslide. This overwhelmed us, and John turned to me angrily and said, "Dammit, if we had stayed at Joe McCormick's Club, Smith would have been elected."

My system of not looking is reminiscent of the strong belief in prenatal influence among the women on the East Side during my childhood.

Yes, this was a serious problem with pregnant women. They were deathly afraid of accidentally staring at anyone or anything that would harm the unborn child. The East Side was full of stories about the woman who gave birth to a midget because she had "mislooked herself" at a passing carnival, and a red spot on the face of a child was supposed to have resulted from the mother's clasping her hand to her face in fright—and at that very spot.

When the pregnant woman had to venture into the street, she would often take along a relative who had to be on the alert every step of the way. The relative would say, "Look away, there are a couple of dogs running this way." American movie audiences have laughed a million times at that old scene where the wife tells the husband she is pregnant and husband grabs a chair and insists she sit down. Well, this was no laughing matter in a Jewish home. It was both law and tradition that the pregnant woman be pampered. She was even guarded from bad news of any kind. It was always feared the slightest disturbance would result in a deformed or misshapen child.

Many pregnant women would hire a good-looking child of a neighbor (a boy of course) to run an errand ostensibly, but actually to get her fill of "looking." And, fat kid with black curly hair that I was, but "beautiful" by Old World Jewish standards, that's where I came in—for a dime.

# Four hundred million years of life

1. Algae
2. Fish
3. Reptiles
4. Birds
5. Mammals
6. Dinosaurs
7. Saber-toothed tiger
8. Discovery of fire
9. Invention of the wheel
10. The alphabet
11. Code of Hammurabi
12. Moses, the Bible
13. Homer
14. Socrates
15. Jesus of Nazareth
16. Magna Charta
17. Printing press
18. Shakespeare
19. Declaration of Independence
20. Einstein, Atomic Age
21. Point Four
22. Sputnik

The next major step will be the exploration of uninhabited planets, and communication with inhabitants of other galaxies. People will live to approximately two hundred and fifty years and they will look back upon the history of war in the same way we look back on our primitive ancestors' eating human flesh. The population of Earth will have expanded from two and a half billion to about one hundred billion in 2557; but the occupation and settlement of uninhabited planets in space will have been going on for nearly three centuries. Eventually Earth will become a sort of repository of the archives and art works of all civilizations. Folks will visit Earth from all over space to have a look around; scholars will spend interesting years here doing research for their books.

One of the holidays is sure to be Passover. We will always celebrate Passover, which even now has a history of nearly thirty-five hundred years. The Fourth of July also will be celebrated by the billions of people throughout the planetary systems. It will have been America that tipped the scales of the balance into the true Humanism, because of two things—the Declaration of Independence (political freedom) and Point Four (all men are brothers).

It is quite possible that Passover and Fourth of July may be combined into one observance, since the perspective of history will have made it clear that they had always been one and the same holiday.

## America—a sexual Sahara?

I THINK the flaw in the Kinsey Report was not in its method, and neither do I question its validity. But we could not achieve proper perspective unless we had similar "reports" from among other peoples of the world—Britain, France, the Middle East, Scandinavia, Russia, India, China. And I have a suspicion that America would not only prove to be sexually immature, but quite definitely undersexed in terms of the entire sex culture and activity.

We are on the go constantly. A three-day holiday and millions and millions of people are on the move; and millions more do not wait for any holidays; it is "go, go," and "let's drive," and "let's visit," and just—"let's go."

This tremendous mobility may have something to do with our own problem, of course—the frustration and the immaturity that results in the overemphasis we see all around us.

A prostitute and brothel-keeper with many years of experience in the city of Shanghai wrote a book in French some years ago which could not be sold in the United States. In general, her classification placed the Hindu on top of the list as a lover, followed by the Chinese, the Malayan, the Japanese; and then came the men of the West, with the American either last or next to last; which would tend to confirm two things: the American "mobility" and the Hindu poverty.

Man starts out with three "spokes in his wheel of life": food, shelter, and sex; and when he loses one of these spokes he is in a bad way; and if two are gone, it is rather hopeless. But when there are literally hundreds of spokes, those provided by a very high standard of living—music, art, participation in politics, charities, public affairs, a whole network of clubs, societies, fellowships, churches, etc., the loss of the sex spoke is no longer fatal.

Basically man's greatest problem, with respect to sex, too, is this unending drive to prove himself.

There is no answer to this, of course, but there is most certainly a fairly well-trod avenue of relaxation which is achieved by many more fortunate men than you would suspect. This fortunate man is one who, at some time in his life, has been thoroughly convinced by a woman that he was indeed "all right." But this is not as simple as it sounds. It takes a most special kind of convincing to ease the mind that is forever in doubt. And of course this cannot come about, not in one million years, through promiscuity, which actually compounds the problem.

And so the vicious circle goes round and round; and he finally tries to get elected secretary of something, or maybe get to sit on the dais once in a while; all of which does actually bring some measure of temporary relief.

## Inevitable hour

WE ARE all sailing under sealed orders, and the very "completeness" of Death frightens most of us whenever we allow ourselves to think of it.

In the words of Thomas Gray:

> The boast of heraldry, the pomp of pow'r,
>     And all that beauty, all that wealth e'er gave,
> Awaits alike th' inevitable hour:
>     The paths of glory lead but to the grave.

I do not hold with the school of thought that directs the overwhelming sympathy to the "survivors." Somehow I feel sorry only for the one who is put into the grave. I loved my mother as much as the next man loved his, and the day I walked out of the hospital and knew she was dead I thought to myself, "How can I ever stand this?" But time is a great healer. A few weeks later I was at the Polo Grounds yelling for the New York Giants. Of course death is a great shock to the relatives and loved ones left behind; but in the morning "joy cometh as usual," and you go about your work. For a little time you take particular note of the memories of the departed, but eventually you resign yourself to the inevitable and continue to wage an endless battle in which you must lose, assured of nothing but that someday you too will lie still, your chest not moving. Then at lunchtime some friend will say you were a nice guy, and a few weeks later, a few months, maybe, it's all over.

> Perhaps in this neglected spot is laid
>   Some heart once pregnant with celestial fire;
> Hands, that the rod of empire might have sway'd,
>   Or waked to ecstasy the living lyre.

> . . . . . . . . . . . .

> Full many a gem of purest ray serene
>   The dark unfathom'd caves of ocean bear:
> Full many a flower is born to blush unseen,
>   And waste its sweetness on the desert air.

# A nice place to live

THE "greatest place in the world" for each of us is where he earns his livelihood. One of the most important words in our lives is PARNOSSEH—livelihood. You cannot beat that for a word.

During the war the *New Yorker* magazine had a cartoon showing a young GI looking at the Taj Mahal and saying, "That's nothing compared to the new post office back in

Moline, Illinois." The joke was on the *New Yorker*, because to that boy the new post office in Moline meant father, mother, sweetheart, past, present, future, and PARNOSSEH. What's the Taj Mahal compared to that?

It is many years now since I stopped sneering at the fellow who says, "New York is a great place to visit, but I wouldn't want to live there." And why shouldn't he say that? The fellow is earning a LIVELIHOOD in some other city, which is HOME and family, and friends, and a sense of belonging, and yet he has the imagination and the sense of values to *want* to *visit* New York. I think, if you carefully examine that statement again, you will agree with me that it is a very great tribute to New York.

# Our delegate to the fair

As SCIENCE keeps conquering the degenerative diseases, it seems apparent that we must either crowd one another off the earth or begin to populate the other planets. Science has spent no time figuring out how Earth is to accommodate between fifteen billion and twenty billion people, but it has spent a great deal of time figuring out how to travel in space. Eventually, I am convinced, we will colonize the planets which are habitable. Communications will improve and we will have stellar radar so we can talk with one another.

Two thousand years from now there will be a Planetary Fair, much like national capitals today have a World's Fair. When that time comes, Earth will be asked to contribute some product that best represents it. The best representative we could send is a little girl between the ages of four and nine. At that age little girls are without guile and are much neater than little boys. Little girls are a joy to look at, and they have a wonderful curiosity about people and places. I don't know that Earth's little girl will necessarily win the heart of the universe, but, when some stellar inhabitant asks, "Why do you live on Earth?" he will best understand by talking with a little girl. This is our best.

# Getting old

THE teen-ager thinks her thirty-year-old sister is middle-aged. A young bride wonders if sex life continues at all after forty. The politician is stunned when the party leader tell him in caucus that he is too old to run again. Age is relative and imperceptible to the individual. And we want to believe we're only as old as we feel.

So women call themselves "girls" even though they are in their fifties and their husbands say they are going fishing with the "boys." But every once in a while we are caught up and realize we aren't girls and boys. I know a lady who realized it one day when she walked past four boys in a snowball fight and heard one cry, "Watch out! Don't hit the old lady."

The imperceptible process of age has a point which, once passed, cannot be retraced. I knew I had passed that point and was getting old the day I noticed that all the cops looked so young.

# He misjudged me

ON A TRIP to New York an old friend of my father's—one of the last survivors of his generation—asked me to accompany him to a lawyer's office "to talk for him." I met him on a corner on the edge of the Lower East Side, and we walked past all the pushcarts, and suddenly the old gent disappeared. When I found him he explained why he had fallen behind—he was eating a pickled tomato he'd bought from a pushcart and he didn't want to embarrass me. The old gent misjudged me. If there was anything in this world I wanted to do, it was walk beside an old bearded Jew eating a pickled tomato.

## The lonely ones

HAPPY is that man who has learned the value of solitude. But do not confuse solitude with loneliness. They are entirely different.

I have seen many lonely people in my life. Many of the lonely people spend their time "recalling." When I was a hotel clerk I remember them standing at the desk alone. "I used to come here twenty, thirty years ago," they said, "I remember when there was only one elevator, and the stairway was in the back." Eventually people stop listening because lonely people have a tendency to repeat themselves. And when the lonely people recognize that folks have stopped listening, they go to the bar for a drink and there they find new people who will listen for a little while, but eventually they, too, stop listening. And some of the lonely people become alcoholics, but their quest for someone to listen goes on.

I suspect that the wonderful work of Alcoholics Anonymous may be attributed to the fact that it provides a forum for the lonely ones—a forum where the folks listen to one another.

## Visitors

I GET everybody—Presbyterians, ministers, Negroes, Catholics, Jews. When they call up and say, "Mr. Golden, I'm at the bus station," I know I'm in for it. The radicals all come to the bus station. The other guys come to the airport.

# The ultimate reality

PEOPLE never discuss their salaries publicly, or their income, or their patrimony. People make a successful effort never to discuss money in front of friends or relatives, because money in our society is the ultimate reality and to discuss it is to reveal oneself.

# No more flirting

THE flirt has disappeared from our culture. "Flirtation Walk" would be an anachronism today. The word "flirt" itself has become as obsolete as the word "woo." Who woos today? Today it is all a cut-and-dried proposition and significantly the famous hotels have cut down on their "promenades" and "alleys" and have now left only their registration desks. Good evening and—sign in.

The new generation does not know what it has lost—those days of the thrilling "preliminaries."

# Women and philosophy

A FEW charming ladies have shaken angry fingers in my direction because I wrote that women are not interested in philosophy. I believe that women are by nature more "practical" than to involve themselves in the abstractions of natural science. Sinclair Lewis once wrote that his first marriage (to a nonprofessional) was a failure, because he was never able to convince his wife that he was working while sitting in a chair looking out the window. Xantippe was always looking for Socrates with fire in her eye—"Why don't you stop hanging out with that bum Alcibiades—try doing something useful for a change." Of course let us be fair about it. Many a man has used that philosophy dodge to get out of work. The wife did all the work while the husband spent his life poring over books, which did not always contribute anything to our intellectual advancement. Put it to a test. I dare you. Just get up enough courage to say to your wife, "Honey, please don't bother me for a few hours, I want to do some thinking." First your wife will split her sides laughing, then she'll reach for a broom handle.

# Rats would take over

IN THE last act of that famous play *R.U.R.*, the scientist is looking out the window as the robots are mopping up the last of the humans who had created them. Presently he says sadly: "It was a fine thing to be—a man."

When and if the atomic "robot" which man has created mops up the last of us, I believe that, of all the other animals living on this planet today, the rat will take over. Of all living creatures, except man himself, the rat is the most resourceful when it comes to survival, the most adaptable to his environment. All the efforts by man to exterminate him have proved unsuccessful, and each rat produces between twenty and fifty new rats a year. Originally the brown rat which we know in America entered Europe from China in the thirteenth century. He all but exterminated the black rat, which carries with it the dreaded bubonic plague, and then sailed across the Atlantic. Today there are at least one hundred and fifty million rats in the country, and, according to agricultural experts, they cost at least one million dollars a day in feed. There is no way we can estimate what rats cost us in other ways—in diseases, damage to property. After four hundred years of warfare against them, we have not found a successful method. Exterminating experts will tell you they cannot use the same poison over any prolonged period in the same area. The rats catch on quickly and through some system of communication or careful observation the deadliest poison becomes useless. The rats have been known to leave in a body, returning a month or two later. Is it possible that they have some method of "government"? The rat is everywhere at home and he'll eat anything—soap, glue, tobacco, paint, bone, all of which makes him everywhere dominant as well as everywhere dangerous. This ferocious beast is the one enemy who has kept the fight with man, through all the centuries, absolutely even—a draw.

# My duet with Meredith Willson

THIS talented man Mr. Meredith Willson (*The Music Man*) called me long distance and was kind enough to say he enjoyed my story about Hymie buying a suit on the East Side. Mr. Willson mentioned another essay of mine. It was the story of my affection for Rossini's great requiem for the Catholic Church, *Stabat Mater* ("See the weeping Virgin Mother . . .") and how I played it five or six times and how my neighbor's secretary asked my secretary, "Why does your boss play that Jew music all the time?" And at this moment Meredith Willson burst into the "Inflammatus" part of the *Stabat Mater*. He has a beautiful voice and I joined him. And so, my friends, let it be recorded that "Music Man" Meredith Willson and I sang a duet over long distance. And can you imagine the fun we'll have together after such a beginning?

# The saloonkeeper

THE saloonkeepers represented the backbone of organized charity in the days before community chests and charity federations. Irish Catholic saloonkeepers had very much to do with the building of St. Patrick's Cathedral. The Jewish saloonkeeper helped keep up the neighborhood Talmud Torah (Hebrew School) and the home for the aged. The saloonkeeper was not only the easiest touch, but his establishment was the first call the committee made when something was needed in the neighborhood, like giving someone a decent funeral or putting up bail for a wayward boy.

# To parents and grandparents

THINK only in terms of the magnitude of the universe, and only then will you have the proper perspective. We work hard, we think hard, and we worry hard—all "for the children." And one day the son will be sitting in the bosom of his own family and he will say: "My father was rather a tall man." And if you are floating somewhere in the ether you will say: "Is that all I get out of it? Is that all I get for the time I got up in the middle of the night to get a doctor when he was sick?"

Of course that is all you get out of it. And this is good. Reverence for the past is important, of course, but the past must not lay too heavy a hand upon the present and the future. It is good to work hard, think hard, and worry hard—for the children, for ourselves; and, if, years later, all you get out of it is: "My mother was a good cook, too"; just figure it as a bonus. Let us not worry about our obituaries. Let us only hope and pray that our children survive us.

PART 4

*Artists and the
Big Story*

# The newspaper game and the Big Story

EACH generation believes that the news events of its time are the most world-shaking of all history, but the Big Story remains the same.

It is the story of a bride, of the winner on an Irish Sweepstakes ticket, of an ax murder, of a child killed by fire, of villainy and courage, of Don Larsen's perfect game in the World Series, of the so-called "love triangle," of the death of a man who lived down the street. . . .

It is the story of the human heart.

And the newspaperman, whose job it is to seek out this story, is much misunderstood.

Many a newspaperman winces when a layman refers to him as a "writer." Actually a writer is a novelist. This is not to say that we do not have many brilliant journalists, reporters, editors, analysts, economists, muckrakers, pamphleteers, sociologists, and propagandists—all writers in the sense that they communicate their ideas and their experiences through the printed word, in books, newspapers, pamphlets, broadsides, and magazines; but "writer" is really a designation which belongs to the creative artist.

The layman looks with awe on the by-line in his newspaper. Some of our great reporters and editors have their names attached to their material, but on most daily newspapers the by-line, in itself, is not too important any more. Quite often a reporter, just out of journalism school and on his first job, will get a by-line when sent out to write up the late developments at the Y.M.C.A. This is not to say that this stuff is not important. It is as necessary as the morning headline, but many men who really are the kings of a news room seldom see their names in print. These are the rewritemen and deskmen. The young reporter will go out to interview a celebrity at the airport. He writes the stuff in his little book; drinks a Coca-Cola; revises what he has written; walks over to the library to look up a word or a quotation; tears it all up; chats with a couple of friends about this and that; gets over to the office and writes the story; looks it over; corrects it; maybe writes it over again; and finally turns it in. The job of the deskman is a little more intense. The phone rings about ten minutes before the paper goes to press. On the other end of the line is a sheriff, or a policeman, or a part-time correspondent of the newspaper. In great excitement, the caller says that there's been an accident on the highway; above the din of passing traffic, ambulance and police sirens, the caller pours out names, places, circumstances, and other details; a click in the ear, and the deskman rolls a piece of paper into his typewriter; he has to record the names of the occupants of the car; who was driving; who was hurt; which hospital the injured were taken to; the first officer on the scene; arrests, if any; home addresses of the occupants; where they were going; any other car involved; who was driving that one; and on; and on; and in three or four minutes the story has to be in the hands of the printer, with the proper heading in perfect shape; and everything had better be accurate right down to the middle initial.

Reporters and deskmen, however, share one distinction. They never "have it made." You can be the Ace for years, but *one* item, a carelessly checked story, and nothing that has gone before means a thing. There are no erasures once the edition hits the streets, and there are very few second chances. I guess that is one of the reasons the business is so fascinating. There is no challenge like it. It is probably the most valuable occupation known to our society. And this fascination, inconsistent with the remuneration involved, has been transferred to the general public. Hardly a man alive with common sense and red blood hasn't seen himself at one time or another as a reporter.

If I were managing editor of a metropolitan daily newspaper, the first thing I would do would be to throw out at least 50 per cent of the syndicated junk. To fill this valuable space I would use my own staff of young men and women. I would turn them loose in the state, county, and city in search of the Big Story. As a case in point, there are at least ten newspapermen here in Charlotte who not only can write better than Robert Ruark and Constantine Brown, but who have more education and far more intelligence.

And I say this as a member of the fraternity of syndicated columnists, myself.

The trouble is, most of the columnists lose sight of the Big Story.

I sold newspapers as a boy on a busy corner (Norfolk and Delancey) of New York. The days were filled with great events: "Archduke Ferdinand Assassinated"; "Russia Mobilized"; "England Warns Kaiser"; "Germany Invades Belgium"; "Hindenburg Smashes Russians at Tannenberg"; "Von Kluck Reaches Suburbs of Paris."

The reader grabbed the newspaper out of your hands before you had a chance to fold it properly. But these were not the real banner days. Not by a long shot. On the days you had to go back two or three times to get more papers the headlines were "Society Girl Found Dead in Opium Den"; "Another Murder in Hell's Kitchen"; "Police Lieutenant Becker Electrocuted."

And, by far the biggest day of all was when Leo Frank was lynched down in Georgia. I remember that the Yiddish papers that day had front page streamers in red ink, which I had never seen before.

The *Manchester Guardian* recently concluded that newspaper readers are interested in the same type of story on both sides of the Atlantic; and that the most stimulating newsbill (equivalent of our tabloid headline) is the announcement of a story concerned with any one of these interesting subjects—murder, sex, dope, kidnaping, or children.

James Gordon Bennett grasped the idea when, as editor of *The New York Herald,* he decided to cover a murder story. A prostitute was found dead in a sleazy rooming house. In accordance with the custom of the 1850's, this should have been a one-line item among seventy other reports on an inside page. But Bennett put a screaming headline in his paper, "Prostitute Found Slain," and ordered his artist to draw a picture of the body showing a naked leg dangling over the side of the bed. That headline and the dangling leg ushered in a new era in American journalism.

If you were asked to list the great American news stories, you would think of the Lindbergh kidnaping; Leopold and Loeb; the disappearance of Charlie Ross; the disappearance of Dorothy Arnold; did Nan Patterson kill Caesar Young in the hansom cab in Central Park? the Girl in the Red Velvet Swing; and a great many others, including the marriage of Grace Kelly and Prince Rainier.

The news and photo coverage of this last-named wholesome event is worthy of a study by an expert psychologist.

One of the greatest story plots of all time, in all history, in all languages, in all religions, in all cultures is the Cinderella theme. In every play, novel, story, movie, article, and speech, humankind is forever trying to seek out the wonderful story of the one who comes upon the good things in life—suddenly—as if by magic.

And, of course, the Rainier-Kelly wedding was Cinderella come to life, and among the greatest stories ever told.

What interested me particularly was that so many people, in their complete absorption, cried out, as if in desperation: "I am sick and tired of reading so much about Grace Kelly."

It is only when a story completely overwhelms you (you are afraid that you are actually losing contact with reality) that you resort to this protest, often stopping strangers on the street in order to keep a firm grip on yourself: "I am terribly sick of reading so much about Grace Kelly"; the implication being that you are eager to get back to the speeches of Everett Dirksen. But the symptoms are well known and the protesters cannot hope to fool the news and wire services, the experienced reporters and managing editors.

*The New York Times* is the most consistently excellent newspaper in the world. It is also one of the finest American institutions, along with Harvard, the New York Yankees, and the Supreme Court. The *Times* has an unvarnished integrity. It maintains correspondents in every nook and cranny of the globe. It will report the price of hemp on the Bombay exchange.

The *Times* lists the names and titles of every diplomat, statesman, ruler, potentate, president, or cabinet member who comes to New York each day, records at what hotel he registered and what ship brought him. When a thief is arrested the *Times* always gives the name of the arresting officer. If Kenyon beats Oberlin, the *Times* explains what a surprising upset this is. Yet the real proof that the *Times* understands the real news is that it has never failed to include the full Sunday section of brides. Often it runs into extra pages. The entire section is devoted to pictures of girls in wedding gowns and each one of these stories is as freshly written as the next. In fact, to read through this section is to take a deep breath of fresh air. The *Times* knows this. The human story still is a bride.

Or a murder . . .

I remember how my second son, Harry, Jr., dug into murders some years ago when he was police reporter for *The Charlotte Observer*.

Harry's most interesting murder story involved a respected businessman held for the murder of his wife. One morning at 7:30, Richard Russell called the police and told them he'd found his wife murdered. The police found Mrs. Russell in the basement, scantily clad, with her head beaten to a pulp. The coroner established that the woman had died some five hours earlier. In their investigation police found a pair of trousers belonging to Russell which had been cut up into strips and flushed down the toilet. Further investigation revealed that the woman had been killed in the bedroom she shared with her husband and dragged feet-first downstairs. The police, in arresting Mr. Russell, alleged that he had spent those five hours between the time of the killing and his call to the police "cleaning up" the place. But, the police claimed, he forgot to clean the blood spots on the ceiling of the bedroom. The man's stenographer was also taken into custody when the police discovered a stack of love letters. But hours of questioning failed to shake Russell's story that his wife had been killed downstairs while he was sleeping upstairs. All this time everyone was waiting patiently for the "confession."

In Charlotte we have two big daily papers—*The Charlotte Observer*, the morning paper, and *The Charlotte News* in the afternoon, and naturally there is the usual rivalry between the two news rooms. All through these days of the Russell questioning, Harry, Jr., was praying that Russell would confess on "his" (Harry's) time (4:00 P.M. to midnight) instead of on *The News'* time (6:00 A.M. to 4:00 P.M.). But actually I doubt whether good reporters really want the fellow to confess. If he confesses the story is over. On the other hand, without a confession, they can keep writing good stories, and Harry, Jr., went to town. He described the color of the wallpaper in the bedroom where the murder had taken place, the pictures on the wall, the clothes in the closet, the quality of the mattress, etc. Those are the things people want to read, and those are the things that make the newspaperman.

(The fellow finally copped a plea at his trial, but by that time Harry was busy covering a grand jury investigation of the police department, and his colleague, Kays Gary, covered the trial.)

My own selection of the all-time American news story would be the one that concerned Miss Elizabeth Borden, the New England marm with the thin lips, who was accused and tried for murder of her father and stepmother. The story has been told a million times and has been made into drama, comedy, opera, and even a ballet (*The Fall River*

*Legend*). And for the first decade of this century the teachers found it difficult to teach "Twinkle, twinkle, little star . . ." because most of the kids were filled with jingles such as:

> Lizzie Borden took an ax
> And gave her mother forty whacks;
> When she saw what she had done,
> She gave her father forty-one.

All of these stories are part of the human drama and there is nothing to be ashamed of because they absorb our interest.

Recently a convention of news editors voted for the all-time big story and first on the list was the "Discovery of America by Christopher Columbus." Leaving out matters of faith and religion, it would be hard to dispute that choice —but only in perspective. The newsboys of Europe did not shout, "Extra! Columbus Discovers a New World." Only a few people were interested, and the only question they asked was, "What did he find there?" The great mass of the people took the news just about as we took the news that Admiral Byrd had discovered Little America near the South Pole. If Europe had a William Allen White at the time the Columbus story broke, I am sure he was getting all the attention with an article on "How Old Should a Child Be Before He May Be Whipped?"

As a boy, I kept a scrapbook of the leading news story of each day from July 1, 1914, to November 11, 1918. I used those old-fashioned notebooks and when it was all over I had about fifteen of them.

In later years, I discovered that the Big Story in every instance was on the other side of my important clipping.

On the other side of the clipping which told of the loss of Lord Kitchener on the H.M.S. *Hampshire* was an announcement by the Borden Milk Company that it would put up milk in sanitary bottles, no more dipping out of the can at the grocery.

On the back of the photo showing the Kaiser Wilhelm and his five younger sons on parade, I found an advertisement of John Wanamaker calling attention to boys' "going-back-to-school" wool suits at $7.95.

Here is a photo of General Joffre in conference with David Lloyd George and on the other side a box score of a game between Cleveland and the Red Sox. The score was 4 to 1. Ernie Shore was the pitcher for Boston, Bagby pitched for Cleveland, and Hooper hit a home run.

There are photos of the Belgian Ambassador Emanuel Havenith arriving in New York; the Irish nationalist John E. Redmond appearing before Parliament; the story of the death of "Austria's Aged Emperor," and a photo of the German submarine commander who had sailed across the Atlantic.

And behind each of these world-shaking events was the more important story; a fire on Twenty-third Street and Tenth Avenue—twenty people were dispossessed by the flames but they found refuge next door at the public baths.

And a statement by Carrie Smith, regional president of the W.C.T.U.: "If there were no drinking, there would be no war."

Behind the news story of a new offensive in the Meuse-Argonne, I read that Father Francis Joseph O'Brien, a recent graduate of the Iona Seminary in New Rochelle, had been appointed to his first parish on 116th Street.

This was the real news of those war years. Because this was the everyday life of the people.

Thirty-five years from now, despite the Khrushchev pronouncements, the twirling sputniks, and artificial planets, the Big Story will still be about people who struggle to pay the rent and get up the tuition for a girl in college.

The story is about people who lose jobs and find better ones. How they go off to hear a first sermon of the new priest, and how they raise their families, and how they die.

And the moral is, don't paste up your scrapbooks with that old-fashioned white school paste. It is a terrible problem trying to unpaste them without tearing the clippings. And thirty years from now you'll be interested only in "what was on the other side."

On his way to and from the Globe Theatre, William Shakespeare could see the tall sails of the *Golden Hind* in which Sir Francis Drake had circumnavigated the globe.

The poet was beginning to reach toward his creative powers when the Spanish Armada was destroyed and the first Elizabeth ushered in Britain's age of Gloriana.

Yet Mr. Shakespeare, who "held a mirror up to life," never mentioned a single one of these events.

Instead, he was busy with the Big Story, the human drama: the story of good children and unkind children; the story of noble men and of cowards; and the story of the mother who upsets her son by remarrying too soon after the father's death.

Think of the many empires that have been won and lost since that afternoon when Cleopatra sailed down the Nile, draped in a cloth of Venus, under a canopy of gold, to meet her lover, Mark Antony:

> Age cannot wither her, nor custom stale
> Her infinite variety. . . .

Shakespeare meant, of course, that "age cannot wither" the Cleopatra story. He knew then what all good reporters know now, that the Big Story is not of our technological wonders, nor of the enchantment of unknown lands.

The Big Story is rather of the mysteries of the human heart.

# Memorable events

YEARS after a memorable event or performance, you find more people who saw it.

This is not really bad, and if such people are caught in a discrepancy, it would be the height of boorishness to contradict them. It merely shows interest and imagination.

After all, what is the person putting over? He has become enamored of an idea or of a personality and he sees himself as having been there. So what? Has anyone been hurt? In fact I believe it is a good thing.

I have found that invariably the people who "weren't there" can tell the story much better than the actual witnesses. So in the end, mankind really benefits.

I remember the time when the Yankee baseball pitcher Carl Mays killed the Cleveland captain-infielder, Ray Chapman, with a pitch. I was a devoted follower of the game in those days, and not only could I tell you the first name of every ballplayer's father, but I could give you statistics on each game right down to attendance. On the day Chapman was killed the attendance at the Polo Grounds, where the Yankees used to play, was seventy-five hundred. But even that was a round figure. They always added a couple of thousand on slow days. Today, I'll bet that at least half a million New York baseball fans will tell you they witnessed the tragedy.

A memorable event occurred at the Metropolitan Opera House one day. Since I *was* there I cannot for the life of me remember whether it was a matinee or an evening performance, and I have forgotten the date except in approximate terms. I'll leave all those necessary details to be ironed out by the vast army of people who weren't there as I proceed to remember:

Whenever there was a change in the program, occasioned, for instance, by a singer's developing a sore throat at the last minute, the opera people used to place a printed notice on each seat, announcing that "Due to the indisposition of so-and-so, someone else will sing such-and-such." On this occasion, as we took our seats, we read the announcement that due to the sudden illness of Pasquale Amato, his understudy, a Mr. Lawrence Tibbett, would sing the baritone role in *Pagliacci*. Poor Pasquale—he sure got sick at the wrong time! The audience rose as a man to cheer Mr. Tibbett on to a great career as an artist.

# The underground shelter

ON THE morning of May 8, 1902, the City of St. Pierre on the Island of Martinique in the West Indies was as peaceful as any other prosperous community of 40,000. The mayor was preparing a speech of welcome for the visit of the governor, M. Moutet, of the Republic of France.

That morning was to become one of the most important dates in science, and, of course, the most important date in the history of the island.

On that day, as usual, there were several ships in the harbor—one, an American oil tanker, *The Maurice,* and the other a passenger liner, the Canadian S. S. *Roirama,* bringing tourists and goods from Canada and the United States. Summer heat begins early in the tropics and the temperature in St. Pierre that day had passed the one-hundred mark.

As the master of the S.S. *Roirama* walked the streets of St. Pierre, he waved a greeting to the United States consul, Thomas Prentiss, whose mansion was only a few blocks from the pier. "I'll bring my son over tonight; it's the first time he's sailed with me," shouted Mr. Scott, the *Roirama's* master, and the American waved acknowledgment in happy anticipation of a pleasant evening.

While the heat was intense, the sun was obscured by black clouds of smoke pouring from the volcano Pelée, six miles west of St. Pierre. But this did not alarm the citizens of the island city. As long as the oldest inhabitants could remember, this volcano had acted up every year—a few days of angry black smoke spouting, and then peace—Mount Pelée would settle back to normal.

Mr. Scott of the S.S. *Roirama* did not call on the Ameriman Mr. Prentiss, because, before the day was over, everyone was dead—with but one exception—every man, woman, and child; every animal! everything with a breath of life in it. Not only Mr. Scott, the ship's master, but his son on

the ship itself was dead, because the disaster twisted the two
ships in the harbor like so much paper.

And it all happened in exactly four minutes.

The horror struck at ten minutes after eight o'clock in the
morning. Clocks found in the wreckage weeks later had
stopped at that hour. What had happened was that the
black smoke of the volcano Pelée, without warning, had
changed to fire, and the entire mountain blew its top and
burned like a Roman candle. Within a few minutes the
eternal fire of the earth poured from Pelée in huge vapors
of gas and flame. Thousands of the dead were found later
with their clothing intact, but lungs burned in a single breath
of the flaming vapor. Hundreds and hundreds of men,
women, and children were found in natural positions of
eating, sitting, and sleeping, but their bodies at the slightest
touch disintegrated into piles of white ash.

So intense was the heat that it was impossible to identify
the dead, because ashes now blown into sizeable heaps
throughout the desolate city represented the remains of
human beings, animals, property, wood, iron, and steel.

But one person living in St. Pierre at ten minutes past
eight on the morning of May 8, 1902, was alive five minutes
later. Months afterward, an official survey disclosed that
40,892 citizens of St. Pierre had died in those four minutes
of natural horror.

The one survivor was Auguste Ciparis, a Negro who had
been convicted of assault two years before. He had been
imprisoned in one of the ancient underground dungeons of
St. Pierre. He had another twenty months of confinement
to complete his sentence. At the first flash of light, he had
crouched low in his underground cell. At one time flaming
lava had seeped into the dungeon, but it had already spent
its intense heat and he had been able to smother it.

One week after the disaster, searchers heard a faint cry
from the walls of the prison and they found Ciparis, hungry
and thirsty, but untouched by the killing flame. A pardon
from the governor followed and the Negro lived on until

the year 1921. Nature's wrath had spared only one man—sentenced to prison by the society it destroyed.

One had lived where 40,892 died within four minutes. All of history fails to record an escape more miraculous.

# The *Titanic*

MGM made a dandy movie on the sinking of the *Titanic*. (Eighteen months before the movie, I wrote a story for *The Carolina Israelite* based on the transcript of the Lord Reading investigation into the disaster of April 15, 1912. The movie was a coincidence of course, and a pint of bourbon would settle all claims I have on MGM.)

Anyway, the picture followed the true story as faithfully as possible. A man *did* actually put on women's clothing to get into one of the lifeboats, but he was not discovered by anyone at the time. He confessed and killed himself years later. Records of the steamship line and other evidence pointed to the truth of his confession. Naturally the picture would be expected to side-step the testimony concerning Sir Cosmo and Lady Duff-Gordon. They left on Lifeboat Number 1, which, with a potential capacity of forty persons, had actually taken on twelve, of whom five were passengers and seven members of the crew. Sir Cosmo gave each member of the crew a five-pound note, and the allegation was made that it was paid as an inducement not to turn back and pick up people. Then the investigation revealed something about Sir Bruce Ismay, the owner of the line, who kept the radiogram from the *Baltic* which warned of icebergs. The charge was that Sir Bruce wanted nothing to interfere with the speed record he was after. Anyway Sir Bruce was saved by the *Carpathia* and—think of the happy surprise—he had two heavy trunks with him "saved" too. But six hundred of the seven hundred and nine third-class immigrants were drowned. More than fifteen hundred perished.

An Englishman stays to the last, hip-hip cheerio, and all

that, don't you know! This time, however, it was not an
Englishman, but an American Jewish woman, Ida Straus,
who stuck to the last. Offered a lifeboat, she said that she
had spent a long time with Mr. Straus and she saw no reason to be separated from him now. Anyway, Sir Bruce's
trunks probably took up too much room.


# Why Mussolini attacked on Easter

MUSSOLINI made a deal with the Albanian mountain chief-
tain, Zogu, who later made himself King Zog I. For sur-
rendering the sovereignty of his small kingdom Zog was to
receive financial support for his army, roads, schools, three
hundred miles of railroad, and a new palace for himself.
But, in the middle 1930's, there was no smarter cooky than
old Zogu. He seemed to sense that everything was on a
temporary basis, including Mussolini himself. As fast as
Musso sent him his monthly allotments, King Zog sent the
dough flying into banks at Istanbul, Paris, London, Zurich,
and New York.

All of this took some doing. Mussolini was not entirely a
dope, and Zog had to play the game carefully. He established a system of espionage and communication. As soon
as he got word that the Italian ambassador intended to pay
him a call, Zog whistled for his mountaineers who had rehearsed their act so thoroughly they could have mixed
cement in their sleep. Thus the Italian ambassador always
saw Albanians flapping around in their ballet skirts, busy as
one-armed paper hangers with hives—guys were mixing
cement, others were looking through surveyor's glasses,
measuring, yelling, giving orders, carrying bricks, measuring
lumber, and running hither and yon. Everybody was
busy until the Eyetalian was out of sight. Then old Zog
went back to his bankbooks, and his mountaineers went back

to the hills and their beloved distilled drink known as "kvatt." Once a non-Albanian took a drink of kvatt and actually succeeded in pulling his head off his shoulders with his bare hands.

Like the proverbial husband who is always the last one to know, the truth finally caught up with old Benito. But Musso was up against quite a problem. How could he tell the cheering mob under the balcony that he had just been made the prize sucker of all time by an Albanian mountain chief with a ballet skirt? Mussolini spent many sleepless nights during that winter of 1938 and spring of 1939. Here he was—the Caesar who made the trains run on time, now taken for the buggy ride to end all buggy rides.

Of course it wasn't one hour before Zogu found out that Musso had found out, and then began the strangest part of this fascinating bit of history. Zog knew that Mussolini was staying awake nights figuring out how to get his hands on the mountain king. Zog had ten high-powered motorcars stationed in front of his palace, arranged so that he could get away at a moment's notice. The cars were always loaded with gas and oil, and there were three shifts of trusted Zogu mountaineer chauffeurs. Zog conducted daily rehearsals of the getaway into Yugoslavia. But now Mussolini also knew about the motorcars. He knew too that Zog had trained a special battalion of mountaineers to handle the escape with everything timed to the split second—one man was assigned to removing the towel racks from the palace, another man was to take care of the silverware, and so forth. (Actually correspondents later reported that the Zog party had removed doorknobs from the palace, all the furnishings down to the Venetian blinds, nine cases of toilet paper, and ten full-length wall mirrors—he didn't leave Musso a stick.)

Mussolini could have taken Albania any time he wanted, of course, but it was not Albania he was after. He wanted his dough (estimates range from ten to fourteen millions). Benito knew that if he ever got his hooks on Zog, he would have a good chance of getting back the money.

Finally the break came. There was happiness in Rome that night, when Mussolini confirmed the rumor. The truth of the matter was that Queen Mathilda, Zog's wife, was very, very heavy with child, and the blessed event was due at any moment. Now it was Benito's turn to rub his hands. He checked with his staff officers. He knew that the battle had been won. He found that the cruiser which he held in readiness to grab Zog could get to the Albanian coast in four hours. A regiment of marines could be at Zog's palace in Triana exactly two hours later—six hours, that's all—how could he miss? All he need do was wait for the word from his espionage agents that Mathilda was having labor pains —and the invasion would begin.

At last, Mathilda took to her bed. The obstetrician was summoned, and Mussolini glanced at the calendar. A cold shiver went down his spine. It was Sunday, April 7, 1939 —and of all things—Easter Sunday. Musso had signed a concordat with the Vatican. His capital city was the center of world Christianity, but now fat Benito was set to invade a friendly neighbor on the most sacred day of the Christian year! But there was not a moment to lose. He gave the order and the Italians sailed against Albania.

But what was Zog doing this Easter Sunday morning? Of course he had left nothing to chance. During the previous forty-eight hours he had constructed a huge hospital-truck with special springs, an operating table complete with surgical supplies, and cabinets loaded down with most of Albania's medical supplies. The moment Musso's cruiser set sail, Zog's mountaineers went into action. In less than two hours, Zog, his wife and child, doctors, nurses, and mountaineers were on their way to Yugoslavia and then on to Hungary, and the home of Mathilda's parents. When Musso's marines arrived at the palace they found it literally stripped bare. Zog had even take the lawn mowers.

And so years after Mussolini had been hanged upside down and dragged to his grave with grappling hooks, old Zogu was buying up another mansion—this one on Long

Island in New York, and no doubt somewhere on the grounds at this very moment, some kvatt is being made by the man who came out best in World War II.

# The great books

READING without thinking is worse than no reading at all. Memorizing how many people there are in Tokyo or how long it took to build the Eiffel Tower is of little or no use at all. No one did anything in this world who was not a thinker.

That is why I am a bit skeptical about the current popularity of "Great Books" courses. Unless the books are studied and understood, the whole thing is useless. If a man read only one book all his life, and if it made him think, it would be worth more than having a smattering of a thousand works.

Of course many of the lists of the great books are made up by people who haven't read them at all. This is not as bad as it sounds. The list maker understands that a certain book is considered one of our great classics and it is enough that he has this sense of awareness.

My own list of books is not based on any idea that they should be accepted as the great books. I list them only to provide the titles of the books that have meant so much to me. These books are part of my life. I keep them at arm's length at all times and not a month goes by that I do not read some portion of them, in some instances for the one-hundredth time.

First, the Bible. The Bible is man's greatest literary expression. No writer has ever written a more perfect short story than the Biblical tale of the "Woman Taken in Adultery"; while the story of "Moses and the Ten Commandments" is so wonderful a narrative that it has become part of the consciousness of the entire human race. Has any

artist ever written a novel as perfect as the story of Ruth?
In eight or nine ordinary pages you have the story which
establishes the status of women and the laws of inheritance
among the Hebrews. And so the story builds up through
Samuel, Saul, Jonathan; right up to the supreme figure of all
history and literature, King David.

Next is Shakespeare. I have concentrated on fifteen of the
plays.

It makes you feel good, too, to have a few books of the
collected plays of George Bernard Shaw. I read the prefaces
all the time with an occasional dip into *Saint Joan* and
*Major Barbara* for favorite passages.

*Plutarch's Lives* would come next.

These and the other books I list here are my textbooks.
In other words, I open them all the time, perhaps to read
a single chapter or only a footnote, for example, the footnotes in Hume's *History of England;* Lecky's *History of
European Morals* and Gibbon's *Decline and Fall of the
Roman Empire* provide a wonderful opportunity for a liberal
education.

Another one of my textbooks is *History of Civilization in
England,* by Henry Thomas Buckle. This man died at the
age of forty-one; he had written only two volumes of what
might have been the best of all histories.

Neither have I been too far away from Carlyle's *The
French Revolution, The Rise of American Civilization* by
Charles and Mary Beard, and a book I wouldn't part with
for anything, *The History of the Intellectual Development
of Europe,* by John Draper. I once memorized an entire
chapter of Henry George's masterpiece, *Progress and
Poverty;* and I know *Leaves of Grass* by Walt Whitman.
And I often reread portions of *Abraham Lincoln* by Carl
Sandburg.

Novels, too, are important to me—*David Copperfield,* by
Dickens; *Père Goriot,* by Balzac; *The Scarlet Letter,* by Haw-
thorne; *The Grapes of Wrath,* by John Steinbeck; and *Jean
Christophe,* by Romain Rolland.

Years ago I went through a long period of reading the mythology of the world. To this day I envy the person who has yet to read Sir Thomas Malory's *Morte d'Arthur,* and the Norse mythology which I remember came in a great big book called *Twilight Tales.*

Some years ago I bought a copy of *The Anatomy of Melancholy,* and this is a particularly valuable volume because there are footnotes with translations of the many Latin phrases. Here is a man, Robert Burton, who, back in 1621, sat down and recorded everything he had in his giant brain, including some of the finest philosophy ever written.

Another one of my textbooks is *The Martyrdom of Man,* by Winwood Reade. His uncle, the novelist Charles Reade, is better known, but Winwood's one book is a masterpiece.

No one who loves the English language should be without Benjamin Franklin's *Autobiography. What a remarkable man!* It was one of the first autobiographies in which the author told about the problems of day-to-day living in personal terms. The best description is to call it a book of wisdom. I picked up an extra paper-bound edition a few years ago, and found that they had expurgated (God help them) a few passages of this great work, and I thought to myself, "What a cockeyed civilization that sells hundreds of novels with four-letter words on every page, and expurgates some of the most noble sentiments ever recorded in the language."

I must say something about another of my beloved books; a work by Luigi Luzzatti, *God in Freedom,* translated from the original Italian, *Dio nella Libertà.* Luzzatti had been professor of public law at the University of Rome, and eventually became prime minister of Italy.

*God in Freedom* is the philosophy of law in its relation to man's struggle for religious freedom. The range of the book is enormous.

I think that the books which played the greatest role in shaping the thinking of mankind include the Pentateuch. And in the eighteenth century before Christ, Hammurabi, the king of Babylon, wrote the regulations known as the *Laws of Hammurabi*. It set the course of mankind for many generations. Egypt produced one of the great books which is known as *Book of the Dead*. It is a collection of biographical data of Pharaohs, and was compiled at the death of each ruler. Then we have the epics of Homer, which gave unity to the disunited Greek civilization and actually laid the foundation for the magnificent Greek culture. India of course is represented by "The Institutes of Manu"; and from China we have the sayings of Confucius; then back again to Greece with Plato's *Republic* and Aristotle's *Politics;* and finally the Gospels of Jesus of Nazareth.

In every nook and corner of this world, wherever two or more men have met in peace, their greeting and their conversation was, to some degree, influenced by one of these books.

Of course I am aware that there are many wide gaps in my reading. I know very well the high place in the world of letters occupied by Goethe, but I know little of him or of Schiller.

I suppose that prejudice plays a part in all of this, too. I once read an article by Tolstoy in which he said that Shakespeare was not a good writer; in fact, he claimed that a certain Mr. Tucker of Boston, Massachusetts, was a greater writer than Shakespeare; and this soured me on Tolstoy. Mr. Tucker was pamphleteer for the anarchists of America, but his political affiliation did not sway me; it was only that Tolstoy said he was a better writer than Shakespeare. This, I know, is a silly prejudice. It would be like disregarding the wonderful stories of Sherlock Holmes because Sir Arthur Conan Doyle was serious about his ability to talk with the dead. I lost on this Tolstoy deal, I know.

I did not pay the slightest attention to Jewish history until the advent of Adolf Hitler, and then I went at it with the fanaticism of a convert. I had gone to a meeting to "Boycott Nazi Germany," and I was given an assignment to see the heads of several department stores. One told me that they bought a lot of canary birds from Germany and what would happen if a customer wanted a canary? Another said that they had sold millions of dollars worth of Dresden china and what would happen when a customer broke a saucer and needed one to complete the set? But none of this discouraged me.

I once sat down to read the *Universal Jewish Encyclopedia*. I know how silly it sounds for a man to claim that he has read an encyclopedia, but that is exactly what I did. A couple of hours a day, and within a few months the job was done. I did not miss a single item, from volume one, "Aaron to Azuli," through the ten volumes to "Spicebox to Zweig." I knew this would be a good investment. What I did was to create an inventory, and one which is not even taxable.

Our people are known as the "People of the Book." It is the Book and other books which have sustained us, and books laid the foundation of this entire better world in which we live:

> There are abandoned corners of our Exile,
> Remote, forgotten cities of Dispersion,
> Where still in secret burns our ancient light,
> Where God has saved a remnant from disaster.
>
> —CHAIM BIALIK

# Who is a great artist?

I STAND in awe of music lovers who worship at the shrine of the three B's—Bach, Beethoven, and Brahms. My own three "B's" are Mozart, Rossini, and Verdi. I think that Mozart and Shakespeare were the two supreme artists of the human race. And they had much in common. Neither Mozart nor Shakespeare said: "Oh, me, I'm in love and must write a poem," or "I am suffering and I will now express my feelings in my art." Essentially we can call them the super-reporters of the human race. They were writing stories as they saw them, and once in a while a special feature. You want wedding music? Okay, this is what wedding music should sound like. Mozart did not build his art around himself. He stood apart like the great artist who paints a landscape. This is it. This is the land, and these are the people who inhabit the land, and these are the everyday problems of human existence.

We haven't the slightest idea what Shakespeare himself thought about politics, religion, love, sex, and human relations. We do know that he reported all the emotions of which humans are capable, that he drew a full-length portrait of each of us which is as true today as it was in his day. Shakespeare and Mozart painted the pictures as they saw them. If they had a headache or if a girl stood them up on a date, we do not know it.

Shakespeare and Mozart had a sense of life, and that is why each is one of us, now and always.

To digress for a moment, I think a love of music is acquired like anything else. Training, training—as Joseph Pulitzer kept saying about good reporters. Listening, listening—to learn to appreciate and love good music. In my home the phonograph was going day and night, like in so many other homes on the East Side. I played "Mi chiamano Mimi" (My Name Is Mimi), sung by Lucrezia Bori, so often that I learned the Italian words (not an easy thing to do from an opera record), and I learned to love Lucrezia Bori with a devotion that has lasted through life. Another great favorite in those days was, "Lo, Hear the Gentle Lark," sung by Alma Gluck "with flute obbligato." That was a tremendous favorite on the East Side because Alma Gluck was an immigrant Jewess from Romania; Reba Fiersohn was her name. My father loved everything Alma Gluck sang, and one of the records, a duet with Louise Homer, was "Whispering Hope," a magnificent piece of work.

My father would have been surprised at his enthusiasm if he had known it was a Christian hymn.

Perhaps I should list here some of the music I learned to cherish.

These are my favorite operatic arias:

Tenor: "Je crois entendre encore," from *The Pearl Fishers* (Bizet).

"O Paradiso," from *L'Africaine* (Meyerbeer).

"La donna è mobile," from *Rigoletto* (Verdi).

Baritone: "Madamina! Il catalogo," from *Don Giovanni* (Mozart).

"Credo in un Dio crudel," from *Otello* (Verdi).

Soprano: "Una voce poco fa," from *The Barber of Seville* (Rossini).

"Caro nome," from *Rigoletto* (Verdi).

"Mi chiamano Mimi," from *La Bohème* (Puccini).

Duet: "Là ci darem la mano," from *Don Giovanni* (Mozart).

"Solenne in quest' ora," from *La Forza del Destino* (Verdi).

Quartet: "Bella figlia dell' amore," from *Rigoletto* (Verdi).

Quintet: "E scherzo od è follia," from *The Masked Ball* (Verdi).

Sextet: "Chi mi frena," from *Lucia di Lammermoor* (Donizetti).

I think the greatest recording ever made was "Solenne in quest' ora" with Enrico Caruso and Antonio Scotti. The second best was a Spanish melody, "A la luz de la luna," sung by Enrico Caruso and Emilio De Gogorza.

There was nothing wrong, either, with Caruso and Schumann-Heink singing "Ai nostri monti," from *Il Trovatore*, or Caruso and Rosa Ponselle in the "Miserere" from the same opera.

The first time I heard these records was when my cousin Joe, who lived with us as a boarder, bought a phonograph. The phonograph and his opera records were his most valued possessions and he guarded them with zeal and devotion. Every time he left the house he warned one and all against anyone's playing the phonograph in his absence. It took a little skill to play the thing anyway. You had to have a steady hand in applying the needle to the record and you had to be very careful not to overwind the machine itself. Eventually this whole business became a great problem with Joe. The moment he entered the house he rushed immediately to his phonograph and records and cried out in distress, "Aha, somebody has played the phonograph already." We then realized that Joe was leaving some secret marking on the machine or among his records; and we responded accordingly. Before we touched anything we studied the situation very carefully, taking mental notes of the exact position of the machine, the direction of the horn, and the records as we found them. But this did not work. Somehow Joe always knew. The machine, as I recall it, had a headpiece in which you put the needle. This was a comparatively small but most important part of the phonograph. Finally, when Joe went out to work or in the evening to a meeting to hear Morris Hillquit, Algernon Lee, and the other Socialists of the day, he would unscrew that headpiece and hide it. This made it very tough, and we often spent an hour or more looking for it. We found it, of course, and Joe finally gave up. He just took that part with him wherever he went. I take a more tolerant view of the whole business today.

In those days Joe was a shipping clerk. Every dollar he could spare went for opera records and in those days they cost from $1.50 for a ten-inch record to as much as $6.50 for the Sextette, and, of course, you did not begin to live until you had acquired the Sextette. I have forgiven Joe a thousand times for hiding that phonograph headpiece. Instead I am eternally grateful to this immigrant workman who introduced me to the opera.

And Joe has been a workingman all his life. In recent years he and his wife have operated an old-fashioned candy store and newsstand in South Ozone Park, New York. They have both worked night and day, sending their children to college and seeing them married off. I haven't seen Joe in a good many years, but I am sure of one thing. Candy store or no candy store, somewhere very close to him are a phonograph and albums of Caruso, Alda, Bori, and Scotti.

Now, why have all these artists meant so much to me? Who is a great artist?

Well, for just one example, Julie Harris is an artist.

What a wonderful thing to see an actress in these days without big breasts who can hold her audience by the sheer magic of the spoken word—the slight movement of the hand, or a tilt of the head. After you see her in *The Lark* you finally believe in the story of the Maid of Orleans.

She was a most convincing prostitute in *I Am a Camera*, and now she makes you believe in saints in her playing of Joan of Arc. If we can produce a Julie Harris, what's a little miracle like the "voices" of Joan of Arc? I'd love to drink wine out of her slipper.

But to get back to the question of who is a great artist, I say it is the one who imposes least on his audience. Obviously when a girl takes her clothes off on the burlesque stage, it may be pleasant and all that, but that's just the point. Captive audiences do not go hand in hand with art. And here I refer to captive audiences attracted by writers, actors, artists who appeal to prejudice, fear, hate, sex, and murder. In old vaudeville days some of the acts had various props to win audience approval. A song, "Mother Is Your Best Friend," would turn the trick, or waving an American flag at the end of an act. I remember one lousy act used to unfurl a backdrop showing Abraham Lincoln in a Father Abraham pose, holding his hand over kneeling Negroes. It always brought down the house. But these were harmless props. Many writers use props which are not harmless.

Let me make this point by citing two Southern writers—

Thomas Dixon of North Carolina and Ellen Glasgow of Virginia. They were contemporaries. Mr. Dixon's audience was, let us say, at least thirty thousand times larger than Miss Glasgow's. Of course I include in this Dixon audience the people who saw (and are still seeing) *The Birth of a Nation*. This was one of Mr. Dixon's more rabid novels known as *The Clansman*, which did its duty in stirring up racial feeling and in the creation of the Ku Klux Klan of the 1920's. The point I make (I'm no prophet, it's already happening) is that long after Mr. Dixon and *The Birth of a Nation* are completely forgotten, Miss Glasgow's novel *Barren Ground* will be resting in honored places on the shelves of libraries and homes of the English-speaking world. Miss Glasgow did not impose on her audience. She was the true artist. *Barren Ground* was the first Southern novel that lifted the South out of space and into time.

It's interesting that in the end the people themselves know best. It takes time, but as high as they raise a Mickey Spillane or a Thomas Dixon, after a while they blot them from memory with a vengeance. "Art alone endures."

(Note: Wildacres, Dixon's mountain project, is now the site of the B'nai B'rith Institute of Judaism. An ironic development that could happen, of course, only in America.)

## Lincoln and Pericles

WHEN Abraham Lincoln was asked to speak at Gettysburg, he knew it was only a polite invitation. The principal speaker was Edward Everett, a Unitarian clergyman and United States Senator. Everett was the best speaker of his day and Lincoln had no wish to encroach upon what would no doubt be a milestone in American letters.

Lincoln's few words were only protocol. At the ceremonies, Everett spoke for one hour and fifty-seven minutes and Lincoln for a few minutes, and Lincoln's Gettysburg Address will live forever.

When Everett was introduced he bowed low to the President, then stood in silence before a crowd of fifteen thousand people that stretched far out to the limits of the cemetery field. He had earlier rehearsed a portion of his speech to make sure that his voice would carry to the edge of the crowd overflowing the adjoining wheat field. Mr. Everett began low: "Overlooking these broad fields now reposing from the labors of the waning year, the mighty Alleghenies dimly towering before us, the graves of our brethren beneath our feet, it is with hesitation that I raise my poor voice to break the eloquent silence of God and nature." It was the effort of Everett's life and by the standards of the day a perfect oration. Then came the President's turn. He fumbled for his steel-rimmed glasses, put his high stovepipe hat on the floor beside his chair, took out a wrinkled piece of paper, and began: "Four score and seven years ago our fathers brought forth on this continent, a new nation, conceived in Liberty, and dedicated to the proposition that all men are created equal . . ." an echo of a few other speeches made before him at Sinai, and at another place in Palestine they called "the Mount," and eight minutes later this speech was finished, ". . . that government of the people, by the people, for the people, shall not perish from the earth," and the President sat down.

Yet, to Everett's credit, he was the first to realize that Lincoln had transcended politics, protocol, and matters of state and had entered history and literature. Everett understood at once the supreme eloquence, and, in praising the Address, which met with only desultory applause, said it was a second Periclean Funeral Oration.

What Everett referred to was the speech Pericles delivered when he spoke over the mass grave of the Athenians who had first fallen against the Spartans.

The war was the Peloponnesian War (the Peloponnesus was the peninsula of which Sparta was the capital) and the year was 431 B.C., the first year of the war.

The Athenians, following their custom, gave a public

funeral for soldiers who had died in battle. All of these soldiers were laid in a public sepulcher, each in a separate coffin. There was always one extra coffin, which represented all the missing soldiers—our unknown soldier is a tradition we have borrowed from the Greeks. After the prayer and benediction, a prominent citizen was asked to read a eulogy; Pericles, who had been, and was to be again, the ruler of Athens, was asked to fulfill this formality. Next to the Gettysburg Address, Pericles' is the shortest funeral oration on record (it is about four pages long) and it and the Gettysburg Address are two of the greatest expressions of the human intellect.

Pericles started by saying that he wished the reputation of the many brave men were not imperiled in his mouth to stand or fall as he spoke good or ill. He went on from there to praise Athens which, he said, was "the school of Hellas." Then he said:

> We throw open our city to the world and never by alien acts exclude foreigners from any opportunity of learning or observing, although the eyes of the enemy may occasionally profit from our liberality. . . . We cultivate refinement without extravagance and knowledge without effeminacy, wealth we employ more for use than for show, and place the real disgrace of poverty not in owning to the fact but in declining to struggle against it.

It was for Athens that these soldiers, he went on, had died. "But," he said, "heroes have the whole earth for their tomb and it is only the love of honor that never grows old, and honor it is, not gain, that rejoices the heart of age and helplessness."

The speech is preserved for us in the *History of the Peloponnesian War* by Thucydides. Thucydides was a general in this war, but was later fired by the Athenians for arriving late at a battle. It was no fault of his own, but in his history he does not excuse himself. He is a historian much like Sir Winston Churchill, writing flawlessly about a war in which he played a major part.

When Pericles finished his oration, the mourners turned and walked away, just as they did when Lincoln finished. Both men, so aptly compared by Edward Everett, were by destiny the leaders of their nations and both were eventually sacrificed. And both walked into literature by performing in a simple way a minor duty of state, a eulogy over the dead.

Back on November 19, 1863, there was at least one other observer perceptive enough to appreciate the greatness of Lincoln's little talk.

*The Chicago Tribune* was right.

*The Patriot,* a local paper at nearby Harrisburg, said, "The President acted without sense . . . so let us pass over his silly remarks."

*The Chicago Times* said, "The cheek of every American must tingle with shame as he reads the silly, flat utterances of the President."

The correspondent for the London *Times* wrote: "Anything more dull and commonplace it would not be easy to produce."

A reporter for *The Chicago Tribune* sent home the following dispatch: *"The dedicatory remarks of President Abraham Lincoln will live forever in the annals of man."*


# The Ghost of Cherry Street

I observed the High Holy Days at the famous Spanish-Portuguese Synagogue in New York, Shearith Israel (Remnant of Israel), on Central Park West. In the vestibule of this oldest Jewish congregation in America, I saw the grinding mill that had been on the property of its first edifice on Mill Street. A year or two after the congregation was founded

in 1655, the Jews of New York were given permission to
bury their dead in their own cemetery. The earliest deci-
pherable date on a gravestone is 1683.

(At a meeting some months ago I was heckled by a white
supremacist. "When did you come to the South?" he wanted
to know, and I told him: "I came in 1655.")

George Washington had a residence at 1 Cherry Street.
This Cherry Street had received its name from the cherry
gardens in the vicinity, but, in modern times it became the
very symbol of poverty. If you lived on Cherry Street, you
were very poor, and you were also very tough. In a report
by the Association for Improving the Conditions of the Poor,
we find that Cherry Street had sixty tenement houses in
which there were rooms fourteen by nine feet with one
window, and each room housed an average of seven people.

John Hancock lived at Number 24 and Edgar Allan Poe
at Number 18. Mr. Poe was a reporter at the time, and he
patronized Anderson's Tobacco Shop at 26 Nassau Street. A
beautiful salesgirl there by the name of Mary Rogers was
a favorite of many of the great men of the day. Washington
Irving and James Fenimore Cooper were also among her
customers.

Mary disappeared and her body was later found, dis-
figured, floating in the Hudson River. The crime shocked the
city, and Edgar Allan Poe wrote a story about it, *The
Mystery of Marie Rogêt*.

The facts came out two years later. Mary Rogers died as
a result of an abortion. The abortionist and the young lover
had become panicky and had disposed of the body. The
woman who had attempted the operation was arrested for
another crime and confessed about Mary. She did not know
the name of the young man who had brought Miss Rogers
to her, and there was never a clue to his identity.

In my day we all heard about "The Ghost of Cherry
Street." In an old tenement, voices kept coming through the
pipes and they chased tenants out. The people, social workers, and philosophers went down there to investigate, but

nothing came of it; the tenement was abandoned and finally destroyed.


# Evelyn Nesbit Thaw

I SAW a photo of Evelyn Nesbit Thaw in the newspaper not long ago. It showed her modeling with clay—a sculptress. The caption gave her age as sixty-one and she was still a beautiful woman.

Just think of all that has happened since the murder trial of her husband, Harry K. Thaw. That was in the year 1907. In those fifty-two years we have had at least a thousand years of history, maybe more. Whole dynasties disappeared. The Hohenzollerns, the Hapsburgs, the Romanovs, some of the lesser royal houses, Alfonso of Spain, Ferdinand of Bulgaria, Marie and Ferdinand of Romania, the whole Ottoman Empire was shattered, and a modern Turk came along who, in five years, eliminated habits of two thousand years, the fez for men and the veil for the women. Poland was still split among Germany, Russia, and Austria in accordance with an agreement signed by Frederick the Great, Catherine of Russia, and Maria Theresa of Austria, but Poland rose and fell twice during those fifty-two years; then split up again, and now back again to darkness. Whole countries disappeared, new ones were born. Some went through the processes of birth and death twice. And the personalities! Wilhelm, Franz Josef, Joffre, Foch, Clemenceau, David Lloyd George, Woodrow Wilson, Hindenburg, Ludendorff, William Randolph Hearst, Pershing, Einstein, Mussolini, Hitler, Lenin, Stalin, rose, filled the world with thunder, and disappeared—all within those same fifty-two years. Millions of people were murdered in incinerators and lime kilns; whole populations moved from one country to another. Other millions had no country any more—were chased from one border across another. Then there were Sir Winston Churchill, General Eisenhower, Franklin Delano Roosevelt, Harry Truman, the United Nations; Israel became a sovereign nation after two thousand years; there were the wonder of the movie camera, the automobile, the airplane, and television. And there were the sinking of the *Titanic,* the Iroquois Theatre fire, the Triangle fire which helped establish trade unionism. Those fifty-two years had Clarence Darrow fighting for the underdog; they also had William Jennings Bryan and Teddy. The soapbox radical in 1907 was egged because he demanded workmen's compensation, and within fifty-two years a Republican President of the United States demanded more social security and more old-age pensions.

And I guess to Evelyn Nesbit Thaw, modeling clay out in California, the whole thing seemed like yesterday.

Fifty-two years ago, the President of the United States was someone way off in the distance, like a king or something, and you thought of him in personal terms only once in four years. The biggest piece of news was the trial of Harry K. Thaw. Everything was local, down the block, around the corner, the union hall, the corner saloon, and the band concert in the park. Those were the big things. When you thought of government you thought of the local member of the Board of Aldermen, or maybe your assemblyman. The local picture has changed in those fifty-two years. The states' rights boys are hanging on for dear life, but it's a losing battle. A governorship of a state used to be a tremendous proposition. Eventually the office will be occupied by a professionally trained administrator, like the city managers in so many of our cities. The governor will be a $25,000-a-year state manager, and he'll be hired by a committee of the Legislature. All eyes are now on Washington. The fellow used to stand in line every Friday night to get a three-minute audience with the district leader or his member of the Board of Aldermen. Today that same fellow says: "What will Ike do?" "And what about Nehru?"

In 1907 life was the shoeshine stand on the corner, and you took a walk on Sundays. You may have lived in a big city, but actually it was a small village. You knew the homes that had a sick child, or a wayward daughter, or a genius son. If we ever spoke of a foreign country it was always in terms of the geography lesson at school. You said, "Paris, France"; "London, England"; "Tokyo, Japan." Today every garage mechanic speaks trippingly of Paris, Rome, Cannes.

Journalism has changed. Our whole concept of sex and life has changed. I was reading a story of the trial of Harry K. Thaw in 1907 by Irvin S. Cobb, the great humorist, who was a correspondent representing a string of newspapers. The story told that when Evelyn Nesbit Thaw came to a particular point in her testimony everybody in the courtroom began to cry, and even Irvin S. Cobb could not hold back the tears. Do you know what Evelyn Nesbit Thaw said that made everybody cry, including the judge, the jury, and Irvin S. Cobb? She told about Stanford White (the murdered man). "He took off my clothes," she said.

But don't laugh at that now, because that's the whole trouble with everything. Irvin S. Cobb lived a life of honor and of humor, and let us envy him that in his time the only thing there was to cry about was—Evelyn Nesbit Thaw, fourteen, being undressed by a fat old man.

All of this came about in fifty-two years, and I'll tell you a secret. With all that has happened, if the trial of Harry K. Thaw were on today, it would still be on Page One.

So with all these dynasties and reforms, disasters and personalities, what remains? The same thing remains—the Big Story—LIFE—the relationship between a man and woman; a jealous husband; a beautiful woman; a secret and confession —those are all still part of the Big Story.

And now, after all that, I should at least tell you about the trial of Harry K. Thaw, shouldn't I?

Harry K. Thaw, whose doting mother gave him all the money in the world, fell in love with the show girl, Evelyn Nesbit, whom artists called the "most beautiful girl in the world." She was eighteen when she married Thaw, who was the heir to millions of Pittsburgh, Pennsylvania, dollars. Evelyn Nesbit was eighteen, but she had already "tasted of the bitter dregs of life," as they used to call it in 1907. When she was fourteen it appears that Evelyn and her mother had been befriended by America's number one architect—Stanford White, of the firm of McKim, Meade, and White, builders of the Washington Arch, dozens of mansions for millionaires, and designers of the Panama Canal. White was a fat, middle-aged màn known as a *"bon vivant"*; a 1907 term for wolf. Evelyn's mother accepted White's friendship and let the fat millionaire pay for Evelyn's singing and dancing lessons. She also dressed up Evelyn in middy blouse and sailor hat to "go pose for that nice old man."

Now it's four years later. Thaw, erratic as hell (in later life he used to whip young boys with a hairbrush), is in love with Evelyn. He woos her and wins her for his wife. Thaw probably married Evelyn for the thrilling experience of hearing about Stanford White and what all he did, because, from the first day, Harry K. was obsessed with Stanford White and—"I demand that you tell me the truth—it wasn't all platonic, was it?" Evelyn was being driven crazy by these constant demands of her husband, so she confessed: "No, it wasn't all platonic." She gave Thaw the details of her seduction, how one afternoon after she had finished posing, fat old White gave her a glass of champagne and removed her middy blouse. She remembered that the champagne tickled her nose—and then all went black. She blacked out twice a week like this for nearly a year up in Stanford's penthouse—and that was indeed that.

On June 25, 1906, Harry K. Thaw murdered White. He shot him during an intermission of a floor show on top of old Madison Square Garden. White had designed the building, and that's where he died with his boots on. Thaw handed the pistol to the person closest to him and, with considerable originality, said: "He had it coming." The trial was a sensation. It had everything. The murdered man was an international figure; the killer, a millionaire playboy; the girl, a famed beauty; and Thaw's mother was right beside him with all the millions at her command to save him. She sacrificed more than money. She took the stand and swore that her son had always been mentally unbalanced. That's quite a thing for a mother to do. There were over one hundred witnesses, and for the first time psychiatrists—they called them "alienists"—played an important role in an American courtroom. After all the testimony was in, the jury found itself hopelessly deadlocked, and when they were polled they stood seven for conviction, five for acquittal. At the next proceeding, Thaw was permitted to plead to an indictment which sent him to the State Hospital for the Criminally Insane, at Matteawan, New York. After a few years of incarceration, Mr. Thaw escaped in a milk wagon, and after some maneuvering by lawyers, judges, authorities, and mother, the matter drifted out of the courts and out of the headlines. Thaw lived on a farm in Virginia until his death about a dozen years ago.

The story lasted five full years—almost right up to the day when a Serbian high-school student shot and killed the Archduke Francis Ferdinand, heir to the throne of the Austro-Hungarian Empire, which started the ball a-rolling.

In London, Sir Edward Grey, the foreign secretary, looked out the window and said, "The lamps are going out all over Europe; we shall not see them lit again in our lifetime."

## Jewish rye

THE folks up in the Bronx are up to their ears in English muffins. The Jewish rye bread bakeries have been on strike for many weeks. The wives are calling up the husbands to stop off at a delicatessen store in Manhattan to bring home —a rye. Of course, the best thing they can do is bring home a factory rye, wrapped in cellophane, and these synthetics are just not the same thing. When the boy comes home from school, you send him for the rye, and there's no fake wax paper wrapped around it, and it is especially good if the kid

drops it on the sidewalk once or twice on the way home, or
if he plays catch with it with another kid; besides, nothing
but authentic Jewish rye bread has the shpitz (the pointed
end) which is so delightful with a bit of cream cheese and a
heavy slab of lox. Let us hope that the strikers go back to
work, and the folks up in the Bronx are soon relieved of
those English muffins and that fancy wrapping-paper rye.

# The heart recalls

TIN PAN ALLEY said it before Freud:

I want a girl just like the girl that married dear old dad.
I've got you under my skin.
Did you ever see a dream walking?
I'll see you in my dreams.
When I grow too old to dream.
I'm forever blowing bubbles.

And that most gnawing of all fears that has sent so many
men to the couch of the analyst:

I wonder who's kissing her now.

I think the best popular song ever written is "I Wonder
Who's Kissing Her Now." The lyrics are worthy of a Lord
Byron or an Edna St. Vincent Millay:

I wonder if she ever tells him of me—
I wonder who's kissing her now.

There was an entire era of great songs from 1900 to 1912;
it was the day of the music hall; no radio, television, or
automobile; and comic books were not yet important. There
was Girard's great song:

Sweet Adeline, My Adeline,
At night, dear heart, For you I pine.
In all my dreams, Your fair face beams;
You're the flower of my heart, Sweet Adeline.

The great political song was written by Theodore Metz. Whenever Theodore Roosevelt appeared, the band blared forth:

There'll be a hot time in the old town tonight.

Then there was Jessie Brown Pounds' "Beautiful Isle of Somewhere":

Somewhere, Somewhere, Beautiful Isle of Somewhere,
    Land of the true, where we live anew,
Beautiful Isle of Somewhere!

And how about the immortal lines:

Many a heart is aching, if you could read them all,
Many the hopes that have vanished, after the ball.

Another sentimental hit was Monroe Rosenfield's song, "Take Back Your Gold":

Take back your gold, for gold can never buy me.
Take back your bribe, and promise you'll be true.

Man began to sing even before he scratched his ideas on stone. Every man has "a song"—"our song," the lovers call it, but it goes much deeper in our consciousness. You hear a song and it reconstructs the past.

The everlasting popularity of many of our hit tunes is based on this nostalgia. Man's greatest of all possessions—memory—makes songs live for generations.

You will find in this song culture a continuing commentary on our lives, our loves, our aspirations, our hopes for the future.

A thousand novels were wrapped up in one song title: "There's a Broken Heart for Every Light on Broadway." It brings back memories. It establishes the time, the place, the hour; indeed, the very moment.

And so, as we sing "Mary is a grand old name," and "Daisy, Daisy," the poet Bayard Taylor has already explained: "Each heart recalled a different name, but they all sang Annie Laurie."

> Maxwellton's braes are bonnie
> Where early fa's the dew
> And 'twas there that Annie Laurie
> Gave me her promise true.

## Only-in-America Department

AH, WHAT a wonderful country this is. I delivered some lectures at the Southern Senior Judaea at Camp Blue Star, Hendersonville, North Carolina. It was a sort of workshop on the 1954 celebration of the three hundredth anniversary of Jewish settlement in the United States, and, as I finished my first lecture on that noble man George Washington, the two hundred Jewish high-school boys and girls from all parts of the South—from Lumpkin, Georgia, to Memphis, Tennessee —rose as one to give me three cheers—in Hebrew. "Hay-daad, hay-daad, hay-daad." George Washington would have been pleased. I replied to the cheers in Washington's words, written in the summer of 1790 in a letter to the Hebrew Congregation in Newport, Rhode Island:

". . . May the Children of the Stock of Abraham, who dwell in this land, continue to merit and enjoy the good will of the other inhabitants; while every one shall sit in safety under his own vine and figtree, and there shall be none to make him afraid. May the Father of all mercies scatter light and not darkness in our paths, and make us all in our several vocations useful here, and in his own due time and way everlastingly happy."

# The Associated Press

MY FAVORITE story about the mighty Associated Press concerns Sam Davis, a Nevada string correspondent, who interviewed Sarah Bernhardt for *The Carson Appeal*, his own little paper; for *The San Francisco Examiner;* and for the A.P. The actress liked him so much that, when her train was ready to leave, she put her hands on his shoulders, kissed him on each cheek, and then squarely on the mouth. She said, "The right cheek for *The Carson Appeal*, the left for *The Examiner*, the lips, my friend, for yourself."

Davis displayed no trace of bashfulness. "Madam," he exclaimed, "I also represent The Associated Press, which serves three hundred and eighty papers west of the Mississippi River alone!"

# One hundred years of the American novel

1856:—"She has canceled all her social engagements."
1880:—"She is in an interesting condition."
1895:—"She is in a delicate condition."
1910:—"She is knitting little booties."
1920:—"She is in a family way."
1935:—"She is expecting."
1956:—"She's pregnant."

# The Charlotte Coliseum

WHEN Titus completed the Roman Colosseum, five thousand animals were killed as part of the dedication activities. This act was followed by five hundred pairs of gladiators fighting each other to the death.

When Charlotte dedicated its six-million-dollar coliseum in 1956, Billy Graham, the evangelist, just made a speech.

We have come a long way.

# The time capsule

WHEN a new important building goes up there is the usual ceremony of sealing a crypt in the cornerstone, "to be opened in the year 2059." The crypt contains copies of the daily newspapers and other pertinent documents. Of course, there are many imponderables connected with this procedure. For one thing, we are not sure that the affairs which seem important to us will interest the people in the year 2059. Some time ago they tore down a century-old building in Charlotte and in the cornerstone was a list of the members of a local fraternity. Naturally, this was important to the people who sealed the crypt, but frustrating to those who opened it with such trembling hands.

# The North Pole

THE Russians claim they are the first to have crossed the North Pole. They maintain no one reached it until they sent two aviators over it in 1938. We know this is propaganda. The important thing is not who reached it but who's going to figure out how to farm it. The funny thing about the North Pole is that there has always been a great dispute about who was the first to get there. Admiral Robert E. Peary is usually credited with having reached it in 1909. But when Peary returned from this successful expedition, he found that Dr. Frederick A. Cook, who had been a surgeon on Peary's 1891 expedition, had just filed a claim that he got there before

Peary. Dr. Cook insisted that he had reached it on April 21, 1908. After a long investigation (after all, no one left footprints), Dr. Cook was adjudged wrong. Peary was the discoverer. But was he? The story is that he left the ice-bound expedition ship and set off on foot for the Pole some one hundred miles away. He was back in a couple of days. He and his party were piped aboard by the captain of the ship who stepped forward as Peary came up the gangplank and said, "Congratulations, Admiral, on having reached the North Pole." Peary never said he had or hadn't reached the Pole. All he did was shake the captain's hand.

# Gala night at the Met

WEARING a sixty-nine-cent sweater and carrying my schoolbooks, I used to take my place once a week in the line at the Met as soon as school let out at 3:00 P.M.

By 6:30, I could sell this favorable spot for one dollar and wait at the end of the line again until 8:15, when the Met put standing room on sale.

After a few weeks, I had a steady customer. A little woman looked for me and she always had the dollar bill inside her glove.

Once she said to me, "You weren't here last week."

And I said, "It was a Jewish holiday."

And she said, "Oh."

It was too bad I was not yet a reporter because it would be nice to write about her, her name, her history, her education, her interests, and her needs.

When I got a little older I noticed that many of the regular subscribers in swallowtail coats and ermine wraps would leave at the end of the first or second act, probably to go to the Waldorf or Delmonico's or Sherry's. One evening I asked a departing gentleman for his stubs. For some reason he appeared to be overjoyed when he gave them to me. When the third act began I could almost reach out and touch Frances Alda. This gambit gave me an insight into the comparative popularity of the operas. I was always certain of a front-row seat for *Lucia di Lammermoor, Rigoletto,* and *Aïda.* For *Carmen, Samson et Dalila,* and *La Bohème,* it was fifty-fifty. I never got a stub for *Tristan und Isolde* or *Don Giovanni.*

# PART 5

# From Clam Chowder
## to Shakespeare

# Eisenhower and the Republicans

THERE is one lone hostage down in Washington and his name is Dwight D. Eisenhower. He is all alone and surrounded. In a sense, he has been double-crossed. He is the only person in Washington not responsible for his present predicament. Back in 1950 every political hack and ward heeler started flying across the Atlantic to importune Eisenhower to run for President. They promised him he could be the kind of President he wanted to be. He was lulled by these promises and he decided to run.

Everybody voted for Eisenhower. Management voted for Eisenhower. Labor voted for Eisenhower. The Negro voted for Eisenhower. The white supremacist voted for Eisenhower. It reminded me of an old-fashioned Jewish wedding. Everybody cried but each one was thinking of something else.

Now management is mad at Eisenhower because they say he is really a New Dealer; labor is mad at Eisenhower because he did not amend the Taft-Hartley Act; the Negro is mad at Eisenhower because he did not step into the vacuum between those who said "tomorrow" and those who said "never," and the white supremacist is mad at Eisenhower because he sent the troops to Little Rock. But it is worse than this.

The professional Republicans are mad at Eisenhower. They are blaming him for their defeat at the polls in 1958.

All of the magazines fell victim to this Republican propaganda that it was Eisenhower who really lost the 1958 elec-

179

tion. The magazines said that Eisenhower did to the Republican Party in six short years what Franklin D. Roosevelt and Harry Truman couldn't do in twenty.

All of this is nonsense. Dwight D. Eisenhower performed wonderfully for the Republican Party. Whatever happened to it is not his fault. They could not have won without him in 1952 so at least he gave them that. And despite the fact that he was a man in his middle sixties who had suffered a heart attack followed by a serious operation, he ran again in 1956 when it was obvious to everyone that he would rather have retired.

Before commenting on Eisenhower's performance as President, let's get into the matter of why Eisenhower made it in the first place.

General Eisenhower's popularity, even before anyone knew what he stood for, rested squarely on the human instinct to follow the "Big White Father." The fact that Roosevelt's elections suited me does not alter the fact that his political success was also due to this primary urge in the hearts of men to transfer the burdens and worries of state and society to the shoulders of a leader. The social, economic, and political advances we have made were not because this concept had ever failed, but rather because once in a while the Big White Father turned out to be a Lincoln, a Gandhi, or a Roosevelt. It was sheer luck.

The nation's temporary disenchantment with Harry S Truman (but he's now growing in stature every day) was due to the fact that he wore a colored sport shirt and interrupted the pinochle game to ask, "Do you boys think I did the right thing today?" He was the man who told a civic club, "There are a million men in the country who could handle the job of President." That is just the thing *not* to tell the people. They want a man in a cape, or with a riding crop, someone aloof from the crowd, who looks and acts like he can "fix" everything. The people have too much on their minds to worry about fellows like Truman who sit around the cracker barrel annoying them in asking for advice. First of all there's a World Series, with football right around the corner. In addition there are Superman, automobiles, and a little over three hundred million comic books to be read every year. Plenty to take care of without discussing "policy" with Truman.

To be sure, there were other factors that made Eisenhower successful politically. Let us examine what happened in the South.

It is a sad tale.

I heard former Governor James F. Byrnes introduce candidate Eisenhower from the steps of the State Capitol in Columbia. Such enthusiasm you never saw. The huge crowd was in a festive mood. They would finally get rid of *that Truman*. How they hated *that Truman*. *That Truman* who was always talking about civil rights.

Of course Roosevelt had also talked about civil rights, but that was different. There was something about Roosevelt's Navy cape that reminded Southerners of dueling pistols, magnolias, and the old plantation. Anyway an aristocrat could talk about civil rights without stirring up anything.

But *that Truman*. When a fellow like that begins to talk about civil rights something had better be done about it. And when the reporters asked the I-like-Ike fellows why they hated Truman so, they merely spluttered, "That Truman."

So, in Columbia, Mr. Byrnes shouted, "I give you the next President of the United States," and as the band began to play that song, General Eisenhower grabbed the microphone and shouted, "I always stand up when they play 'Dixie.'" And pandemonium broke loose, women wept for joy, and the male folks hugged each other.

And then General Eisenhower went on to the White House to "stand up when they play 'Dixie.'" The first thing he did was tell the Southerners to desegregate the public schools, then the Administration took a heap of money away from the Port of Charleston, and there was a strong rumor that the folks would lose the Army camp at Fort Jackson, and on top of all that came "civil rights." The South's I-like-Ike boys would have been far better off if they'd heard the counsel of my mother: "Don't ever go looking for bargains."

Now, what was happening all over the country in that first Eisenhower campaign of 1952?

Like the doctor who "cures" himself out of patients, the Roosevelt-Truman administrations had "chased" millions of their voters from the slums and alleys and congested cities into the upper-middle-class suburbs and developments, and part of the social pattern of this transformation is to "vote Republican." It was bound to happen sooner or later. There were thousands and thousands of people who couldn't make a five-dollar check good fifteen years before who were now paying one thousand dollars dues in a country club. The tip-off to this tremendous impact upon our economy appeared in the census of 1950. Nassau County in New York (Republican) had gained 38 per cent in population since 1940. The increase in the big city of New York (Democratic), was 6 per cent for the same period. This is not an isolated instance by any means. The Nassau Counties, the Longview Terraces, and the Fairmount Gardens throughout the country gained in the same proportion at the expense of the lower-middle-class and middle-class apartment populations.

The Republicans charged during the campaign that all of this was due to "the wars," but it goes much deeper than that. I am sure that the Republicans would be the first to acknowledge that all that talk was nothing more than campaign oratory, otherwise it would place them in the silly position of claiming that America cannot enjoy or sustain a high standard of living unless there is a war. Thus they would be nullifying the basic tenet of their own faith—that our system is the best yet devised by man. Of course it is, and we should be generous enough to let the Republicans get off the hook by forgetting what they said in the 1952 campaign. I am sure they'll never say that again. Our system is the best, but it needed a bit of shoring up, and Roosevelt and Truman did it. They saved capitalism for America; but they did more than that, they laid a solid foundation, which as years pass, will give Americans the greatest sense of security ever known by human beings on this earth.

After the oratory of that first Eisenhower campaign was over, what happened?

Well, someday a good writer will sit down and record the events immediately following the inauguration of 1952. There will be a lot of humor in the book. The writer will attempt to fathom the streams of consciousness which surged through the minds of the men who took over the government after twenty years of Democratic administrations. *"This is it,"* they said. For twenty years the Republicans went up and down the land crying "Havoc!" The United States was going to the dogs, down the drain of creeping socialism. Too much spending. Taxes were too high. Individual initiative was dead. Private enterprise was on its deathbed. The late Senator Taft once said, "Our deficit is three and a half billion dollars. If it goes to four billion, we are through."

Finally the Republicans took over. The boys rolled up their sleeves. Now to get the country back on an even keel. Both-feet-on-the-ground stuff. Lucky for the country that the first measure the Republicans put over was the hard-money policy. I say lucky, because the reaction came so fast and so decisively that the Republicans had to reverse their field and go back to the Roosevelt-Truman policies. What the American people said in effect was, "Listen, President Eisenhower, we elected you because you are a fine man, but that doesn't mean we want you to disturb anything."

And President Eisenhower soon got the point. In his State of the Union message in 1955, he said casually, albeit significantly: "It is well to recall that we have developed in our country a fiscal system that tends to cushion or offset a decline in private income." An unkind Democrat would say, "Where do you get that 'we' stuff?" It would be unkind to ask the President to name those "we's"—fellows like Franklin Roosevelt, Harry Hopkins, Robert Wagner, Leon Keyserling, and dozens of others, mostly fellows who never met a payroll.

And so it went. And many years from now historians may record the Eisenhower Administration as one of the most important in the entire history of our nation. And its importance will have very little to do with accomplishment as such. But, in its broader aspects, I believe that liberals for a generation to come will hail the Eisenhower presidency as one of the great milestones in the history of human relations and economic advancement, because the Republicans *ratified* the Roosevelt New Deal and the Truman Fair Deal. They stamped their approval on the most momentous economic reforms in the history of government.

Just think back on what all of this means. For twenty years we had fellows threatening to "move out" of the United States because of Roosevelt and Truman. The "doubts" would have been with us always. But finally the opposition came to power and what happened?

We all know that Eisenhower, Wilson, Humphrey, and Dulles did not touch a single hair on the head of the New Deal Fair Deal, and in fact added to the certification by pleading for *more* welfare and recommending *bigger* social security.

Who can doubt for a single moment that this is part of America's true greatness? It has happened throughout all of our history. Mr. Jefferson was a thorn in the side of the Federalists while he was out of power. But once he became President he found it necessary to borrow from his archenemy Hamilton and so he, too, in his term ratified much of the conservative (Federalist) policy. He spent many a sleepless night worrying about the Louisiana Purchase. Here was a territory bigger than that which we possessed as a nation, but Jefferson was not stubborn where the destiny of America was concerned, and in making the purchase he exercised the very executive power of the central government which he had argued against so valiantly and for so long. Then the Jeffersonian "reforms" were ratified in turn by succeeding administrations and finally along came Andrew Jackson who knew all about executive power, and who wove the entire fabric of both conservatism and reform into the American blood stream. It was probably the stroke of destiny that an Eisenhower and a Republican Administration came along when they did to put the stamp of ratification upon the noble ideas in human relations which had been advanced by Woodrow Wilson and Al Smith and carried out by Roosevelt and Truman.

Well, now that it's practically over, it can be said that the eight-year Republican Administration had its historical compensations. But it does not by any means follow that we would have been in approximately the same place if we, the American people, had had the wisdom and imagination, either time, to elect a Governor Stevenson.

On the contrary, we would doubtless have been further down the road in the quests for economic security *and* a basis for world peace—the basic goals of our time, and perhaps of any time.

I have always thought it the height of naïveté to hear someone say, "I always vote for the man, and not the party." When you voted for General Eisenhower you voted for the Republican Party. The General himself made that very clear. On the broad basis of history, going back seventy-five years, the party thesis is the only one that really holds up. The Democratic Party has always had the broader outlook in America's relation to the rest of the world. It was Republican isolationism that brought us so many troubles after World War I. Since the "industrial revolution" after the War Between the States, most of the social and industrial legislation from workmen's compensation to social security has come to us from the Democratic Party. On three or four occasions, the Republican Party initiated restrictive immigration legislation against the opposition of the Democratic Party. Because of its cosmopolitan background the Democratic Party has been in a better position to deal with depressions, poverty, and social injustice. In the social and economic advancement of America, Republican laissez faire and status quo were beaten down after bitter struggles by such men as Grover Cleveland, Woodrow Wilson, Franklin D. Roosevelt, and Harry S Truman.

Despite the way it all turned out, the fat cats who wanted

Eisenhower in the White House have no legitimate complaints about how he defended their policies. Long after they realized that a balanced budget was impossible if not ridiculous, Eisenhower and Jim Hagerty were still talking about it. As soon as they were in the driver's seat, the professional Republicans knew that "creeping socialism" was here to stay; they knew that if they so much as suggested tampering with social security the working people who got them to Washington were going to get them out just as quickly. But Eisenhower was still braving the blasts and talking about too much spending and how important was individual merit. The New Deal and the Fair Deal were the way things were going to be.

The astute professional Republicans saw this immediately. Still they let Eisenhower fight the conservative battle.

And about politics, it wasn't Eisenhower who decided to become the first lame-duck President. The professional Republicans, Taft and Bricker, decided that long before they asked him to run. They were determined to beat F.D.R. for a third term even though he had been elected four times and was now gone. Eisenhower did as well as any man could do who knew, at one point in his incumbency, that a few months or years hence, the law dictated that he could not possibly be in power. A two-term President has now become a six-year President. The last two years—nothing.

But even if he had campaigned with the energy of Dick Nixon, a man twenty-five years his junior, things would still have been the same.

The Republicans are no longer exciting.

They are like the serious speaker at the fund-raising dinner who has to follow George Jessel. The audience has been long lost. They've seen George Jessel. Now they're going home.

The people loved Eisenhower, but they never loved the Republicans.

This is a hard thing to admit—that you are not loved. The Republicans are not going to admit it.

# No more clam chowder

WHEN Fiorello La Guardia became the reform mayor of New York he said: "No more turkeys for Thanksgiving." He referred to the old Tammany vote-getting system of distributing turkeys, coal, paroles, matzos, clam chowder, boat rides, and wedding presents. The implication, of course, was that now you would get one-hundred-per-cent honest government.

But politics, like love, will find a way. Soon the big fellows learned how to arrive at their goal via a different route and the only discernible difference was that now the "peepul" didn't even get their clam chowder.

Very little is new in politics. Today we have all these one-hundred-dollar-a-plate dinners to collect campaign funds. In the old days they called these dinners excursions. Tammany Hall used to run excursions at five dollars a ticket. For a boat with a capacity of four hundred, they sold four thousand tickets. You weren't expected to go on the excursion, and of course you couldn't go. In the end Tammany sachems would notify some orphanage to bring the children on the excursion. They alternated between Catholic and Jewish orphanages, and hardly anyone of the four thousand ticket buyers put in an appearance. I left out the Protestants, and I do not want you to get the idea that there were no Protestants in Tammany's New York, but most of them were in the Silk Stocking District and voted Republican, except when there was a strong Socialist in the field, and then the Republicans united with Tammany on one candidate to beat the Socialist. There was a Socialist by the name of August Claessens—a brilliant fellow, full of sound humor, who kept winning elections. Finally the Republicans united with Tammany on one candidate and still Claessens won, even on top of everything the Tammany vote-counters could do. In this one election the Socialist's margin of victory was something like two hundred out of a hundred thousand votes, and Mr. Claessens sent a telegram to the Tammany headquarters saying he felt guilty taking an election with such a small margin of victory—suppose we have a recount to make sure; and Tammany Hall sent word back—Hell, no, you win.

Tammany did not distribute any literature. Tammany worked at the precinct level. The way Tammany worked it was to have one of the precinct bigwigs take a nondescript office with an old battered desk. They always took an office at least two flights up. The idea was that if any precinct worker did not have the energy to walk up two flights, he or she would not do them any good. One desk, one chair, and two spittoons. One thing about Tammany clubhouses, there were always plenty of spittoons. On the designated day the precinct workers lined up outside. The chief sat at his desk with a map of the district in front of him and he gave instructions to the worker. He paid off, usually thirty dollars, and said: "Buy yourself a ten-cent notebook and a pencil and mark down the names of the people you visit in your precinct. Go inside and ask them one question—'How old are your children?' When the people ask you why you want to know the ages of children, just tell them—the *Democratic* candidate wants it for his record for future jobs. Tell them you know nothing about it, that you are merely a solicitor for the Democratic Party."

There were variations. Often, the question would be: "Is your husband working, and if yes, does he like his job?" This enabled the housewife to indulge herself in all sorts of dreams for the future, and of course to vote Democratic. In a fancier neighborhood the "question" would veer away from children and jobs and the solicitor might ask, "Are the streets in your neighborhood being cleaned properly?" Of course they weren't and the answer was always no. Then the canvasser would say: "Mr. So-and-So, the Democratic candidate, wants to find out about it." The workers made no promise, and no further statements. The precinct worker jotted down the name and asked his question. The rest was left to the imagination of the voter, and it meant votes.

In the poorer neighborhoods, of course, the services offered by the politicians were more direct. The Tammany district leader always had a connection with the undertakers in the neighborhood. In these districts undertakers and saloon-keepers were the key politicians, while in the fancier districts the florist always had a finger in the political pie. The Tammany chieftains would keep close tabs on who died—and before the body was cold they sent a flunky over with flowers and condolences. Tammany district leaders would immediately send a hearse over to the address of the deceased, a donation from the Tammany club. Often two Tammany men would be fighting for the leadership of the district. Then they went all out in their "social services." One rival would have a spy inform him of the kind of wedding present the other bought for a newly married couple and he would buy a more expensive present. Often the word of a death would reach the two Tammany rivals at about the same time and each would send a hearse. The undertakers would then race through the streets to see which hearse would get there first. Once two hearses arrived at the same moment and there was one grand fight. The two undertakers were slugging it out on the sidewalk and then the folks came out of the saloons and were soon taking sides. Everyone was in it except of course the corpse. But later on, on election day, he voted too.

Of course in the old days the political bosses were more powerful than today; and paradoxically it was Roosevelt who really clipped their wings. In more ways than one, the Roosevelt-Truman administrations established conditions which cut their own Democratic throats, as far as winning elections is concerned. For example, these great political machines thrived because they offered the social and welfare services which Roosevelt and Truman incorporated into government. Make no mistake about it. You hear all about the Tammany Hall "crooks," but their real strength came from the fact that they "served" the people. Certainly there was no idealism involved, and it is true that they were interested in only one thing—the vote; but the fact remains that a poor

girl with an illegitimate child had no place to go for advice
and help except to the district political club. When a man
with a flock of children lost his job, Tammany sent him a
basket of food, a half ton of coal, and maybe found some
part-time city job for him to tide him over.

There were Tammany clubs all over the city and on
Friday nights the leader "held court," dishing out the jobs,
working papers, peddler's licenses, instructions on how to
become a citizen and where to get free English lessons, relief, coal, matzos, and getting some young delinquent out of
the workhouse a week or two before he had served his full
time. Roosevelt and Truman, during their twenty years, succeeded in making all these services part of legitimate government business and today the big city machines are but shells
of their former structures.

Yes, things have changed. Today it costs a minimum of
a half-million dollars to mount the most modest campaign
for United States Senator. A "hot" congressional race cannot
even get off the floor for less than fifty thousand dollars per
contestant. The Tammany system of collecting thousands of
five-dollar contributions involved far less risk to the process
of democracy than our present method whereby our candidates depend upon large individual and highly interested
contributors.

The irony of this situation is that it would be perfectly
safe to say that the decline of Tammany Hall began when
the organ-eye-zation changed its own almost foolproof system, and when the Irish sachems began to meet at the
University Club on Fifth Avenue instead of in the back of
Pabst's saloon on Fourteenth Street. When Al Smith put on
the high silk hat and had lunch with the Du Ponts it was the
beginning of the end, a far cry from the height of his political
power when he sold tickets to the Oliver Street Chowder
Party in front of Bacigalupo's undertaking establishment.

The peddlers and small merchants who paid their five
dollars were politically wise very early in the game. At that,
it took the Tammany Irish quite some time to get the point.

When an Orthodox Jew learned that these Chowder tickets had something to do with clams (as unkosher as the pig itself), he was not likely even to put the ticket in his pocket, but gave it to the first Italian he met. After a while the Irishmen saw the light and the campaign tickets for the East Side, instead of Chowder, called for a "Boat Ride up the Hudson." These folks who had only recently .spent two months crossing the Atlantic Ocean in steerage were not about to take a boat ride up the Hudson, but at least they did not have to wash their hands in three waters after handling the ticket.

The United States Senate committee which looked into the problem of campaign contributions would do well to look into the old Tammany Hall system. Today's Republicans and Democrats could sell plenty of five-dollar tickets to an assortment of projects from a golf tournament to a book review. (The best campaign speech in the history of American politics was Governor Stevenson's speech in Richmond, Virginia, in the 1952 campaign against Eisenhower, when the Illinois Governor discussed the work of Ellen Glasgow.)

Another feature of the Tammany system would be worth looking into. The organization had a paid employee stationed at the marriage-license bureau. As soon as a couple came in to get their license, this employee relayed all the pertinent details to his district club. By the time the couple arrived home the Tammany wedding present was already there waiting for them, usually a set of dishes. When Bill Devery (who said he only takes honest graft) ran for district leader he said: "If you want something from the voters you've got to give the voters something, and I have today laid in a stock of two thousand pounds of beefsteak, fifteen hundred quarts of clam fritters, and three thousand pounds of candy for the kids."

It would be foolish to assume too cynical an attitude about Bill Devery's campaign platform. This man definitely "fulfilled his obligation" at the moment the last clam fritter was consumed. Not so with the fellows who give twenty-five hundred to fifty thousand dollars to a candidate. This "obligation" is fulfilled only when the candidate finally closes his eyes. So my friends—three cheers for Tammany.

## Senator Jolly and André Gide

ALEXANDER HAMILTON, Leonardo da Vinci, Jean Duvois (who fought arm in arm with Joan of Arc), and Nancy Hanks (Lincoln's mother) were all illegitimate.

One can't help thinking of these heroic figures every two years when Senator Wilbur Jolly of the North Carolina Legislature tosses in his usual bill proposing sterilization of mothers who have had two or more children out of wedlock.

Jolly's folly was aided in 1959 by Dr. Rachel Davis, a freshman legislator.

The bill they jointly propose has its humane aspects. Twins don't count as two births—but as one.

Jolly. What a wonderful, happy name. How can a man with the name of Jolly want to mutilate young bodies or deny a girl the possibility of a happy married life?

The motives that guide Senator Jolly and Dr. Davis are good motives. They have the welfare of the community at heart. Their bill, they hope, will avert abuses of the State Welfare Law which undertakes support of illegitimate children. Many women, says Senator Jolly, are using illegitimacy as a means of livelihood. If this be true, what about sterilizing the fathers?

The answer, of course, is that the pappies of these illegitimate children are not working in collusion with the mammies. The birth of illegitimate children has nothing to do with the existing welfare funds. If North Carolina stopped all welfare funds, illegitimacy would not abate one whit. In fact, before the first established charity in Chaldea there were illegitimate children. Illegitimate children are not "encouraged" by welfare funds. Nonsense.

Furthermore, Mr. Jolly won't save the state one cent. In medical and legal fees alone, North Carolina would more than triple its welfare disbursements. Jolly's accomplishment would be to move Mount Sinai to Raleigh. He will outdo the Pharaoh of Egypt and Herod of Judea—because they only proscribed the first-born male child. Senator Jolly wants to keep the law "sensible." If your IQ is under 70 you must submit to the sterilization.

Adolf Hitler had just as sensible a bill, but young women were dragged screaming and fighting and clawing to the sterilization block and were finally subdued, and they suffered the indignity and humiliation and cruelty because the state ruled they were mentally unfit along with the senile and the feeble-minded. Then they became racially unfit, and then it wasn't only sterilization, it was cremation.

Mr. Jolly and Dr. Davis will insist they are only after the bastards.

But it is well to remember that it was vouchsafed only to Galahad to find the Holy Grail out of which the Lord Jesus had drunk wine—and Galahad, though the illegitimate child of Lancelot and Elaine, was the knight born with the spiritual power, alone of all the noble kings and knights in Christendom, to look upon the Grail.

No man ought to deny the future, and the future, Mr. Jolly, at least according to the French writer André Gide, belongs to the bastards.

# Why I am a monarchist

LORD ALTRINCHAM misses the point when he criticizes Queen Elizabeth's little speeches as "a pain in the neck." As I see it, this young lord is the real "pain in the neck."

It is precisely these little speeches—"We are moved . . ." or, "Now let us all clap hands . . ."—which attest to the strength, the wisdom, and the greatness of the British Constitutional Monarchy. There is no better way to dramatize the wonderful principle, "The Queen reigns, but does not rule," than with these little speeches which the wise men of Windsor Castle write for the Queen (God love her).

My monarchist leanings, of course, probably go back to the days on the Lower East Side of New York when each of the coffeehouses frequented by Jews from Austria (Galitzianer) had a big portrait on the wall of Kaiser Franz Josef. The Romanian coffeehouses had portraits of the beautiful Queen Carmen Sylva, while the Russian Jews had to settle for Count Leo Tolstoy.

But I have often thought what a wonderful thing it would be if we made a queen of the United States, within the framework of our Constitution, of course. I think we would even permit her to marry whatever young man might become her Captain Townsend. This change would not cast any discredit upon the memory of those noble men of 1776 who founded this republic. It would merely be an acknowledgment, based on more mature judgment, that people must have a symbol. In the absence of a unifying symbol, they go wandering after all sorts of demagogic odds and ends such as Father Coughlin, Huey Long, and Joe McCarthy. Heaven only knows who will be the next one.

There is another advantage. We could build a planned nobility from segments of American life. The Queen would probably create a few original Dukes of the Realm—Paul Hoffman of Studebaker, Walter Reuther of the United Automobile Workers, and David Dubinsky of the International Ladies' Garment Workers. Later on she would probably add Carmine De Sapio of Tammany Hall and Jacob Arvey of the Cook County political machine.

Lord Bryce once said that a Tammany Hall district leader had more power than the King of England and it is interesting to note that Tammany followed the same symbolism that is used by the Crown. This was known as the Fourth of July speech. Usually the Hollywood script writers show the Fourth of July speech in a rural setting, a watermelon-cutting of the Elm Street Baptist Church. This is completely erroneous. The Fourth of July speech was invented by Tammany Hall in New York City. I doubt whether those Irishmen received engraved invitations, "decorations are to be worn," but the sachems would gather around their speaker with the symbol of their office, a huge medallion suspended from a heavy gold chain and resting on a red, white, and blue silk sash across their chests.

Then the speaker: "And the great American Eagle spreads its wings, from the rock-ribbed coast of Maine to the Golden Gate . . ."

The sad part of this story is that President Eisenhower, who is indeed the political leader of our nation, often makes the same "And now let us all clap hands" speeches and, with all due respect to a great soldier and a fine man, if I am to have merely a symbol, I'll take Princess Margaret and that gold coach.

# The boys used to get rough

IN THE long run, it's probably good for the country that there's less and less emphasis on the private lives of the candidates.

This development tends to focus attention on the real issues.

Also, the candidates, some of whom, after all, become our leaders, are a lot better off.

Now, take the presidential campaign of 1884. There, sir, was a campaign!

And the worst tactical errors ever made in American politics were made by James G. Blaine, Governor of Maine and the Mr. Republican of his day.

The Democrats nominated New York's great Governor, Grover Cleveland, for the Presidency.

The Democrats sang a song:

> Blaine, Blaine, James G. Blaine,
> The continental liar from the State of Maine.

Wherever Blaine appeared on the platform, a few in-filtrated Democrats raised a chant: "Burn this letter. Burn this letter." This referred to a Blaine scandal of a few years before. Some people in high places used the ugly word "bribery." There was a congressional inquiry which settled nothing except that Mr. Blaine was a great orator. The facts were presented as follows: the Fort Smith and Little Rock Railroad had received some public lands, which they were restricted by law from selling for more than two dollars and fifty cents an acre, since they had received the land as a government subsidy. It was charged that Congressman Blaine had maneuvered a vote to remove this restriction. Anyway, the railroad did sell the land at tremendously inflated figures and the charge was made that Mr. Blaine received railroad bonds valued at $125,000 as payment for his services in the deal.

Whatever the actual circumstances, the letter issue was a real one, of course, since it reflected on the candidate's conduct of public office. There were a few other legitimate issues, on both sides. It was later that things got rough.

Mr. Blaine weathered the railroad-deal storm by his oratory and by the testimony of a railroad executive who denied Blaine had been bribed. However, an accountant up in Boston produced a letter which Mr. Blaine had written in which he had mentioned disposition of some bonds he had received and on the back of the letter Mr. Blaine had written, "Burn this letter." So, during the campaign, he heard the phrase at every whistle stop.

But let's get to Blaine's tactical errors in the campaign.

Despite the "letter," the Republican Blaine had a big head start over Cleveland. The Republican Party was rubbing its hands in anticipation of carrying New York, Cleveland's home state. But poor Blaine had a friend, a Presbyterian minister named Samuel D. Burchard, and Burchard cost Blaine New York and the Presidency.

One afternoon in October, several clergymen met in New York's Fifth Avenue Hotel. They were all friends of Blaine, and Burchard was among them. The tired Blaine arrived, made cursory remarks, and left. But, at this little meeting, Burchard called the Democratic Party the "party of rum, Romanism, and rebellion."

Blaine's first tactical error was in not repudiating this remark. He had a chance to do so that night, before the morning *Times* was out. Blaine did not see anything wrong in the remark, and, besides, Burchard was his good friend and he trusted Burchard's judgment.

But the alliterative Burchard had handed the Democrats verbal dynamite. At the time, the country was afflicted with a wave of anti-Catholicism. There was an anti-Catholic press, which published cartoons of priests that would make most of us blanch today. Blaine had not only offended the Catholic population of New York, but also the thousands of non-Catholic liberals among the Protestant and Jewish fellowships, and the Democrats made sure that every city in America was "placarded with the insulting alliteration."

Later, of course, Blaine was forced to repudiate the statement. But it was too late.

Having made one tactical error, Blaine blundered into another hoping to recoup. The Republican Party released the news that Cleveland had fathered an illegitimate child.

Ten years before, in 1875, Cleveland, who was one of our two bachelor Presidents, then the sheriff of Buffalo, had met Maria Crofts Halpin, a good Episcopalian widow with two grown children. She worked in a very fancy Buffalo dress shop and was fluent in both music and French. Cleveland was about thirty-seven and Mrs. Halpin about thirty-five. The last thing, I imagine, these two expected from their union was issue—but issue Mrs. Halpin had, a son. Cleveland did not want to give up his bachelorhood, or maybe he had doubts, or maybe he just didn't want to marry Mrs. Halpin, even though she spoke French. He acknowledged his responsibility, nevertheless, and undertook support of the child and Mrs. Halpin.

When the Republicans released the news, they said that no man's daughter was safe with Cleveland in the White House. The Democrats were stunned and called the charge a canard. But Cleveland was a smarter man.

"Tell the truth to the people," he said, and that statement made him President.

Mr. Cleveland reminded the voters that Mrs. Halpin had passed the age of eligibility of being a man's daughter. "I am not now and never have been a celibate," he said.

Cleveland won sympathy and the Republicans were looked upon as tattlers. More than that, the ministers started to line up against Cleveland, and, although we Americans call ourselves a great religious nation, the best advice an officeholder can get is to see that, in general, the ministers are not on his side. A blue Sunday has never yet won an election.

Paradoxically, however, Cleveland owed a lot to the great Protestant preacher, Henry Ward Beecher, who campaigned actively for him. It was the Reverend Beecher who delivered the blow that took the heat off the scandal. In a campaign speech, the famous churchman said: "If everyone in the State of New York who erred in the same way as Cleveland were to vote for him, he would carry the state by a sweeping majority."

At that, Mr. Cleveland won by the narrowest of margins. He carried his home state of New York by 1,200 votes, and New York's electoral vote was the difference between defeat and victory. His popular majority was only 60-odd thousand in slightly less than ten million votes.

Some politicians felt that the Republicans' greatest mistake was breaking the story too early in the campaign, thus giving the Democrats plenty of time to explain it truthfully and permitting the whole thing to go stale by election day.

Some people have said since that the dirt of the campaign

wasn't Blaine's fault. If that's true, Blaine deserved to lose, for he exercised no control over his party.

To make the story interesting, though, right after the Republicans publicized Cleveland's indiscretion, the Democrats came to Cleveland with a similar plan. They said there was something fishy about Blaine's marriage.

Blaine had been married by an itinerant justice of the peace in Ohio, and when he and his young bride moved to Maine a few months later, they were married by a minister in a church service. A few months after this second marriage, Mrs. Blaine gave birth to a child. The Democrats wanted to charge Blaine with having got a girl into trouble and having married her because of it.

Cleveland was not only a shrewd politician but a gentleman. He knew the charge's only effect would be to offend Mrs. Blaine and the Blaine children. Further, he believed the charge was a lie. He refused any part in the plan. *He told his party that, if such publicity were condoned, either with official approval or connivance, he would resign from the ticket.* Thus he not only disavowed his participation, but, by effective protest, made it impossible to employ such tactics in the Democratic arena.

How bad the tactical errors Blaine made are more or less evident in the fact that he did not ascend to the Presidency.

Since his time, there has been less emphasis on private and personal affairs of office seekers, not because most of them lead blameless lives—but because they have learned their lesson.


# Shakespeare, Marlowe, and Dirksen

I was thinking of Calvin Hoffman's theory that Christopher Marlowe was the author of the Shakespeare plays, and my reflections brought me, curiously, to the Honorable Everett Dirksen of Illinois, the Republican minority leader in the United States Senate.

The Marlowe theory is based on the fact that Christopher Marlowe was a literary genius, and even staunch Shakespeareans have said that if Marlowe had lived to middle age, he might have produced works as great as Shakespeare's. But, says Calvin Hoffman, Marlowe did live to middle age. His murder in a tavern when he was still in his twenties was a fake—someone else, probably a vagrant, had been killed off in place of Marlowe. Marlowe was facing arrest for heresy (atheism) and a rich patron arranged this method of saving Marlowe's art. After the authorities had been satisfied that he was dead, says Hoffman, the rich patron took Marlowe to his castle where the playwright wrote the plays and arranged with an obscure actor to sign them. This obscure actor was William Shakespeare. So goes the Marlowe theory.

Like the Baconian theory, Mr. Hoffman's theory raises a similar question. The man who wrote those plays was not an ordinary craftsman, and we have dozens of pieces of evidence, particularly in the sonnets, that the author had a strong hunch he was writing immortal stuff. How then could a man, emotional enough to write that poetry, sit still in a castle, year after year, and witness the acclaim that came to these works even during the lifetime of William Shakespeare? Fear of arrest? Nonsense. It seems to me that the fellow would have shouted from the housetops, "I am the true author of *Romeo and Juliet, Hamlet,* and *Macbeth.*"

But this is all nonsense. We heard the same thing about Lord Bacon. How Bacon was a noble and therefore it was beneath him to acknowledge the fact that he wrote for the theatre. In his later years Lord Bacon was convicted of a felony, so this whole theory collapses, although it never really went high enough to collapse. A judge (Lord Bacon) who was convicted for taking bribes certainly would have also confessed to the "crime" of having written *King Lear* and *Julius Caesar*.

But it is really not necessary to go into details concerning all these theories, because they all start off with one basic error. Whether it is Bacon or Marlowe or Lord Vere de Vere; all the theorists start off by saying, "We know nothing of Shakespeare, therefore . . ." and they go into their mystery story. We then proceed to get involved in all sorts of arguments when, as a matter of fact, the premise upon which this "exploration" is founded does not have a leg to stand on. Who says we know nothing of William Shakespeare? We know when and where he was born. We know that his father was a glover and a man of some eminence in the affairs of Stratford-on-Avon. We know that his mother's name was Mary Arden, that she came from the town of Wilmcote, and that her family had property. We know when Shakespeare married, the name of his wife, when his children were born, his daughter Susanna, and the twins, a boy Hamnet and a girl Judith. We know when Shakespeare went to London, when he became an actor, and when he wrote his plays. We know the order in which he wrote them and when and where they were produced and who published them. We know who his friends were, and his associates. We know that in 1592 the famous dramatist Robert Greene, already outstripped by young Shakespeare, wrote of the "upstart crow"; a mere actor, who dared to enter the profession of writing plays. We know what investments Shakespeare made, and finally we know when he died; that his son-in-law, a doctor, was called in during his brief and fatal illness, and we know where he was buried, who attended his funeral, and how he disposed of his property.

What else is there to know of a man who died on April 23, 1616?

Do we know one fiftieth as much of Senator Dirksen whose name appears in the public prints every day of our lives? I am sure that Mrs. Everett Dirksen is a charming and cultured woman, but I doubt whether one thousand people in all this world know her maiden name. Yet there are high school and college students in every nook and corner of this planet who can tell you about Anne Hathaway of Shottery, and how Shakespeare married her when he was eighteen and a half years old.

What Everett Dirksen thinks of Shakespeare, if anything, we do not know. But what William Shakespeare thought of Everett Dirksen is as plain as anything can be. He has drawn him full length in the character of Polonius: the statesman flapping around in every room of the castle, listening to this, eavesdropping on that; running with every bit of good news to the king in the hope that in the telling thereof he will also get the credit for its creation; a man full of pious phrases and wonderful clichés, "to thine own self be true," and everything is always "all right"; a man always smiling and looking wise but completely lacking in sentiment and humor or a new idea.

# Speaking of unions

THIS perilous American decade attempted to measure patriotism by the degree of hatred a man could mount against the communists or the extent to which the communists claimed they hated him. But this test involved the complete renunciation of logic as evidenced by the fact that trade unionism was denied the advantages of this fascinating horror. For there is no established institution in our culture which the communists hate more than organized labor.

The communists do not let generals or admirals or schoolteachers or novelists or millionaires excite them, but they cannot abide trade unionists. This hatred reaches as far back as Karl Marx who did not expect that trade unions would help at all the revolution he wanted to sweep over Europe. Lenin actively worked *against* and inveighed *against* all unions in his pamphlets.

No visiting communist wants to talk to a shop deputy. When communists go backstage the last person they want to talk to is the Equity representative. They don't want to banter with George Meany or David Dubinsky. The proprietors and the managers are toys in their hands, but the union men are cobras. The unionists will not talk to the Russians about coexistent foreign trade or mutual scientific advancement. The unionists want to talk about political freedom and the right of workers to organize, strike, vote, change jobs as they see fit, and go where they please within their country; and this the communists have not, will not, and dare not discuss.

Of course we hear things about unions today which would indicate that many people longed for the days when the governor could call out the militia and chase strikers off into the hills. But even the most medieval manager doesn't want that day again. He's done too well since men and women organized themselves into unions. We forget too often the terribly precarious position of the employer himself in the brutal industrial jungle before the unions. We forget too often that organized labor increased the profits for free enterprise in the same proportion that they raised the wages of their workers. But unions could not do what mankind itself has not yet been able to achieve, to remove from the hearts of some men a misdirected drive for power for the sake of power itself, and for the sake of satisfying greed and a perverted need for comfort.

It is obvious that we do not always understand mankind, and unions we usually understand least.

When I was a boy my older sister worked in a sewing shop on Greene Street in New York. She worked nine hours a day, six days a week, and earned an average weekly wage of fourteen dollars. I visited her shop often on errands such as bringing her an umbrella when a heavy rainstorm blew up late in the afternoon. I saw the hundreds of her fellow workers performing various operations in the manufacture of ladies' petticoats and other undergarments. It was a time when the employer had not yet learned that his best customers were sitting right there in his shop. Today the girls in the organized sewing shops spend more on lipstick alone than my sister and her co-workers of 1915 were able to spend on their entire wardrobes.

In those days when the teacher asked a boy what his
father did for a living, the boy answered without humor or
guile, "My father is a striker." Everybody's father was a
striker, which brings me down to the present time in the
South. When I see the mill-workers in my state of North
Carolina driving to work in automobiles (and at home they
have refrigerators, TV, and electric washing machines; and
their wives go to garden clubs and beauty parlors), I always
say to myself, "Little do you know how much of this you
owe to those pioneer strikers of forty-five years ago." And
the most amazing development of all is the fact that important advantages of belonging to a union trickle down to
the hundreds of thousands of unorganized workers who pay
no dues. One of the largest manufacturers in my state once
revealed his secret—how he keeps the union out: "I make
sure that I am always five cents an hour ahead of the sons-
of-bitches."

## Is there a Jewish vote?

THE political preferences of the Jewish voters, of course,
are determined by the same factors as those of the rest of
the American citizens—geography, occupation, trade-union or
employers' affiliations, economic status, etc. If an avowed
anti-Semite ran for public office, all the Jews outside the
insane asylum would probably vote against him regardless
of his party label; just as the bankers would gang up on
any candidate who was in favor of abolishing banks. Which
reminds me of the time the late Senator Willis Smith ran
against Senator Frank P. Graham, and in the run-off, the
Smith managers produced printed surveys which indicated
that most of the Negroes had voted for Graham. The Smith
managers were indignant about this. Their idea of the true

American patriot was the fellow who voted against his own interests. Who does that?

Up in Boston, a Roman Catholic has a five-hundred-to-one better chance of being elected mayor than either a Protestant or a Jew. In many of the Southern states, neither a Catholic nor a Jew nor a Negro can hope to become governor, mayor, or sheriff. In some of our states in the Northwest you must have a Scandinavian name to win votes at the polls; while in New Mexico it helps if your name is of Spanish origin. Bankers, cattle raisers, bottlers, and members of the American Medical Association vote as groups for what they believe to be in their own interests.

But though group interests occupy such a prominent place in the picture of democracy at work, let it not be hastily concluded that all these groups are selfishly concerned with their own welfare solely. Such a conclusion would be incorrect, because most of the American groups, whether they be business, cultural, or religious, go to the polls in the sincere belief that their interests coincide with those of the country as a whole.

Which brings me back to the "Jewish vote" and the ubiquitous Arab student who asks the same question at every open forum around here on the Israel-Arab situation: "How about the Jewish vote?" Now this is funny. The Arabs who do not even have a word for "ballot" have suddenly become experts on the democratic system of voting. But are we not foolish to argue this on their terms? Why not a Jewish vote where the interests of Israel are concerned? Suppose the Saudi Arabians had a fight with Scotland, whom would the Scottish Presbyterians around here vote for—the Saudi Arabians?

But when the Arab student sneers that the "Jewish vote" influences the policy of our government in the Middle East, he shows a complete ignorance of our history and traditions. It presupposes the idea that if there were not any Jewish voters in America, the United States would automatically support the Arabs. Why? There is nothing in our history to remotely support such a contention. Incidentally, the state of Israel is the first country in the Middle East where a new foreign minister is escorted to his inauguration by his predecessor. This has not yet happened anywhere in the Arab world. When a new king or a new minister takes office in the Arab world his predecessor is either dead, or in jail, or if he is lucky, he was able to make it to Switzerland in time.

## Tactical error

POLITICIANS never admit to making mistakes. If they make a mistake, they say it is a tactical error. And many tactical errors have been made. Thomas E. Dewey made a tactical error when he charged that Franklin D. Roosevelt sent that destroyer back to pick up Fala.

It was a tactical error on two counts. First of all, Americans love dogs and the average voter would have sent the entire Pacific fleet to retrieve a stranded dog.

Second, and more importantly, it let Roosevelt make satiric capital of Dewey during the famous Teamsters' Union Speech: "And they have even attacked my little dog Fala . . ."

When Roosevelt finished that speech, the election was over.

## La Guardia's platform

EARLIER in his career, the late Fiorello La Guardia, Mayor of New York, had been elected to Congress on the Republican ticket. When the Republicans of New York brought him news of his nomination, the "Little Flower" made a speech as follows: 'Thanks for the Republican nomination. I am a Republican, but I stand for the Republicanism of Abraham Lincoln; and let me tell you fellows something—some of you Republican leaders east of the Mississippi know as much about Abraham Lincoln as Henry Ford knows about the Talmud."

# The visit of Anastas Mikoyan

IT WAS a dilemma for some of our editorial writers. Mr. Mikoyan put them on the spot.

He met only with the fellows who have both feet on the ground, the fellows who meet payrolls. On one day he visited with Henry Alexander, president of J. P. Morgan & Company; David Rockefeller, vice-chairman of the Chase Manhattan Bank; Mr. Weed, head of Anaconda Copper; Devereaux Josephs, chairman of New York Life Insurance Company; Mr. Sheperd of the First National City Bank; it got better as he went along. And not a do-gooder in the bunch, nor a brain truster, nor a liberal.

For thirty years now the communists have systematically killed socialists, Social Democrats, trade unionists, and liberals; and they succeeded in encouraging the ultraconservatives in our country to help them—by trying to silence the liberals, the only truly effective enemies of Bolshevism. *The Jewish Daily Forward* was the pioneer! If, God forbid, the communists came to America, the first ones they'd kill would be Norman Thomas, Frank Graham, and David Dubinsky.

Throughout Eastern Europe, wherever the communists have established their hegemony, they have always come to terms with the ultraconservatives while eliminating the liberals and the do-gooders. They made peace with the directors of the Skoda Munitions Works; but they could never make peace with the socialists Jan Masaryk and Mr. Benes.

They can never make peace with the men of ideas—the individuals.

## Woman suffrage

Mrs. Arthur M. Dodge, president of the National Association Opposed to Woman Suffrage, issued this official statement one day in 1913: "Woman suffrage will make women indecent. It was for anyone there to see at the parade yesterday, the marchers for women suffrage wore no petticoats, and their skirts actually clung—well, it was awful."

## Rockefeller won by a blintza

A few years ago I offered a new idea to eliminate prejudice. I suggested a National Cheese Blintzes Week (with sour cream), and now along comes this dynamic Republican Nelson Rockefeller who used the idea to win the election over Governor Harriman in New York.

Mr. Rockefeller toured the Lower East Side of New York and proved beyond any doubt that his appreciation of blintzes with sour cream was much greater than Harriman's. In fact this young Rockefeller demonstrated that he was a master in conducting a political campaign. On Rivington Street he bought a salami, wholesale—a five-dollar salami for three dollars. *The New York Times* reported that a jealous customer upbraided the delicatessen man, "For Rockefeller he gives discounts."

Luckily the Republicans have a Jewish attorney general, Mr. Lefkowitz, who guided Rocky directly to Ratner's Dairy Restaurant on Second Avenue and Sixth Street, where they produce the best cheese blintzes in the country, with sour cream, and when Rocky came out of Ratner's with a smile that stretched from ear to ear, he was as good as elected.

Which suggests to me that it would be a good idea if I prepared a campaign menu for New York candidates for mayor, Congress, Senate, and governor. This would enable the politicians to clear the air and get down to basic issues:

Monday: Knockwurst and sauerkraut
Tuesday: Blintzes, sour cream, and a side dish of kasha varnishkass
Wednesday: Minestrone and pizza
Thursday: Corned beef and cabbage
Friday: Fish all day
Saturday: Southern fried chicken, and a side dish of chitterlings

This would take care of the Germans, the Jews, the Italians, the Irish; all the other Catholics; the fancy Southerners on Madison Avenue; the Negroes in Harlem; and finally, on Sunday, the candidate can take care of the upstate left-footers with a New England boiled dinner with two different kinds of pie for dessert.

# Adlai Stevenson

"I HAVE not sought the honor you have done me . . . I have asked the merciful Father, the Father to us all, to let this cup pass from me. But from such dread responsibility one does not shrink in fear, in self-interest or in false humility. So, 'If this cup may not pass from me, except I drink it, Thy will be done.'"—(Acceptance speech, 1952 convention).

Adlai E. Stevenson is the *only* candidate for the Presidency, victorious or defeated, since the middle of the nineteenth century, whose campaign speeches can be read seven years later without the slightest embarrassment to himself, his friends, and his party.

# Shakespeare on the coming political conventions

WHEN he campaigns:

> His promises fly so beyond his state
> That what he speaks is all in debt; he owes
> For every word.

After he's elected:

> His promises were, as he then was, mighty;
> But his performance, as he is now, nothing.

When he wants to be "drafted":

> Bid me run,
> And I will strive with things impossible . . .
> Now humble as the ripest mulberry . . .
> And dress'd myself in such humility
> That I did pluck allegiance from men's hearts,
> Loud shouts and salutations from their mouths,
> . . . That's the humor of it.

PART 6

*To Mae West
and Truck Drivers*

# Queen Liliuokalani, farewell

DESPITE the excitement and enthusiasm over Hawaii's becoming a state, no one recounting its history has mentioned Queen Liliuokalani, Hawaii's last queen.

Perhaps we have neglected Liliuokalani because of a sense of guilt.

Liliuokalani was a tall, forbidding woman, every inch a queen. She ascended the Hawaiian throne in 1891, the year her American husband, John O. Dominis, the military governor of Oahu, died. She succeeded her brother Kalakaua, whose control of the country had been removed bit by bit by American interests. In order to protect Hawaii against British marauders, Kalakaua had signed some sort of reciprocal treaty with the United States, but America would renew it only on the condition that it receive rights to Pearl Harbor. Liliuokalani saw Hawaii gobbled up by this sort of diplomatic attrition. When she became queen, she wrote a new constitution, one section of which read that no foreigner could be considered a citizen and allowed to vote unless he was married to a Hawaiian. A week later the streets of the Hawaiian capital were filled with United States Marines and the royal palace was put under guard. Queen Liliuokalani was informed by courier that a provisional government had taken over because of her unconstitutional acts. This provisional government was headed by Sanford B. Dole, the pineapple king. Liliuokalani tried to bring her side of the story to President Harrison, but he went ahead with a treaty of annexation. President Grover Cleveland threw the treaty out but later recommended that Hawaiians be given the choice of self-determination. Sanford B. Dole refused outright to turn the country back to Liliuokalani. Instead he imprisoned her, had her court-martialed, forced her to sign a Commie-style confession, and made her abdicate. He did not assign her an American lawyer to present her side before the court-martial, but did let her confer with some Hawaiian flunkies who worked for him.

Cleveland pardoned her so that the death sentence was not carried out and Liliuokalani made a trip to Washington to retrieve her personal lands that the Americans had seized. These lands were valued then at six million dollars, and it was land that had been claimed and worked and owned by a long line of Liliuokalani's ancestors. No soap. The government denied her petition, but they did grant her a pension of one hundred and seventy-five dollars a month.

It was during this trip that Liliuokalani was evicted from the Waldorf-Astoria Hotel in New York. She transported a carload of pets with her wherever she went and the Waldorf couldn't take it.

Liliuokalani died in Honolulu in 1917. She was eighty years old. She died still hoping to regain her throne. She was a cultured woman and she had many talents, among them a strong predilection for poetry. She wrote hundreds of Hawaiian songs, among them *Aloha Oe*.

She certainly had to be in love with Hawaii to have written those songs.

> Farewell to thee, farewell to thee,
> Thou charming one who dwells among the bowers,
> One fond embrace, before I now depart,
> Until we meet again.

# Herbert Bayard Swope

THE death of Herbert Bayard Swope ended the career of one of America's greatest newspapermen. Mr. Swope did his most valuable work as executive editor of the old *New York World,* and many of his ideas and crusades brought tremendous influence to that famous Pulitzer newspaper. Two years after Mr. Swope left the *World,* that grand old New York daily was no more.

Swope's biggest story came in 1911, when, single-handed, he struck out against "the system," an alliance of New York City police and the underworld. He broke the story of the great Rosenthal-Becker case.

Herman Rosenthal was a gambler and like the other fellows operating gambling houses, brothels, and narcotics concessions made his regular payoff to the system—crooked politicians and corrupt police officials.

But this Herman Rosenthal had the perverted idea that he was bigger than the system and this was a very serious mistake. Herman also liked to see his name in the papers and this was another mistake.

Police Lieutenant Charles Becker was a big fellow, who, except for his devoted wife, could not claim a single friend in the world. Those who worked with him disliked him as intensely as those who feared him. In 1911 Charles Becker was promoted to the command of the Strong-Arm Squad, which extracted confessions, spotted stool pigeons, and the like, and from then on Becker's history was written in graft, blackmail, extortion, and blood.

There were not only regular payoffs but also special assessments, and because of one of these assessments, Herman Rosenthal was killed and Becker died in the electric chair. Lieutenant Becker had sent word to the gambling-house operators that he needed an extra five hundred dollars from each as a defense fund for one of his henchmen who was in jail for murder. Rosenthal balked and then Rosenthal squealed. He went down to the district attorney's office and offered to reveal the story.

Rosenthal had agreed to tell all to the newly elected district attorney, Charles S. Whitman, and the date was set for Monday morning, July 17, 1912. But Rosenthal never got to see Whitman. At 2:00 A.M. Monday morning, Rosenthal was killed as he stepped out of the Metropole Café (still standing and now the excellent Rosoff's Restaurant on West Forty-third Street).

If Herbert Bayard Swope had not acted swiftly that night the system might have been able to cover the trail of the gunmen and Lieutenant Becker would have entered another murder as unsolved. But within an hour, Mr. Swope had gotten District Attorney Whitman out of bed and had taken him to the West Forty-seventh Street police station, and the license of the murder car was recorded.

During the entire investigation and subsequent trial, Herbert Bayard Swope stood beside District Attorney Whitman. He wrote his press releases and managed every move of this interesting drama.

It wasn't long before Baldy Jack Rose, a professional stool pigeon for Lieutenant Becker, saw that he was being thrown to the wolves and decided to turn state's evidence. Within a few weeks, all the gunmen were in custody and thus began one of the greatest trials in history. Many organizations and individuals came to the aid of Lieutenant Becker, and arrayed against Whitman were some of the most famous attorneys of the New York Bar—men like Max D. Steuer, Bourke Cochran, John W. Hart, and John F. McIntyre. Rose and Vallon were the main witnesses for the state and much of the defense strategy was to try to nullify testimony given by confessed murderers. Whitman produced dozens of witnesses from Broadway who had dealt with Becker in having their illegal operations protected. And, of course, what always counts with a jury, even more than the word of a witness, is the telltale evidence that the man being tried has a hundred thousand dollars in the bank saved out of a police lieutenant's salary of, in those days, one hundred and ninety dollars a month.

The trial resulted in the conviction of Becker and the four gunmen—Whitey Lewis, Lefty Louie, Gyp the Blood, and Dago Frank. And after many legal maneuvers which were to take another year and a half, the five men went to the electric chair in Sing Sing for the murder of the gambler Rosenthal. Whitman was elected Governor of New York, and, but for the fact that he was defeated for re-election by the up-and-coming Democrat Al Smith two years later, he would have certainly been considered for the Presidency at the convention which nominated Harding.

On October 10, 1920, Herbert Bayard Swope, in the *New York World* wrote another story with this lead:

> The Old Ku Klux Klan of Reconstruction Days has been revived. Hooded night riders in long flowing white gowns parade the thoroughfares and bypaths of the South in dark hours when innocent people are abed.

Mr. Swope then began one of the most effective crusades in the history of journalism. He used six of his finest reporters to gather information in every state in the country where the Ku Klux Klan had a Klavern. One of his own stories helped break the back of the organization of bigots. It was a report of a Klan meeting in New Brunswick, New Jersey, and he used the most effective of all weapons— humor. It is hard to write humor in a story about hatred, but Mr. Swope and his reporters got the idea across.

All authorities agree that the *New York World* campaign of pitiless publicity and brilliant writing helped smash the Klan. By 1930 its membership had shrunk from four and a half million in 1924 to nine thousand.

May Herbert Bayard Swope rest in peace.

# My baseball days and Ty Cobb

TY COBB, the Georgia Peach, was the greatest ballplayer who ever lived. He began where all other ballplayers left off. He had a special place in my heart, along with Enrico Caruso, Franklin D. Roosevelt, Winston Churchill, Irving Berlin, Al Jolson, and John Barrymore.

I once heard a Columbia University professor deliver a lecture on Ty Cobb. He said that if Cobb had entered banking, he would have been the leading banker in America; if he had gone into politics, he would have become President; he was a born leader, a man who would always win; he would have been in the number one spot of whatever field of endeavor he chose.

As far as teams were concerned, of course, I was always a New York Giants' man.

On warm spring days we walked from the East Side to the New York World Building on Park Row to watch the baseball game on the electrically operated board. I also saw many a game during the summer vacations. I found that I could see the game at the Polo Grounds and get back in time to sell newspapers to the home-going factory workers. On the Bowery at Houston Street was a large bakery which sold pretzels to the Polo Grounds concessionaire, Mr. Harry Stevens. We kids in the neighborhood alternated in delivering those pretzels, and I got the job as often as any of them. The pay was twenty-five cents for the errand and ten cents carfare, plus the privilege of seeing the game. The pretzels had to be delivered by twelve o'clock; with the game not scheduled to start till around three P.M., but the only chance you had of seeing the game, without paying, was to stay inside the park. However, I did not sit in the stands for three hours just twiddling my thumbs like a dope. I moseyed around, got to know the players, ran their errands and made myself useful in many other ways around the clubhouse, and once I even helped the groundkeepers put the tarpaulin down over the infield during a sudden shower before game-time. I became friends with the Giants' captain, Larry Doyle, and players George Wiltse, Al Demaree, Leon Ames, Otis Crandall, George Burns, Buck Herzog, and Jeff Tesreau, and received many a smile from the aloof but kindly Christy Mathewson himself.

There was a billboard behind the centerfield bleachers advertising flypaper: "Last year George Burns caught 198 flys, but Ajax Flypaper caught 19 billion, 865 million, etc., flies." A good advertisement. I also recall a lady with a very large black picture hat sitting in the front row of the center-field bleachers, and often on weekdays she was all alone out yonder, and just as the Giants took the field, you could hear her battle cry in every corner of the Polo Grounds, "Come on, Artie," and the shortstop Arthur Fletcher would wave his glove at her, everybody would applaud, and then the first visiting batter stepped up to the plate. Probably Mr. Fletcher's wife or sister. There was a big player by the name of Heinie Zimmerman playing third base and the fans behind him rode him unmercifully. Once Zimmerman ran up to the stands in New York and socked a guy for calling him names. That personal touch in baseball is gone. It is more of a business today.

The Giants represented the New York of the brass cus-pidor—that old New York which was still a man's world before the advent of the League of Women Voters; the days of swinging doors, of sawdust on the barroom floor, and of rushing the growler.

The Yanks also played in the Polo Grounds in those days and the star attraction was the famous Hal Chase, who played first base for a while. Later he got into trouble with gamblers, but that was in the National League. Among the Yankee players I knew in those days was a pitcher by the name of Ray Caldwell, who was nuts about Jewish food, and I took him down to the East Side several times so he could eat knishes.

But when the Detroit Tigers came to New York, I did

not go near the clubhouses if I could help it. I didn't want to speak to or meet Ty Cobb.

I wanted it left as it was—just sitting in the grandstand, watching every move of that great and wonderful man.

# My brother Jacob

When my brother Jacob stopped off at Charlotte, he was on the way back North from his annual trip to Miami. As he got off the train he said, "Do you know why I decided to stop off at Charlotte?"

I said, "Well, I suppose it has something to do with seeing me, hasn't it?"

And Jacob said, "Of course, but there is yet a higher purpose," and he told me a story about a landsmann whom we all called Uncle Sholem. Uncle Sholem ran a small grocery store on the East Side of New York, and his sons became successful and he was able to spend his last years in leisure.

One day he came into our apartment in great excitement. His eyes fairly sparkled with joy as he took from his wallet what looked like a theatre ticket. He waved it in the air and said, "I'm going to the Metropolitan Opera House next Monday night," and with that he passed the ticket all around to confirm his statement. Everybody stood around in deep admiration and there was no doubt that there was something contagious about Uncle Sholem's great happiness.

When the first flush of enthusiasm had died down, Uncle Sholem confessed: "Frankly, I know nothing about the opera. I don't understand it, have never been interested in it, and, to be perfectly honest about it, it is not my kind of music. To me good music means only one thing—a good chazan [cantor], but why am I so excited about going to the Metropolitan Opera House? I'll tell you. I am now a little over eighty years old, and I am afraid! I know that the time is not far off when the One above, blessed be His name, will call me; and when I get up there, I am sure He will greet me gently and He will, in all probability, ask me, 'Uncle Sholem, where did you live down there?' and I'll answer, 'I lived in New York,' and the One above, blessed be His name, will then ask me, 'Since you lived in New York, Uncle Sholem, did you ever hear Caruso?' and I am afraid if I answer, 'No,' He'll bring out his big whip and start whipping; and so that was the reason I kept after my sons to please get me a ticket."

And that was the reason, said Jacob, he decided to stop off at Charlotte. He, too, is afraid. Comes the day after one hundred and twenty years, the One above, blessed be His name, will ask, "Jacob, did you go back and forth from Miami every year for sixteen years?" and Jacob will have to say, "Yes," and then will come the question, "Did you ever think of stopping off at Charlotte, North Carolina?" and Jacob was terribly afraid that a negative answer would bring out the big black whip.

My brother Jacob, or Jack, as he has been known most of his life, is one of the most honorable men I have ever known. A year before the New York World's Fair, he bought an expensive lease on the famous old Hotel Cadillac, which was situated on the northeast corner of Times Square, opposite the New York Times Building. The World's Fair was the flop of the century (only Billy Rose made money) and Jack lost a lot of money in that hotel. His lawyers advised him to file a petition in bankruptcy for that single business operation, since it was a separate corporation, but Jack said that he would not permit the tradesmen, suppliers, and banks to lose a penny, and he absorbed the loss in two other hotels in Manhattan which he was operating successfully at the time.

Jack is the oldest in the family. He was born in 1888, and he was followed by two other brothers who died during a typhus epidemic which raged in the empire of Froyim Yussell (Emperor Franz Josef). Then came my two sisters

—both spinsters. For many years, Clara has been operating a ghost-writing bureau and an addressing service, with such clients as the Republican State Committee and the various Jewish fraternal and cemetery societies around New York. Mathilda is a dress designer and creates fashions for some of the Hollywood beauties. I am next to the youngest and the kid is Max—Mendel, or Mack.

Max's first steady job was with the New York Stock Exchange, and after the crash they began to discharge the unmarried men first, and Max was among the first to go. He then took a job with the Metropolitan Life Insurance Company, as an agent with a debit. In those Depression days, many men became insurance agents when there were no salaried jobs in sight at all. But it turned out to be no mere refuge for Maxie. He really went to work at it and today, after some twenty years or more, his income from his renewal premiums alone is quite substantial. When Maxie went into the insurance business, my brother Jack owned and operated two hotels in Manhattan, the Hotel Markwell on West Forty-ninth Street and the famous old Union Square Hotel on East Fifteenth Street. Eighty years before, the Union Square Hotel was *the* hotel in New York. The Prince of Wales, later King Edward VII, stopped there on his visit to New York, and most of the great artists and musicians made it their home when the opera was performed at the old Academy of Music on East Fourteenth Street. Down the block was (and still is) Lüchow's Restaurant, and across the street was the original Tammany Hall, and the Steinway piano plant and concert hall.

Of course, when Jack took over the Union Square Hotel in 1920, it was a different era, and the hotel was no longer first rate, nor even second rate. But Jack stamped his own personality on the establishment and it became a sort of Hotel Algonquin for the Jewish theatrical and art world. Most of the actors of the Yiddish stage, the Jewish artists, journalists, poets, producers, and dreamers either lived there, visited there, or received their mail there.

To me, my brother's purchase of the Union Square Hotel

had a much greater significance than that of a mere business. As a follower of Henry George, I had always regarded the Union Square as a sort of shrine, long before my brother thought of it as a business. It was there that Henry George had his campaign headquarters when he ran for mayor of New York in 1897; it was at the Union Square Hotel that he died suddenly, two nights before election day. The first thing I did when Jack took possession of the hotel was to spend the night in the room where Henry George had died. I sat up most of the night thinking of the men whom George had inspired—Tom L. Johnson, Newton D. Baker, Louis F. Post, Samuel Seabury, Robert M. La Follette, Woodrow Wilson, George Bernard Shaw, Charles Stewart Parnell, Michael Davitt, and hosts of others.

On the pillars in front of the hotel there had been two bronze plaques, one commemorating the visit of the Prince of Wales, and the other a memorial to Henry George. The Prince of Wales plaque had been removed a few years earlier by the English-Speaking Union, and now when my brother decided to tear down the old front and modernize the building, I called up a few of the leading Single Taxers in New York, and James R. Brown, Oscar H. Geiger, and Joseph Dana Miller took the Henry George plaque up to the Manhattan Single Tax Club, where I suppose it is today. A few years ago, I wrote a letter to the late Mrs. William C. de Mille, telling her this story. She was Henry George's daughter, Anna Angela George, who had married the playwright brother of Cecil B. de Mille. Their daughter is that gifted choreographer Agnes de Mille, granddaughter of Henry George, the author of *Progress and Poverty*. Mrs. de Mille wrote me a letter of about four pages, in longhand, and told of the terrible events on that night in October, 1897, when her father died after making about ten campaign speeches earlier in the evening.

Getting back to Maxie and his insurance debit, the first thing he did was to go right down to see brother Jack. This was a natural move and more or less standard procedure with all insurance agents—to see a rich uncle, a brother, or a friend and sell that first policy. Jack, however, held up his hand and said, "No, siree." He told Max that he must make sure that he (Max) intended to stick with the business and make a career of it. "Go out and sell insurance to strangers," Jack said, "and if you are still in the business a year from now, I'll really go to work for you." Maxie did just that. And Jack came through as he had promised.

Jack is the perfect example of the man who does not "live by bread alone." Like my father before him, Jack has missed very little of the passing parade. Politics, history, and the study of people in general have played an important part in his life. With the experience of nearly half a century behind hotel desks on Manhattan Island, you can well imagine how many stories an observant man can tell, and Jack has not forgotten a single incident.

To this day, he can tell you how many votes George B. McClellan received in his race for mayor, he can repeat the opening sentences of Bourke Cochran's address to the jury in the Becker case and, in general, he can recall to you the details of every event of importance in New York during the past fifty years. His success as a businessman is surprising, too, when one considers that he is a genuine good fellow. One day I was standing in the lobby of his hotel while one of his guests, a young woman, was talking with him. After she left, he called me over and said, "You see why a small businessman can never hope to make the money like the big fellow. Now if a corporation owned the hotel, this girl who owes three weeks room rent would have been locked out last week—her room would have been sealed and she would have had to dig up the money to get her belongings; but with a small businessman, it's different. It's more personal. She owes me forty dollars, and she just gave me seven, with a promise to do the best she can, and I thanked her and made her feel welcome."

I've always wanted to know how Jack could tell whether a couple were married or not, merely by watching them stand at the desk. He never missed.

When the Depression hit bottom, and before Roosevelt

put in the Federal Theatre Project, it was really bad for the people of the stage. Practically all the guests in the Markwell, as I have noted, were theatrical people. Naturally, they would much rather have gone without food than to move out. It is all tied up with morale—moving "out of Broadway" is like giving up the stage, and then there is the matter of an established address, where an agent can still reach them. I remember a famous old vaudevillist. She was about seventy-five years old then, and terribly up against it. Jack was kind to her and she lived on and on with no rent payments. One day I saw her standing at the elevator with another woman, and with her cane she was poking into the plaster of the wall and scattering the cement all over the carpet. Naturally she did not see me, because as she kept poking she said, "Let that damn Jew spend some money on the place." I told it to Jack—the lady was living there for free—but Jack laughed it off, saying, "There's nothing we can really do about it, but we must not let it alter our own actions and our own purposes. And anyway we Jews can't ever afford to lose our sense of humor."

There were many guests, however, who were very kind and grateful, and who haven't forgotten to this day.

There was also Lillian Lorraine, the famous Follies beauty. Miss Lorraine pops up in nearly every biography or "as told to" autobiography of a stage personality. Lillian was a beauty. Some called her the most beautiful woman in the world. She was a blonde and words are inadequate to describe her. Ziegfeld was in love with her, and so were many others. According to the autobiography of Mrs. Florenz Ziegfeld (Billie Burke), Lillian was the only one whom she really worried about during the Ziegfeld-Burke courtship. None of these stories, however, tells of the sequel; how nice my brother Jack was to Lillian Lorraine when she really needed a friend. Lillian was (how shall I put it?) fond of alcoholic beverages. It was sad. Once when she was picked up in bad shape, she was brought to her church, the Roman Catholic St. Malachy's on West Forty-ninth Street. St. Malachy's was known as the Actors' Chapel, because most of its parishioners were people of the stage. Miss Lorraine gave Father Leonard a long list of "friends" whom he should call. The list included everybody from William Randolph Hearst to George S. Kaufman. At the end of the list was my name. Father Leonard, a wise man, looked at the list, pointed to my name, and said, "There's the only 'live one' in the whole bunch." He called me and I arranged for Miss Lorraine to stay at Jack's hotel. She stayed for several weeks and then some friends took her away. Later MGM made a picture, *The Great Ziegfeld,* and a smart lawyer attached himself to Lillian. The picture showed Lana Turner falling down a flight of stairs, and Lillian Lorraine (and the lawyer) immediately recognized it as part of her own life story. Lillian had indeed fallen down a flight of stairs at the height of her career. It was on the Amsterdam Roof, also operated by Florenz Ziegfeld, and she became crippled for life. I heard that MGM made a settlement.

The last time I saw Miss Lorraine, I was at the *New York Post.* It was about 9:30 A.M. when a boy came in and said a lady who wanted to see me was out in the reception room. It was Lillian Lorraine, and in very bad shape, too. She said there was a taxi downstairs with six dollars on the meter and the cabby threatened to take her to the police station if he didn't get his money. I went down with her and gave the cabby a ten-dollar bill and asked him to take seven dollars out of it; and to drive her wherever else she wanted to go for the extra dollar. As they drove off, I thought of this greatest of all stage beauties; of the time Ziegfeld had her walk across the stage for the audience to look at. I thought of the time she used to sit on a swing covered with garlands of roses and swing out into the million-dollar audience of the fabulous *Follies;* and as I looked at my three dollars' change, I thought of the wealthy playboys of another era who would have gladly given a thousand times three for the sole privilege of being seen somewhere with Lillian Lorraine. But it was a different era, and a different Lillian Lorraine. I never heard from her again.

I probably haven't told enough about Jack or about Maxie,

for that matter—but there are so many stories, and we'll try and get to them all in due course. Jack is a traditional Jew —he likes to daavin (to follow the orthodox prayers in the synagogue) and he prides himself in being somewhat of an expert on the cantorial music.

It would be hard to find anyone who loves America more.

# The tragedy of Jimmy Walker

BOB HOPE played Jimmy Walker in the movie *Beau James*, and surprisingly the picture had considerable depth. It put flesh and blood into the character of New York's famous mayor.

Jimmy was no Sir Galahad, but neither was he a bad man. He was a product of his era. He had a fine brain, and no politician of his time could compete with Jimmy for thinking on his feet. When he was in the New York Legislature the folks up in Albany went to hear him speak at the night sessions just as they would go to a movie today, for entertainment and relaxation.

Mr. Walker was a ladies' man and a heavy drinker (a devastating combination for any man in public or private life). And this business of being able to "handle the stuff" is plain bunk. I saw him at an important meeting way back during his first campaign for mayor, and he had to be helped down the stairs. One night at the Deauville Club on Fifty-seventh Street I was leaving at the same time and I noticed that the Mayor could not get into his overcoat without assistance.

But he had some great advantages. He came along in a cynical era when everybody was buying bootleg liquor; he had a boyish quality (who dislikes a boy?). Furthermore, he was an Irishman with the gift of blarney in an Irish town. No matter how he conducted himself, Mayor Walker thrilled several million people on March 17 of every year when he broke out of the line of march and ran up the steps of St. Patrick's Cathedral to kneel and kiss the Cardinal's ring. Everybody thrills to such a sight, no matter what his religious faith. It was sort of an annual redemption, or like being "born again," as we Southerners would say.

He was a ladies' man, and he was a bottle man.

And finally these things—and Judge Samuel Seabury with his investigation into the affairs of the Walker Administration—got him. Judge Seabury was a Protestant and an aristocrat, and he dared challenge the integrity of the people's hero. The crowds who came to the hearings cheered Jimmy to the echo. As Judge Seabury sat there piling up the documents, Jimmy said, "Judge Seabury is trying to outdo Eliot's five-foot shelf," a quip in reference to a popular set of books which was widely advertised at that time. The crowd roared its approval. But Judge Seabury had the stuff with which to hang our hero, and the Judge took his time. There were few smarter politicians in America than Jimmy Walker, and the Mayor himself must have known it, too; he must have known that Seabury had him. After the first day's hearings, the reporters flocked around the dapper Jimmy and asked him whether he would engage counsel. Jimmy looked over their shoulders to watch the unsmiling Judge Seabury sitting all alone, forever shuffling those documents; and Jimmy said, a bit sadly, "There are three things in life you must do alone: be born, die, and testify."

Mayor Walker then became a terrible headache for Governor Franklin D. Roosevelt. If Roosevelt did not remove Walker in face of the terrible scandals and corruption Seabury had uncovered, the Democrats of the West and the South would say that the Governor had sold out to Tammany Hall; and if he did remove him, the Irish of New York and Boston would never forgive him. While Roosevelt hemmed and hawed, Jimmy Walker took him off the hook, and resigned.

# Abe wound up with all the money

IT WAS during one of those fabulous years when the duties of our government were more or less evenly divided between Calvin Coolidge at the White House and Wayne Wheeler at the Anti-Saloon League . . .

That Abe Kaplan, a lover of his fellow man, had the foresight and the wisdom to open a speak-easy in a small town in Westchester County, New York—a fashionable suburb on the New York, New Haven, and Hartford Railroad.

Abe's speak-easy was in a basement, about ten or twelve steps below the sidewalk; but strangers had no trouble finding it. All you had to do was look for the policeman's motorcycle. It was always parked out in front, except when relieved by the police prowl car. Both the local cop and the county police used Abe's place to rest from their labors of scaring the daylights out of the Yale boys parked with their dates on lovers' lane, a dark road along the shore of Long Island Sound.

The speak-easy was called The Monkey House, in honor of a famous incident involving Enrico Caruso at the Central Park Zoo.

Abe's place was an eminently respectable speak-easy. He allowed no women to enter. If some suburbanite yet unacquainted with the rules brought his wife along for a moment of relaxation after the movie, Abe offered him his choice. He could take his wife home and come back alone, or he could permit the policeman to drive her home in the sidecar of his motorcycle.

But you must have guessed by now that there had to be something about Abe Kaplan's speak-easy that makes it the subject of a *feuilleton*. It was Abe Kaplan himself.

Upon his return from World War I, Abe operated a taxicab along the Boston Post Road; he married a charming and sensible widow with a little money, and together with his own savings, he opened the speak-easy. Abe had suffered a war wound, a shot through the neck, which caused him to speak in a most delightful stage whisper, and which added tremendously to his charm. A handsome man, he was endowed with an amazing talent for rapid-fire banter, everlastingly crisp and original, with never the slightest trace of an obscenity. Abe reminded you of Al Jolson, in both looks and in rollicking spirit, although he was much better looking.

Yet, despite his wonderful blarney, Abe Kaplan knew "his place." He knew how to stand aside in respectful silence as many of the great men of that era talked over the big deals and their great exploits. And there were indeed some great men in that speak-easy. Mike Meehan, for instance, the famous stock-exchange man, who ran up the common stock of the Radio Corporation of America from two dollars to over three hundred dollars a share. There were another dozen or more Wall Street tycoons—including Guy Loomis. Mr. Loomis had sold millions of shares of a promotion oil stock, only to wake up one morning and find to his amazement that the company had brought in the biggest oil gusher in all history. He was now embarked on an unsuccessful mission of trying to buy back the stock from the suckers before they heard of their good fortune. And Abe would smile with pride as he listened to all this great talk, and he would get out from behind the bar to wipe the tables of other customers; not to intrude of course, but only to show his respect and maybe catch a word here and there from Bill Fallon, "The Great Mouthpiece" himself, who may have been discussing the events of the day with two of his clients, Mr. Fuller and Mr. McGee. And off to another side of the bar was Charles A. Stoneham, who had just bought the New York Giants, and he may have been talking to a few friends of the world of sports, men such as Harry Frazee, or Ross Robinson, or maybe Jack Kearns; and often John McGraw himself would come on up to Westchester County when the liquor began to run low at the Lambs Club in Manhattan.

And Abe would go about his business, wiping the bar, rushing to the mysterious "back" for a fresh supply of liquor; a bon mot at the proper moment; a clever bit of banter at the precise interlude; shaking the dice cup; ringing up the cash register.

"Watch me undress that ten-dollar bill," Abe used to say, until all the great men of his establishment took up the slogan and literally threw the money at him for the mere privilege of saying, "Abe, undress that ten-dollar bill." And the great men would laugh at "their" joke; and so it went in The Monkey House.

And the years rolled along and great changes were taking place in the world beyond the speak-easy.

Thus it came to pass that, one by one, Abe's customers fell by the wayside—committing suicide, going to jail, or just dying of the heartbreak involved in trying to cut the corners a bit too sharply in that silly era. Finally Abe Kaplan remained like the veritable "last man"; the only survivor of a great and peculiar age—the "Armageddon" of 1929.

What happened to The Monkey House? The last time I saw it, it had a fancy "casino" name and it covered acres and acres of the best land in Westchester, upon which stood fashionable hotels and inns, and glass-enclosed dining rooms, with armies of uniformed footmen, bellboys, and waiters.

Only one thing was the same—the policeman's motor-cycle was still parked out front.

# President Herbert Hoover

I WAS sincerely concerned when I read that former President Herbert Hoover had entered the hospital. At his age these matters are always serious. I have an affection for Mr. Hoover. First of all, I have a deep respect for the Presidency of the United States, over and above any partisanship. Second, I admire a man who simply refuses to budge a fraction of an inch in the area of his economic philosophy.

I recall that wonderful news story by Heywood Broun after the first World Series game between the famous New York Giants and the newly arrived New York Yankees. The Giants' manager, John J. McGraw, sneered at the home-run reputation of this left-handed pitcher who had been made into an outfielder. "This Babe Ruth guy hits those home runs in the American League, but he'll find out that this is different," said old Muggsy, who laid out the strategy. "This kid [Babe Ruth] is a sucker for a high one on the inside." And that was that.

Now for the game. It's the first inning and Babe Ruth is at bat. Muggsy McGraw pinches his nose. This means a high one on the inside. Mr. McQuillan, the pitcher, obeys the order and bang, wham, Mr. Ruth hits the second longest home run in the history of the right-field bleachers of the Polo Grounds!

Now it's the fourth inning and the pitcher is another fellow by the name of Bentley, who looks toward the bench. Muggsy McGraw pinches his nose. "Give the bum a high one on the inside." And Mr. Bentley obeys. Wham, bang, Mr. Ruth hits a double which digs a deep trench between the right fielder and the center fielder.

It's the seventh inning and Mr. McGraw is now standing up. Babe Ruth is at bat and Mr. McGraw is ready to give the order: "Give the bum a high one on the inside," and Mr. Ruth swings. Bam, wham, bang, the longest inside-the-park home run in the history of the Polo Grounds.

And wrote Heywood Broun, "Old John McGraw went down with colors flying and with thumb to his nose."

This is what I like about Mr. Hoover. It was all wrong; the whole New Deal, the whole Fair Deal; all the economic and social legislation since he left the White House in 1933 is all wrong; coddling the people and destroying their moral fiber. Mr. Hoover says he was one-hundred-per-cent right in everything he did. Mr. Hoover does not believe that his own "nursery legislation," RFC, banking pool, Credit Corporation, and moratoriums, destroyed the moral fiber of the big fellows. Mr. Hoover believes all of this sincerely and honorably. Like old John McGraw, his colors are not struck and he'll go down like a man, thumbing his nose at the whole post-Hoover world. You have to admire a man like that.

As an intense partisan, it is natural to admire and respect another intense partisan. There's a wide area of trust between us. You can rely on his word because you can rely on his convictions. From the bottom of my heart I wish Mr. Hoover long years.

# April 12, 1945

For the rest of their lives millions of Americans will be able to tell where they were and what they were doing at the very moment on April 12, 1945, when they heard that Franklin D. Roosevelt had died. It was as though time itself had stopped, and as amazing as it seems to us now, the business and entertainment activities of this tremendous establishment of the United States of America practically ground to a halt from the moment he died until he was laid to rest at Hyde Park, New York.

The newspaper announced that the funeral train would pass the Charlotte Southern Railway station around midnight, and about a half-hour earlier I walked toward the station. But I did not get closer than a block away. Thousands of people were there, including hundreds of young mothers with sleeping infants in their arms. No one spoke. People just looked at each other and waited. I had worked my way to the tracks as the funeral train passed slowly, so very slowly, and the folks all around me began to cry. It was an amazing sight. As you looked northward you could see thousands of flickering lights all along the tracks—matches, flashlights—thousands of people had come from their farms and rural homes to watch the train pass.

What was there about Roosevelt?

The thing that impresses me as much as anything else was this great man's amazing flexibility. He could spend an hour with Boss Frank Hague of Jersey City in amicable political fellowship, and the next hour in equal fellowship with Archibald MacLeish, the poet and librarian. He could take in stride, as part of the "game," that sewer contractor in Chicago who shouted through the pipes, "We want Roosevelt," but a few days later he could be discussing Abraham Lincoln with Carl Sandburg. A master politician? There was no one ever like him, and for this alone I can continue to love his memory for the rest of my life.

Mr. Norman Thomas and other fellow "liberals" and socialists have placed important emphasis on the fact that the Roosevelt New Deal was, in effect, the Socialist Party platform of 1904 and 1908. This is true, of course, but I think they miss the point: that only a Franklin D. Roosevelt could have proposed these economic and social reforms into the law of the land. Regardless of the "emergency" the American people would never have accepted economic reforms from the Socialist Party; but they welcomed the same measures when proposed by a senior warden of the Hyde Park Episcopal Church. We saw a confirmation of this fact almost immediately upon the succession of President Truman. New Deal "extensions" or Fair Deal proposals never really got any further than Mr. Truman's State of the Union message. What the Congress and the people were willing to take from an aristocrat, they refused to accept from one of their very own plain folks.

The reformers have played a noble role in American life. In each generation they have kept alive the need for greater individual dignity and greater individual security; but they were always waiting for the time when a fellow would come along whose ancestors had come over on the *Mayflower,* and who had a patrician face and a Navy cape.

So let us reformers keep strong and active. We are bound to get another guy like that someday.

# Clarence Darrow

WHEN Clarence Darrow was seventy-eight years old, he wrote a piece for *Esquire* on how to pick a jury. He was able to contribute the sum total of his fifty-odd years in the American courtroom in this one article. He started off by advising the lawyers to choose a man who laughs, because a juror who laughs hates to convict anyone; to avoid wealthy men, because rich men always convict—unless the defendant allegedly had violated antitrust laws. He then dissected the influence of the various religions upon the character of the prospective juror. He advised that Methodists be accepted as jurymen because their religious emotions can be transmuted into love and charity; but warned against taking Presbyterians because they know right from wrong, but seldom find anything right; and against Lutherans because they were almost always sure to convict. After counseling that one should never accept a prohibitionist under any circumstances, he recommended that the best jurors for the defense were Catholics, Unitarians, Congregationalists, Universalists, Jews, and agnostics, in that order.

What a wonderful man—Clarence Darrow. He picked the wrong time to grow old and to die. How America needs Clarence Darrow today! How he would have stood up against the fakers and shakers of our time! One of the false legends of civilization is that terrible libel upon our mothers and fathers that "anyone can be replaced." Nonsense. Who has replaced Clarence Darrow?

Arthur Spingarn relates that Darrow once asked him whether he should take a certain case which would require a lot of time and expense. "What fee can the accused pay?" asked Darrow. "Oh, he has absolutely no money at all," replied Spingarn. "Well, that settles it," said Darrow, "I'll have to take the case."

How the world has changed since the Old Lion's courtroom days. I was thinking of this when I saw the excellent

play, *Inherit the Wind*, which is based on the famous
Monkey Trial in Dayton, Tennessee. The state of Tennessee
had passed a law prohibiting the teaching of the theory of
evolution in public schools. A group of citizens decided to
test the constitutionality of the law. High-school teacher
John T. Scopes decided to be the principal in this test. He
read a page of a forbidden text, submitted to arrest, and
thus in 1925 America and the world were treated to a courtroom drama that became known as the Monkey Trial.

Offering their legal services to Scopes were Darrow,
Dudley Field Malone, and Arthur Garfield Hays. Behind
them was Henry L. Mencken, having the time of his life.
To aid the prosecution came "the Commoner," William
Jennings Bryan, and in the blistering heat of a Tennessee
July, the battle began. The trial lasted three weeks, during
which Bryan took the stand as a witness for the state and
submitted to a blistering cross-examination by Darrow. As
you would expect, with two such strong personalities, the
issue of the proceedings was completely lost.

Mr. Victor Yarros, a law partner of Clarence Darrow for
eleven years, a personal and intellectual friend for a much
longer period, and author of several books and articles in
most of the liberal publications of the past three quarters
of a century, wrote a letter to *The Carolina Israelite* some
time ago that shed some light on the personalities.

He observed:

Bryan was a Jeffersonian Democrat. He was not, however, an individualist. He sympathized with reforms
and political tendencies which we should now describe
as paternalistic or socialistic. He was a champion of
what we now recognize as the welfare state. . . .

Darrow never adopted nor recognized a label to char-
acterize his advanced politico-economic ideas. He did
not call himself an anarchist—disliking the term and its
connotations. Yet that was the school or group he really
belonged to, had he cared to adopt a suitable label.
He never joined any party, faction or school. He allowed

his views, as expressed in pamphlets and reported speeches to define his position, not really caring very much about logical consistency or what may be called historicity. He had friends in all groups, including religious conservatives. His atheism was not aggressive, and he never offended his religious admirers.

The Monkey Trial was the last public appearance of William Jennings Bryan. He died of a heart attack a few days after the jury brought in a verdict of guilty. Scopes was fined a nominal amount and an appeal was taken to the higher courts. There, with the two forceful characters, Bryan and Darrow, absent, the jurists were concerned not with whether evolution was a correct science or not, but whether the state had the right to prohibit its teaching. By a one-vote margin the conviction of Scopes was set aside and while the law itself was not actually repealed, it became a dead issue.

Much has happened in the world since that day in Dayton, Tennessee. The battle for human freedom, it turned out, was not a battle between the Bryans and the Darrows after all. That is what had fooled us when we split our sides laughing at William Jennings Bryan. The joke, I am afraid, was on us. The sides that were "chosen up" eventually to decide the fate of mankind were not at all what we had expected. The realities bore no resemblance to the black-and-white world of Bryan and Darrow.

Some of us who believed that the struggle for the freedom of men's minds was settled in the Dayton courtroom found it far more complicated. When the chips were down the men of freedom found as many Bryans fighting beside them as Darrows. I admit that I am taking advantage of perspective and history, so hurrah for perspective and history if they contribute to truth.

Life was a breeze in the days of the Bryan-Darrow courtroom battle. Hollywood style. Sweet young girls were sweet young girls and nothing more, and all the villains were dark and swarthy. The Dayton courtroom further simplified matters for us. Bryan leading the forces of darkness, and Darrow, the champion of the enlightened. And Mencken laughing himself sick. All you had to do was slap your thigh and laugh at the story of David and Bathsheba and you automatically became a member—a "freethinker" and a "liberal."

Fifteen years later, this party was over. We discovered that being an agnostic did not necessarily prevent a man from becoming a mass murderer, and that being a fundamentalist did not necessarily make a man a reactionary.

William Jennings Bryan believed in the Garden of Eden and the serpent, but he also believed in the eight-hour day at a time when it was a greater heresy than even Darrow's agnosticism.


# To Mae West and truck drivers

LET us gossips get it off our chest and say that Miss Mae West is sixty-seven years old. Does not this make her all the more remarkable?

For an entire generation Mae West has been a sort of High Priestess of Sex. Yet it is well to note that in her stage and screen careers, spanning nearly a half century, Miss West has been far less obvious about sex than any one of a dozen Hollywood starlets. Miss Jayne Mansfield and the others travel around the country breathing in and breathing out and if they stopped their deep heaving they would be finished. Mae West in all of her career has never bared her bosom, and no one in her audiences has ever seen her ankles. In fact her greatest success has come to her in those Klondike costumes of the 1890's, those full skirts down to the floor with the padding of two or three petticoats, and the picture hat. And even her scripts never have been obscene for the mere sake of obscenity. Actually she has uttered fewer risqué or suggestive lines in an entire generation than

I have heard Bob Hope use in a single half-hour performance.

What then has made Mae West this High Priestess of Sex?

For one thing I believe she is a very great artist. Mae West was as great an artist in her field, trading quips with W. C. Fields, as Sarah Bernhardt was in the recitations from *L'Aiglon* which I heard her deliver at the old Palace Theatre.

Another thing is Mae West's walk. I do not know how this can be done, but I hope that somehow the Smithsonian Institution comes up with an idea that will preserve that Mae West walk for posterity.

But beyond that I believe Mae West's complete supremacy in her field has been due to the fact that somehow she has always suggested old-fashioned sex—MANHOOD, virility, something all men dream about but unfortunately find it necessary to rationalize about at times, with the observation that it belongs only to truck drivers.

There's a wholesomeness about Mae West's sex. It suggests the loud laughter at a Verein picnic in Schutzen Park, or on the annual excursion of the Steamfitters' Union, Local No. 11. There's nothing leering or sneaky about her sex.

Somehow Mae West has been able to communicate this idea for nearly fifty years in vaudeville, on the stage, and in motion pictures; giving the impression that if you even mentioned the word "deviation" she would knock you on the head with her parasol.

And so as we take our leave let us say, "Long live Mae West, and long live the truck drivers."

# Colbert and Crawford

MY TWO favorite movie queens are Claudette Colbert and Joan Crawford. I think they are wonderful. I suppose most of our likes and dislikes are tied up with nostalgia, an association of ideas. A fellow hears a song on his honeymoon and invariably the melody, good or bad, becomes his favorite tune through life. I knew a fellow who broke his glasses in the bathroom one morning and he was fit to be tied. Later that day, the stock market had a sensational rise and he made lots of money. For years, he associated good fortune with his shattered spectacles. Later when his stocks would be going down, he would figure out all sorts of schemes on how to break his glasses so that it would be "an accident" —he'd pick up the pieces and go off to Wall Street as happy as a lark, and as blind as a bat.

I used to go to the Capitol Theatre in New York in its early days. It was the first gigantic "movie palace" in the country. The feature picture was incidental to the program in those days. Erno Rapee was in the orchestra pit, and the stage show was the important event. During one performance a girl came out and sang, "Oh, Dry Those Tears." I do not know her name, and do not know what became of her. For all I know, she may be one of the top stars at the Metropolitan Opera House, or she may be a housewife today, with six children, but I have never forgotten her. And this was not due to some peculiar quirk of my own brain. I remember distinctly that the entire audience gave her a standing ovation; her four-minute appearance on that stage actually electrified five thousand music and theatre lovers. All I remember about her is that she was a thin girl, she wore a white gown, and stood close to the wings of the stage and sang that number. I doubt whether a month has gone by in all these thirty years or more that I haven't thought of that girl and "Oh, Dry Those Tears."

The same principle is involved in favorite movie stars. I saw Claudette Colbert make her stage debut. What a wonderful actress the stage lost because of the big Hollywood money. The name of the show was *The Ghost Train*, and all Claudette Colbert did was scream, but what a scream! Incidentally, *The Ghost Train* was the best suspense play I have ever seen. A year later, Claudette really hit the top. She played with Walter Huston in *The Barker* and was a great success. One of the actors in that show was Claudette's first husband, Norman Foster. She is married to Dr. Joel Pressman today. But Joan Crawford is really the ace. I saw her dance in the early 1920's at the Parody Club, on the same program with Clayton, Jackson, and Durante. Later she danced at the Plantation, another speak-easy in those days, under her real name, Lucille le Sueur. She was great. From there she went up and up; was married to Douglas Fairbanks, Jr., and Franchot Tone; and, through it all, she has never muffed a line or allowed herself to be diverted from her main purpose—to hold onto the top rung of her profession. It takes genius and character to stay on top of your profession for thirty years, and it even takes more than that to stay on top in the most cutthroat, dog-eat-dog profession of them all—Hollywood—and to stay beautiful at the same time. Yes, we should be proud of women like Claudette Colbert and Joan Crawford. I imagine they must get a kick out of watching the others come and go, some of them making a vast noise in the process.

PART 7

## The Vertical Negro
## Opens a Second Front

# The issue in the South

THE issue is not whether a Negro boy or girl can walk to a public school unmolested. The issue is racism. The issue is arguing that all men are created equal and practicing the opposite. The issue is depriving citizens of unrestricted participation in tax-supported institutions. The issue is to allow the Negro to supervise the affairs of your household and care for your children and then place a million obstacles in his path when he wants to vote in an election. The issue is to grant the Negro wearing a white coat unrestricted access to the rooms and corridors of the best hotels and not allow a Negro scientist to sleep in one of the rooms. The issue is to put up the bail when a favorite Negro is in trouble, to respond with generosity to his every plea for funds for his churches, to go overboard now and build Negro schools which are much better than the schools for the whites, to show the Negro every kindness and consideration, to give him everything except recognition as a man, to grant him everything except humanity.

The issue is communication. If we insist upon thinking of one third of our population in terms of "the enemy," then we are fooling ourselves if we do not at least "negotiate." When we made peace with the Japanese, we sat down with Japanese; but governors and members of the power structure have resisted every effort to establish a line of communication. They say that they will not sit down with "extremists," which means Negroes who are in favor of implementing the Supreme Court decision. Two governors have

actually stated it in those terms, which shows how far we
have gone to kid ourselves and obscure the issue. I suspect,
however, that they are afraid of logic. If they believed for
one moment that the Negro leadership would "demand"
the immediate integration of the public schools from one
end of the state to the other, they would establish this line
of communication. It would give them the other 20 per cent
of public opinion which they do not have now. But they
believe no such thing. They fear the Negro leadership would
be logical—"Let's try it here—and maybe we can try it there
in a couple of years." Because, if the truth were known, the
Negro leadership is really the true exponent of gradualism.
Here is a concrete example. I happen to know that, in
Charlotte, the Negro leadership had set for itself a goal—
desegregation in the immediate future of ONE high school;
and the high school they had in mind offered few obstacles.
But in the absence of communication, the school board
"desegregated" five high schools, a token Negro child in
each one.

But they have satisfied no one, least of all the "white
supremacy" group, which now calls the members of the
board Bolsheviks.

The issue is that every Southern governor has stated publicly that racial tension in the South is not hurting the current drive for new industry. This, of course, is begging the
question. When you have to assure yourself that a condition is not doing harm, it is the beginning of a downward
spiral. The more pertinent question would be, "Is the
present resistance to the Supreme Court decision helping
us get new industry?" Try to ask that question of yourself
and double your money back if you do not laugh out loud.

The issue could have been settled. The wise men of Louis-
ville, Baltimore, and St. Louis followed the advice of Macbeth, "If it were done when 'tis done, then 'twere well it
were done quickly."

But in the Deep South it was not necessary to go that far.
The issue could have been settled by the application of
humanity, and by this I do not mean idealism or what some

folks call "do-goodism." On the contrary, the issue could have been settled on a basis of just this:

1. Acceptance of the reality that the Supreme Court will not reverse itself on this issue.

The acceptance of this reality would then enable the South to ask men of good will of both races to accept another reality:

2. There are sections of the South which will not integrate the schools in our generation.

Thus if you grant humanity, if you establish a direct line of communication, and if you accept a constitutional reality, the South can not only silence its critics, but can go on to peace and prosperity, because of the South's many natural advantages, which include some of the kindest people in the world.

## "I paid my dime"

ONE of the most moving scenes I've ever witnessed was a group of Negroes rehearsing in a church basement on the eve of an effort to test integration on public buses in a Southern city.

The Negro minister was an integration leader, and he had arranged a number of folding chairs one after another, in the manner of seats on a bus, and now he addressed the group:

"All you will say when you get on the bus is, 'I paid my dime, I'd like to sit in this empty seat, please.' Do you understand?

"Now, if the bus driver says, 'Nigra, get out of that seat,' you will say, 'I paid my dime, I'd like to sit in this empty seat, please.'

"And if he gets up and stands over you and he says,

'Nigra, didn't you hear me? Get out of that seat,' and he makes a fist, you will say, 'I paid my dime, I'd like to sit in this empty seat, please.'

"Now, you ever going to say anything else?"

And a woman in the group announced, "All I'm going to say is, 'I paid my dime, I'd like to sit in this empty seat, please.'"

"Does everybody understand?" asked the minister. "That's all you're going to say. You're not going to be wrathful. You're not going to be prideful. You're not going to be mean.

"Now, we're going to practice. I'm the bus driver. You two get on. This is my seat and here are the empty seats."

Then the minister turned around in his chair and said, "That seat's for white folks. You got to sit in the back of the bus."

There was silence for a moment.

"Come on," coaxed the minister, "what do you say?"

"I paid my dime," said one of the women. "I'd like to use this empty seat, please."

"I ain't drivin' this bus till you move."

"I paid my dime, I'd like to use this empty seat, please."

"That's all you say. You got it right."

"Preacher," asked one of the women, "what if they don't drive the bus? What if they arrest us? What if the bus don't come?"

"Then we've got to walk to work. You understand?" said the minister. "How far have you got to walk to work?"

The woman spoke up: "I walk eight miles if there ain't no bus. Maybe my feet need a bus, but my soul don't."

## Roots of the race question

IT ALL began with Vasco da Gama, the Portuguese. Now there was a man! The composer Giacomo Meyerbeer (Jakob Liebmann Beer) wrote an opera about him, *L'Africaine* ("The African"), which includes one of the finest tenor solos in grand opera, "O Paradiso." Vasco da Gama sings "O Paradiso" when he sets foot on the African continent. To the real Vasco da Gama, Africa was paradise.

Vasco da Gama had an obsession about Africa. When he was on land between voyages, his house had to face the sea —and Africa. People were afraid of the Dark Continent and da Gama had a hard time getting sailors for his voyages. They all knew that sailing with da Gama meant one thing— Africa. He explored the continent piecemeal. He would sail down the west coast, go ashore, do some exploring, and talk with African native chiefs. On the next voyage he'd go a little farther south than he had been the year before. He kept inching south till one day he went clear around the Cape of Good Hope, only of course it wasn't "one day." The winds and storms buffeted his ship across the bottom of Africa for a month, and half of his sailors died at the pumps. The heart swells up and bursts if you pump water for thirty days without a pause. Now he started to explore the east coast, upward and upward, to talk to African chiefs, and to leave a small blockhouse on shore so he'd remember where he had been. Eventually da Gama sailed into the Indian Ocean and brought the cloves, cinnamon, ginger, and other spices directly to the consumers. Somehow history has slighted this Captain-General Vasco da Gama, because there are two really important stories of exploration—Columbus in 1492, Vasco da Gama in 1499. They both went looking for the same thing. Columbus found the West Indies and thought they were the East Indies. Vasco da Gama found the East Indies and knew they were the East Indies. Both changed the course of world history, as much as any other two men before or since. Because of Vasco da Gama, the great broker-cities Venice and Leghorn closed the book on their histories forever. Siam, Burma, and Shanghai and the whole China trade were opened up to Western civilization.

On each of his trips back to Portugal the populace gave da Gama a parade. The captain-general was up in front on a white horse. He was a very handsome man. He had two hobbies: on sea, Africa; on land, women. These parades always had a few tragedies. Girls and women who knew they had no chance to attract his attention during his short stay did the next best thing to get close to him. They threw themselves in front of Vasco da Gama's horse. This always made the captain-general very sad. It was such a waste. But after all it is much easier to explore the whole African continent than to take care of even half the women in one little village. So Vasco da Gama reluctantly galloped on and did the best he could under the circumstances. Behind him marched his sailors, those who survived the voyage, but they were well taken care of. No nonsense about agreements, double-crossings, arguments, short changings, and "You didn't see it first, I saw it first"—all of which harassed Columbus all his life. Vasco da Gama paid off at the pier. No nonsense. This is yours, boys, and this is mine, and in the parade, we'll just use the stuff that belongs to "them." After the sailors, came the big wagons full of ivory, aloes, cinnamon, ginger, some gold; and in the rear were the blacks. Da Gama brought the blacks from Africa; but let no one call him "a slaver." He was an explorer. Where is the man with imagination, opening up a new continent, who would not bring back some of the natives? In the cities of Portugal these blacks of Africa were objects of curiosity, and the rich families used them as servants. But there wasn't the slightest hint of commercialized slavery yet.

Of course slavery could never be an urban business and could never be profitable even on the castle estates. What difference does it make if you give your freeman servant three dollars a month or give your bondman servant nothing? There's a limit to the number you can use and feed. But working large numbers of blacks on plantations under an overseer, that's another matter. That's where the money was. And now seventy years after Vasco da Gama brought his first blacks to Portugal, Cuba was opening up; all the West Indies were opening up with huge sugar plantations and tobacco and later on cotton. They could use all the blacks they could get, and they never got quite enough.

When I speak of "blacks" and "natives" you may get the impression, which I am afraid is a general impression anyway, that the white sailors and the slavers ran up on the African shore, chased the natives into the bush and up the trees, "tamed" them, and dragged them to the slave ships. Nonsense. Along the west coast of Africa, what they called the Guinea Coast, the Negroes had family life, pretty much as we know it, and they had tribal law, and the administrator (president, king, chief) was not a hereditary position. Yes, the eldest son had a prior claim to the job, *if* he proved himself first. The same was true in Angola and in Senegal from which came most of the ancestors of our Southern Negroes.

The blockhouses which Vasco da Gama built were now put to use for the slave trade, by the Portuguese, then the Spanish, Dutch, English, and French, and then by the peoples living in the New World. The Negroes were not rounded up. They were all stockaded, secured, and ready for shipment when the slavers arrived. Man corrupts man. Men have sold out their own people for an extra slice of bacon. The Negroes of Angola and Guinea and Senegal were human and they, too, produced their Benedict Arnolds and Quislings. And so the slavers established a system of working exclusively through native procurers.

"You are two months late, master-of-the-ship. What delayed you? I had eleven hundred head two months ago, but I ran out of food and had to let half of them go." Then the master of the slave ship would pay off, and the Negro procurer would say, "How come you are giving me only four barrels of rum this time—instead of six?" And the slaver would explain: "You put it over on me last time, black boy, you ran in thirty head on me with sick lungs and more than ten had yaws—if I hadn't thrown them overboard when I did, I would have lost the whole cargo."

And so it went for many years. The plantations in the West Indies and on the American continent demanded more, and the Negro procurers worked faster and faster, first at the rate of about 30,000 a year at the beginning of the eighteenth century, and later as high as 90,000 a year.

A man's slave was his money. If you killed one (under British, Spanish, Dutch, and Portuguese and French law in the New World) it was no one's business. If you killed another man's slave, you paid a stiff fine, usually what the man had originally paid for the slave, with no depreciation for years of use.

Toward the end of the eighteenth century there were rumblings all over the Western world. First, the Protestant Reformation which had played a leading part in the destruction of serfdom in Europe began to catch up with the slave traffic. What delayed it for so long was the fact that the Negro was not thought of as a human being—a man with a soul.

If Theodosius had scattered the Jews throughout Europe as slaves, the result would have been the same as the effects of slavery on the blacks. Instead Theodosius and others made the mistake of their lives! They relegated the Jews to the ghetto—a spiritual, mental, and physical fortress, and what is there to do in a ghetto but read books and practice the art of human dignity?

As it is, the Negro has done well enough. His intellectual advancement with one hand tied behind his back has been phenomenal.

And toward the end of the eighteenth century there were Voltaire and Jean Jacques Rousseau, Thomas Paine and Thomas Jefferson. Light was beginning to seep through. If nothing else, Western man began to question the whole business. Then Christianity took a hand. The early Methodists of England delivered the first telling blow. They insisted that under theological law if a Negro had been baptized he could no longer be kept in slavery. A good beginning. But different factors slowed up each of the religious liberal movements, the Methodists in England and the Baptists in America.

It was not bigotry, per se, to begin with. The Southerners were returning from the war, badly beaten in body and in spirit. It was fairly easy to identify the Negro, the freed slave, with all this misfortune. Then the "victors" stepped in, and they used the Negro to pile humiliation upon humiliation. These Northern politicians and fakers immediately projected the Negro into Southern political life without any preparation, and without any rhyme or reason. Here was the Southern farmer, completely ruined, trying to rebuild life and his home, and he is immediately confronted with Negro members of state legislatures who can't read and write, and who in some cases showed immaturity which would have been comical if it were not so tragic for them and for everybody concerned.

All of this played a part in the tragedy which was to follow—segregation. The coming of industrialization of the section was another factor.

After the Northern politician-faker got through squeezing the last ounce out of it—the playing of the freed slave against the Southern white—he said to the Southerner: "I know it's been tough, boys, but I've got a proposition now. I am ready to leave the Negro dangling in midair. Here's the proposition: get your presidential electors to double-cross Democrat Samuel J. Tilden; have them cast their ballots against the popular vote, and put Republican Rutherford B. Hayes in the White House. I know it's a big price to pay, boys, but I'll turn the Negro over to you, lock, stock, and barrel, and if you want to let off a little steam, I'll not blame you at all."

In England the Methodists were up against a similar situation in different terms. They had succeeded in outlawing slavery by due process. The way it came about was this. Before the Revolutionary War many of the American planters would visit England—the Mother Country—for the same reasons that rich people have visited metropolitan centers since time immemorial. On these trips the planters would take a quantity of their slaves. Slaves for madame, slaves to shine the shoes, hold the horses, carry the packages, and for other chores. One day a Methodist by the name of Sharpe "abducted" one of these Negro slaves, took him before a court, and amazingly secured the decision that slavery was against British law, consequently the Negro was free. That night all the Negroes in England went off— free. But there was no plan, and they wound up roaming the countryside, begging food—and cursing the liberating Methodists. Eventually the English established a home for the liberated slaves at Sierra Leone, where they lived in townships and established a fairly good life. But now a re- action set in all over Europe. A reaction from the French Revolution. If you spoke against slavery you were called a Jacobin—today's equivalent of being called a Red—and that stopped most of the good people dead in their tracks.

In England a large group of slum dwellers paraded with big placards: "Down with Liberty, Equality, and Fraternity."

Thus the theologians left the field of battle—a battle which was rightfully theirs—and they left it to the writers, the crackpots, the do-gooders, and the odd-fish secularists of varying degrees of wisdom and stupidity, opportunism and idealism. And so the secularists, the writers, and journalists carried on the battle, and if *Uncle Tom's Cabin* was a lousy novel and the pamphlets and speeches of William Lloyd Garrison and Colonel Robert Ingersoll were often ridiculous, inflammatory, and stupid, whose fault was it?

And so we had to have a war about it. Before that we had slaves in all the states of the North. But one state after another freed its slaves by statute. Of course they did it because slavery was economically unprofitable in the North. And in a number of states, like New York and Pennsylvania, the effective dates of these statutes were set far ahead to enable a slave owner to take his slaves South and sell them.

On January 1, 1863, President Lincoln issued the Emancipation Proclamation. The Northern soldiers were asking that same old question, "What are we fighting for?"—and Lincoln gave them a cause. The proclamation freed the slaves in all states which were in rebellion. This left slavery untouched in the states and sections not in the Confederacy.

Slavery was finally abolished throughout the nation in 1865 by a constitutional amendment.

It had taken 1,800 years to strike the shackles.


# The Ku Klux Klan—1920 and now

IN THE late summer of 1915, a small group of robed and hooded figures met on Stone Mountain in Georgia and burned a cross.

Southern white, Protestant womanhood henceforth would be protected from being forced into concubinage to the Negro, into the brothels maintained by Catholic monks, and into the factory harems of the Jews.

But white womanhood was not safe from the Klansmen themselves. At the height of the organization's influence in the late 1920's, Miss Madge Oberholtzer took poison after she had been raped by the Imperial Wizard himself, D. C. Stephenson. Stephenson was convicted of second-degree murder; by that time, however, the organization was falling apart at the seams.

But during a ten-year period the Klan achieved quite a show of power in these United States of Jefferson, Franklin, and Lincoln.

The Klan controlled the political machinery of a dozen sovereign states, and a dozen Senators and a hundred members of Congress acted upon instructions from the Wizards.

In the early 1930's I stopped in at my favorite cigar store in Red Bank, New Jersey, and there I met a friend, a Roman Catholic priest. We walked out together. Referring to the manager of the cigar store, I said, "Fine fellow, that Phil Jones, isn't he?" The priest smiled and for dramatic effect leaned down to whisper in my ear: "I saw that fellow lead a gang of Ku Kluxers one night—they marched around my church and finally they burned a cross up the street." We both puffed the cigars and laughed the rest of the way.

Now what made this truly nice man during one stage in

his life decide to march around another man's church and then burn a cross?

The Klan was created by naive and ignorant men, but it did not remain their property for long. Wiser heads saw its possibilities, greedier men saw its possibilities, and political heads saw its potential strength.

During those ten years of Klan power it took in millions and millions of dollars. The membership list was sold by one Wizard to another. One guy, Hiram Evans, got $90,000 for an early list of these frustrated pawns, many of them good men; men with a nervous system, a heart, a pair of lungs; men with a family; men made in the image of God. Evans sold them all, lock, stock, and barrel, for $90,000. And then he sued, said he was cheated, he should have received $143,000. He said the bookkeeper failed to count a few of the sheets with some additional names of Americans.

William J. Simmons was the brains behind the whole thing. Mr. Simmons had been the organizer of fraternal orders and now he hit the jackpot with Mr. Dixon's *The Birth of a Nation* and this Invisible Empire of the Knights of the Ku Klux Klan and he appointed himself Imperial Wizard. He drew up a constitution, the ritual of the Kloran, and created officers—Kleages, Kligrapps, Cyclopses, Geniis, and Goblins. The symbols were to be the American Flag and the burning cross; and in this most Christian land in the world no one told them that the burning cross was a remnant of the Hate-Fire of ancient days and symbolized the burning of God, the God who disappointed and brought no rain, no manchild, no crops, and no good hunting.

In 1920 the Klan began to expand. Simmons hooked up with a couple of hard-boiled publicity agents, Edward Y. Clarke and his fat partner, Mrs. Elizabeth Tyler. Simmons was in charge of fund-raising and the publicity agents whipped up the suckers. Simmons guaranteed his publicity-agent partners eight dollars out of every ten-dollar initiation fee they collected.

At first the Klan was "orderly." Its big parade was on primary day and election day, as a warning against Negro voting. But the publicity team was warning the folks about the *new* Negro, the Negro who returned from the Army and who might begin to think that he was a *somebody*, and then the Klan began to brand the letter KKK on bellhops and janitors who stood up to them with nothing more than, "I have a right to walk down this street." And the Klan posted street signs in small cities of Kentucky, Arkansas, Oklahoma, Georgia, Mississippi: "Nigger, don't let the sun set on your head."

But let us leave the South for a moment. In some instances the Klan power was even more insidious in the North. Indiana was probably the number one Klan state in the Union; and Michigan was strong, and upstate New York, and downstate New Jersey. In the North the Klan exploited fear of the Pope of Rome and of foreign immigrant "hordes." Anti-Semitism was all but unknown in America until the Klan era of the 1920's. America was almost untouched by this virus, which culminated in *The Dearborn Independent*, until after World War I, and the Klan helped consolidate the closing of the gates to foreign immigration. Alvin Johnson, a congressman, devoted all his waking hours to promotion of his bill to stop the flow of immigration into America, and one of his strange allies was Sam Gompers, an immigrant Jew who was afraid of the competition of foreign labor; and the fighters for free immigration were the capitalists and the American aristocrats—each, of course, for a different reason. Ah, America, what a wonderful story.

The publicity agents anticipated every need of the frustrated. They missed nothing. In his earlier Populist days, Tom Watson of Georgia embraced "my Negro brethren," who, he said, were "exploited by Wall Street Jews." When he ran for the Senate he based his campaign on an attack upon the Negro and "his primitive sex appetite," and Watson also delivered a series of venomous lectures on the Pope. The governor of Florida, a Mr. Catts, warned his constituents that the Pope was ready to invade America and establish his Vatican in Florida.

What was the secret of their success? Why did normal,

decent Americans buy the robes and pay the initiation fees to these thieves and hatemongers?

They had a complete package program. Whom do you hate? We got it. This is a pattern which has been part of each of our nativist movements; the Know-Nothings of the mid-nineteenth century, the short flurry of nativism in the 1890's, the Klan in the 1920's, and the revival of the Klan elements in the 1950's.

In 1920 there was a social upheaval. Cotton had been selling at five cents.

Many farmers and sharecroppers were flocking to the cities in the hope of getting work in the new factories. Women were coming into town to work.

Mobility, dislocation, disappointment, and often actual hunger succeeded in whirling these people into the laps of the publicity agents and the Imperial Wizard.

The Ku Klux Klan elements of 1959 are feeding on the fears which have grown out of another social change (the end of legal segregation), and the unemployment in some industries together with declining farm incomes. Up to now they have not made much headway. In fact the recent bombing and attempted bombing of Jewish community centers and temples and Negro churches may be attributed to this inability to consolidate their positions. The press and the police authority are after them, with considerable vigor, particularly in the Carolinas, Georgia, Tennessee, and Florida. There is no central Klan authority and police activity prevents communication among individual groups, and each proceeds on a "project" of its own. What happens is that four or five fellows meet and discuss their mutual disappointments in life, their anger at society. They drink a lot of beer and then the one who works for a construction company and knows where to get some dynamite says, "Let's do something about all our troubles." Invariably they drive across a state line to do their job. The attacks upon the several Jewish institutions is proof of this spur-of-the-moment decision. It has no direct bearing on the integration problem. In Charlotte they attempted to bomb a temple where neither the rabbi nor any of the leaders has ever uttered an expression of any kind on the racial question. If it was an organized Klan attempt to silence a spokesman for his integration views, they might have bombed one of three or four Protestant churches where clergymen have taken a public stand against Jim Crow.

Since these fellows drive across state lines I believe the FBI should enter the investigation. I doubt whether any responsible Southern newspaper or civil or police authority would not accept the experience of the Federal authorities to ferret out these criminals. Dynamite like freedom is indivisible. You cannot isolate it. You cannot separate it. If the attempted bombing of a Charlotte temple had succeeded, it would have set back this growing metropolis by at least ten years. We who travel around the country hear, "Charlotte? Isn't that where you have that big coliseum?" This is better than, "Isn't that where they bombed a Jewish synagogue?"

But because some of the old Klan ingredients seem to be upon us today, it is well that we begin to write about them. All of us should write about them. I do not believe that if we do not mention them, they will go away. This has never worked. The time to study them is now.

# The Catholic showcase

THE Roman Catholic Church has shown it can desegregate its parochial schools in the South without dire consequences. Nothing has happened except the development of a growing sense of pride and a deeper sense of humanity.

It is true, of course, that the comparatively large Roman Catholic cities of New Orleans, Charleston, and Mobile have not made the step yet.

But the Church does offer this Southern showcase of integration, and let us remember that this involves white

Southerners—Virginians, Tar Heels, and South Carolinians. It is worth repeating—nothing has happened. Except on the sports field, there is no socializing. This follows the pattern I knew as a student in New York. I came to the school with a Jewish boy and I went back home with him, back to our block—and the Italian boy did the same, and the Negro did the same, and so did the Poles, Ukrainians, and Greeks; but there was an interchange of ideas in the classroom without which the human mind would still be sitting in primitive darkness.

Up in the land of Senator Harry "massive resistance" Byrd, the Roman Catholics have desegregated St. Benedict's High School for Boys and the Cathedral Elementary School.

In Charlotte, we are the pioneers—even among the Roman Catholics of the South. The O'Donoghue School has been desegregated for three years now, while, in the land of Jimmy Byrnes and Governor Timmerman, in Rock Hill, South Carolina, St. Ann's, with classes up to the eighth grade, has one hundred and twelve pupils, and twelve are Negroes.

It is interesting that in Richmond and in Charlotte the Catholics who send their children to desegregated parochial schools belong to the "power structure" more or less. They are executives and managers. In South Carolina, more than half the white families who send their children to the Catholic desegregated school are millworkers. Thus, at two levels of the Southern culture the Roman Catholics have shown that it can be done.

# In quest of a linotype machine

THE conduct of the Southern Negro in the emotional controversy over segregation will someday be recorded as one of the most noble stories of the human spirit.

It is fantastic that the Negro has not done a single thing

wrong. Over eleven million people, half of whom are illiterate, another third of whom are semiliterate; a civilization of many sharecroppers, truck drivers, and janitors— and they have not done a single thing wrong.

Their houses are bombed, and the Negroes say, "Let's go to church and pray for the fellows who have bombed our houses." A cross is burned on their hills, and the Negroes roast marshmallows in the embers.

It is as if the Negroes had suddenly seen the same vision that inspired the Founding Fathers of America and had become this age's greatest connoisseurs of true democracy.

It involves the process of going to the judge with a writ, and when the judge says, "You have not exhausted all your means of possible relief," the Negro says, "Thank you, I'll start all over again in the morning," and a year later he is back again with the writ, and his children march up to the public school, and they are stopped, and the Negro marches down still another road of peaceful recourse.

Americans of all races, creeds, and social levels will one day rise up with pride and pay honor to this great phenomenon of the human story.

The story really goes back to the 1930's, when it became evident that the Negroes of the South—second-class citizens by law—offered the greatest resistance to blandishments of Communist propagandists. This is all the more remarkable when we realize that the local Communist medicine men automatically promoted the Negro, no matter how unfit for the job, to positions of greatest honor within individual cells. Such promotion had nothing behind it but the color of a man's skin, and therefore was as dehumanizing as legal segregation itself. And the Negroes of the South who fell for this degradation through "honor" were not numerous enough to have filled a respectable telephone booth.

This response is all the more remarkable when we consider the real meaning of racial segregation:

You are fifteen years old, and you have never seen your father in anything but overalls, and you have never seen your mother in anything but a uniform on the way to another woman's home. A car pulls up in your filth-littered yard, and a man shouts to you, "Boy, tell Jim to come at seven o'clock tomorrow instead of eight," or "Boy, tell Nettie not to come tomorrow." And Jim is your father. And Nettie is your mother. So if you take a carton of cigarettes off a truck or get behind the wheel of a car that is not yours—because of the degradation, the lack of self-esteem, the uselessness of trying to prove your individual worth—you know by instinct that a record of even four juvenile arrests will not disqualify you from that job of janitor which is waiting for you.

What are they talking about when Senator Harry Byrd of Virginia and Governor Marvin Griffin of Georgia demand that racial segregation remain part of the American culture? What do they mean by this? Is it a matter of whether a Negro child may or may not go to a free public school? That is only part of it, and a very small part of it. What are they talking about when they speak of racial segregation? They are talking about human degradation and death. Because of the entire system of racial segregation, seven Negro women die in childbirth to one white woman. Because of the system of racial segregation, tuberculosis, which is eighth as the cause of death among the white race, is second as a cause of death among the Negroes. And because of racial segregation, you have that deadening sense of hopelessness among millions of young people who were born to share and contribute to the creativity and glory of America.

And what about the effect on the Southern white children growing up in an atmosphere of evasion? Children pick up the paper every morning and see big headlines: We have a new scheme to "beat" the law. Our attorney general thought up something new to "beat" the Supreme Court decision. Education takes place at many levels: in the school, in the home, in the church, on the street, in the newspaper accounts of the work of the state legislatures, and in the speeches of the governors. How can they tell the children on Monday that to obey the law is the highest point to which an American boy can aspire, and on Tuesday maneuver and connive to get around the law?

And here is the greatest tragedy of all. The South has produced some of the most creative minds of the American civilization, but now creativity has come to a halt. This great civilization is preoccupied with this nonsense about interracial sex, this resistance to a Supreme Court decision, this determination not to grant first-class citizenship to 26 per cent of its population.

This civilization is not thinking about foreign affairs. It is not thinking of the expansion of its educational and health facilities. It is not thinking of the basic strategy of the free world against statism and totalitarianism. No, it is preoccupied with the project of trying to keep a fifteen-year-old Negro girl from going to a public school.

The white man has paid a bigger price for segregation than the Negro.

There is no communication. What the Southerner does not know is that the Negro has intruded himself upon his life. He has intruded himself at every level of his culture. When you set up laws to segregate anyone, you are the one who is enslaved. Booker T. Washington was right when he said, "If you want to keep a man in the gutter, you have got to get down in the gutter and hold him."

In the North, among immigrants who came to America, the Italians built tunnels, the Jews went into the sewing shops, the Czechs went into the coal mines, and the Poles went into the steel mills. They sent their sons to Cornell University, the University of Michigan, and the University of Pennsylvania. They entered the middle class. In the South, they had the black man, and there are huge segments of white Southerners who have done nothing all their lives on account of the Negro.

That Southerner would not do anything that Negroes did because he would lose status. Instead, he hung around the courthouse all his life, running errands for the commissioner. He dabbled a little in rural politics. He would say,

"My wife has a piece of property," and he would draw up new plans, look at them, and tear them up. This did terrible harm to the Southern white man.

Caste has been first, but sexual myth has also played a part in this human drama.

In my state, we have a white high school which has a linotype machine and other printing facilities to teach children this highly skilled trade. There is no Negro school with such facilities.

And so when the white men get together they talk about how the Negroes want to go to bed with white women, and when the Negroes get together they talk about a linotype machine. I have heard about that linotype machine a thousand times at a hundred meetings. And I have yet to hear a Negro, even by the most remote innuendo, even during a thousand unguarded moments, express "desire" for a white woman.

The white man has slept with the Negro woman for two or three hundred years, and now he fears retaliation. This is a great tragedy, and it is also a great insult to the white women of the South. I cannot understand why the white women stand for it—this idea of their men worrying about the matter. But no one seems to get the point. No one seems to be insulted by this thing. If you let the Negro vote and give him equal job opportunity and equal educational facilities, why should the white woman fall for him?

But it is all utter nonsense. In the first place, the Negro has all the "white" women he needs. The white man of the South "gave" them to him. The Negro can pick from a dozen different shades among his own people, all the way from redheads with freckles down to the very blackest of the black. Second, we have learned that, as a race or ethnic group rises in self-esteem, there is not only less crime but less sexual promiscuity. If she knows she can someday be a nurse, or a dental technician, or a stenographer, the day when you can take her to the haystack is over. And self-esteem leads to pride of race. As the Negro enters first-class citizenship in our country, and takes his rightful place in the industrial society, this so-called "mongrelization" which has been part of the culture will finally come to a grinding halt. Exactly opposite to what the segregationist fears will take place.

There was a great calm over the South after the Supreme Court decision. The South was waiting for leadership which never came, waiting for some word from the White House or some word from the state capitals. There was no leadership in the state capitals because the politicians saw an opportunity to ride this issue for another twenty years. In Virginia, Harry Byrd was playing his last card, and he knew it, and the State of Virginia knew it. Harry Byrd rules Virginia like Trujillo rules the Dominican Republic. A quarter of a century ago, we had Cotton Ed Smith, Mr. Heflin, and Senator Bilbo. The fellows today are no different. Their approach is a little fancier, but they are really nothing more than Bilbos in gray flannel pants.

And what is this resistance all about? Why should an old aristocrat like Senator Byrd of Virginia talk like a barber of a mill village when he discusses the problem of one third of the citizens of his state?

Why did the entire middle class turn on the Negro after the Supreme Court decision? In the past, they have organized betterment leagues, and if a Negro ran for public office the only white votes he got were from the best residential sections.

You may be surprised to know that in the 1830's many fellows with goatees, sipping mint juleps on their verandas, made fine speeches against slavery. "Slavery—that's no good. Man is created in God's image." When a reform is not imminent, when there does not appear to be any chance of change, they say good things. But these same fellows, thirty years later, put on a gray uniform and were willing to destroy an entire section of the country to protect slavery.

And the same thing happened with Jim Crow. A lot of people made speeches about how terrible it was, but when the Supreme Court handed down its decision, this was different. To the poor whites in the South, the Negro stands between them and social oblivion. The Negro gives them some degree of self-esteem. Subconsciously, they know the hopelessness of their position, and, if you take the Negro away from them, where will they find self-esteem? They may start voting and joining labor unions.

Without the Negro, the Southern white worker would have to get caste in trade unions. You cannot organize in the South except in some industries which have come from the North and are oriented to a different way of life. In the South, the first thing the boss tells you when the union is trying to organize is: "Do you want to have a Negro working beside you?" Then he shows you a picture of a white working beside a Negro. Always a white woman and a Negro man.

And if, in addition, poor whites start voting, maybe their children will go to Congress instead of Harry Byrd. Trade unions and voting for the millions would make the South an entirely different world. That is why the upper middle class turned the Negro down.

All of this relates to the statement of a woman recorded by a reporter for *Life* magazine outside Central High School in Little Rock as the nine Negro children finally went through the door. This woman gasped: "My God, the niggers are in!" Why should this woman have felt that her world had suddenly come to an end? Actually this woman has been brought up in an atmosphere which tried to give her caste the easy way. While the Negroes were going to the back of the bus and to separate schools and filling the jobs of janitors, this woman had status without money, status without the necessity of voting and without the need to join a labor union.

Still, the remarkable thing about the whole matter is the way the Negroes have responded.

They have just not done anything wrong.

The white woman says: "The Negroes are very happy; they do not want to end racial segregation, my maid told me so." She calls her maid in and says: "Nettie, what do you think of this Supreme Court decision?" And the maid says: "Lordy, Miz Emily, we never sees the paper."

And that night the maid goes home and says to her husband: "Jim, get a move on you with that supper; we'll be late for the N.A.A.C.P. meeting and let's try to put some life into our integration committee this time."


# Long Sam and Deborah

A SIXTEEN-YEAR-OLD girl, Dorothy Brown, of Mooresville (about twenty miles from Charlotte), appeared before a TV audience of millions on the Ed Sullivan program two years ago. It was not a gimmick. The newspaper people had discovered this handsome youngster in a poverty-stricken rural community. It was a pleasure to watch her poise and charm. A dozen New York City reporters, familiar with every known pipe dream of the press agent, were equally impressed with Dorothy, who had been nicknamed "Long Sam."

At about the same time, there was another gracious Dorothy. Her name was Dorothy Counts, and she was fifteen years old, and she was the first Negro ever admitted to the previously all-white Harding High School of Charlotte.

The local school board made a start toward desegregation of public schools in accordance with the Supreme Court decisions of 1954 and 1955. Charlotte's very able Chief of Police at the time, Frank Littlejohn, said: "We'll take this in stride in this city; there'll be no trouble, except, maybe, at Harding High School" (in a low-income neighborhood where the question of caste is so much more significant). And the chief was absolutely right in his forecast, and it was not a pleasant sight.

As the girl walked home after the first day of school, a mob of teen-agers, egged on by a few psychotic adults, followed her with screams and catcalls, and spit at her, and, though they saw the pretty Dorothy who became "Long Sam," Ed Sullivan and those New York City reporters have never, in their entire careers, seen the equal of the other Dorothy's conduct for POISE. The young girl continued to walk down the street, looked neither to the right nor to the left, and never once did she quicken her pace.

North Carolina also produces newspapermen of poise and honor. Kays Gary, of *The Charlotte Observer,* who had really been instrumental in getting the white Dorothy her chance with Ed Sullivan, now wrote a story of this Negro Dorothy. Listen to these words:

> And this is the way she carried her head
> They spat and she was covered with it
> Spittle dripped from the hem of her dress,
> It clung to her neck and her arms and she wore it.
> They spat and they jeered and they screamed
> A boy tumbled out of the crowd and hit her in
> the back with his fist
> Debris fell on her shoulders and around her feet.
> And the posture of her head was unchanged.
> This was the remarkable thing.
> And if her skin was brown, you had to admit that
> her courage was royal purple,
> For how many of us could have taken that walk—
> to and from school?

Like Deborah, the Biblical guardian of Israel, this Dorothy won a major victory for her people. Because such victories are not really won by organizations, nor by literature, nor even by decisions of the Supreme Court. The field of honor in human relations is won only by the dignity of the human spirit. And it happened in Charlotte, North Carolina, on September 5, 1957, where a fifteen-year-old girl took a walk to school.

## An eye-witness account

A NEGRO stands on his porch reading a note which has just come in the mail. It is an anonymous letter, not very important, not even too frightening. It is signed KKK, and it is crudely written, illiterate. It is from a white man who cannot spell a few simple words, and it is addressed to a Negro who teaches philosophy at a Southern university. The Negro counts the misspelled words, and smiles. Now he gently folds the note and places it in his wallet. Uncle Remus is done gone—forever.

## Separate but equal

A NEGRO sharecropper crossed the Mississippi from Arkansas into Memphis, and he went right through the first red light he saw. The state trooper pulled him over.

"What's the matter with you?" he demanded.

The Negro replied, "Yes, sir, I sure did pass that red light. I saw all the white folks using the green one."

## "They want to take over"

THE most damaging phrases I have ever heard run like this:

"They [Catholics or Jews or Negroes or Puerto Ricans] want to take over."

There are countless variations on this, and the repetition of this idea has put thousands at the mercy of the unthinking. These phrases are not only horrible, but untrue. Of the hundreds of Catholics I've known in my life, the only thing a few of them wanted to take over was the sixth race at Saratoga, or maybe a half-acre lot downtown where they think they might make a living selling used cars. All the Jews want to take over is a mink stole for the wife and a few onion rolls at a Miami Beach hotel. And all the Negroes and the Puerto Ricans want to take over is a clean place to live, away from their dirt-littered alleys.

# The Jewish race?

I WOULDN'T worry about using the term "Jewish race." In recent years whenever someone inadvertently used the term, he was sure to get an angry reply, *"We are not a race; we are an ethnic group."* Of course, scientifically, this is absolutely true. Scientists are explicit in their definition—a race is a continuity of distinctive physical characteristcs, transmitted by heredity—the Caucasian, the Negro, the Mongol, etc.

But in the last fifteen years there have been several mountains of pamphlets written to explain that *we are not a race*. This is foolish, and a complete waste of time and money. I would have taken all that money and I would have built little parks with water fountains in at least fifteen cities. The word "race" is one of the most noble words of mankind.

In reference to the Jewish people, of course, it is not a scientific term, but a colloquialism—a figure of speech—which should make us proud. The British are not a race in the scientific sense, but how many times has the great Winston Churchill said, *"We are a hardy race . . ."*?

Can you imagine saying, *"We are a hardy ethnic group"*? Silly. Relax. It's good to belong to the "Jewish race."

# Instruction of children

EVERY Negro mother anticipates the day when she will have to face the child's first segregation experience. Not a pleasant thing, is it? What the Negro mothers tell the kids is that only the uneducated white people are bigoted. This is interesting, and it is too bad it is not more generally known. But I can see how this gives the Negro child self-respect to build on, since he is taught from the beginning that racism is a phenomenon with which only the uneducated are afflicted.

# A switch

FOR many years the stereotype went something like this: "The Jews are traders and businessmen, but they are poor fighters."

Now, with the eleven-year survival of an Israel surrounded by enemies, and the conquest of the Sinai Peninsula in three days—but with a sidelong glance at Israel's unbalanced budget—all of this may be changed: "Them Jews are great fighters, but they are certainly poor businessmen."

# The Golden Pogo Stick Plan

UP IN Detroit there is a motorists' holiday. No tickets are issued. Cars go through red lights, make U turns, and terrorize pedestrians, without so much as a traffic cop's whistle cutting the air.

All of this had a curious beginning. For years the Detroit police force was the Midwest's finest. Negro and white policemen patrolled their beats, kept order, and lived in

amiable professional harmony. But lately, when Negro policemen have come up for promotion, they have been assigned
to the police scout cars. The white policemen objected. They
did not want to ride side by side with a Negro policeman.

So the Detroit cops went on strike. They refused to issue
traffic tickets. All of which made Police Commissioner Hart
pretty hot under the collar. "Intregate or quit!" he announced. But force is not, and never has been, the answer.
If the white policemen will work with the erect but not
the sedentary Negro policemen, the answer is to make all
the policemen in Detroit vertical again. Since they cannot
patrol the whole city on foot, let Police Commissioner Hart
issue pogo sticks. Law and order will again prevail and
errant motorists will be ticketed and the Detroit police commissioner can sleep the sleep of angels.


# Point of order

Down near Mobile, Alabama, the union had won an election at the Courtaulds synthetic plant and they were meeting
at the local courthouse to discuss the contract. One of the
delegates was a Negro.

As the chairman began to read the contract, an officer
stepped up and whispered that it was against the law to have
a Negro attend a meeting with whites. The union leaders
held a consultation and decided to do nothing about it.
Through all this, the Negro sat unconcerned.

The police were having their own problems. A suggestion
to go on in and "pull him out" was vetoed by the chief of
police: "Do you want to have us in every paper in the
North?"

In the room the delegates went on with their business. It
grew hot in the room. The delegates began to shed their
jackets, open their shirt collars. The sweat was pouring off
their brows as they began to fan themselves with the con-
tracts. The only calm fellow in the hall was the Negro

delegate. Just as the chairman had run through the last of the lengthy contract provisions, the Negro finally rose and said:

"Mr. Chairman, I am a little worried about Provisions 3 and 4. Will you please have the secretary read them again? Also, I would like to offer two new amendments to Sections A, B, and F in Provision 5, if you please."

# Profit and loss

THE South spends millions of dollars to provide the Negro with elementary schools, school lunches, transportation, high schools, and even colleges; and on the day the Negro receives his diploma he goes off to Camden, New Jersey, or to Philadelphia, Pennsylvania. Not all the educated Negroes want to be clergymen or schoolteachers within their own segregated society. And the white supremacist says, "We are losing our nigras," but it is not that simple. We lose two thirds of our educated Negroes and he leaves behind his uneducated brother and his old father with arthritis, and so our welfare, charity, and hospital costs go way up, trying to compete with our mounting educational costs in a futile attempt to maintain two separate school systems, which are both dehumanizing and useless.

# Social equality

ANOTHER one of the shadows which haunts the orderly implementation of the Supreme Court decision of May 17, 1954, is "social equality." The shadow is about as real as the ghost I once saw at a spiritual seance some years ago.

There is no such thing. Personally I do not believe life would be worth living in a society of enforced "social equality." There is no such thing in the white race; and there is no such thing in the black, red, yellow, or brown races.

During the period of unrestricted immigration to this country, the poorest of the poor Jews from European ghettos insisted on preserving "yichus" (social status). Immigrants from Poland settled in one section of the Lower East Side, from Russia in another section, and so forth. When a young man called on your sister, the first question did not concern his income or the make of his automobile. The first question was about his social status. Who was his father, and what was the tradition behind the family?

And what about the other groups? Do you suppose an Italian from Milan or Genoa would even be seen talking with a Calabrese, a Sicilian? And the term "shanty Irish"? Who introduced that into our society? The "lace-curtain" Irish, of course!

# My plan to save the quiz show

I THINK perhaps that I could have saved the once-popular television quiz show if they'd put my plan into effect.

Not long before ratings forced them off the air, the $64,000 people called me and asked if I'd go on the program. I told the folks I wasn't their man. I wouldn't have had a chance on this deal. I might possibly get by for two or three questions on Shakespeare. But for the life of me I cannot tell you when Shakespeare's son-in-law died. I once knew the name of the fellow who printed the First Folio, but I dismissed it from my mind long ago.

But then, free of charge, I offered the $64,000 people an idea to help get an additional ten million viewers in the South. Here is the plan:

Put Teddy Nadler in one booth and that Elfrida girl in another booth, and ask them the questions they ask the Negroes in Mississippi to qualify them as voters.

They're interesting questions, like, How many bubbles in a pound of soap?

> *James Grigg Raines, chief registrar of Terrell County, Alabama, said that the five Negroes involved in the Federal lawsuit were denied registration because they failed to read the United States Constitution intelligently: "I interpret the law to mean they must read it so I can understand it . . . every one of them pronounced 'equity,' 'eequity.'"*

# Low man on the totem pole

SOME of the Puerto Ricans of New York are telling their children to keep speaking Spanish so they'll not be mistaken for Negroes.

PART 8

*More Complaints
and Free Advice*

# Instead of leadership

THERE is very little *leadership*. The elected officials wait to see what the Gallup Poll says, and the diplomat takes a taxi ride to find out what "the people" are saying. This idea of the wisdom of the taxi driver is one of America's greatest myths. It is utter nonsense. The taxi driver is universally a hanging juror.

Before Howard Fast left the Communist Party he wrote a book about the Sacco-Vanzetti case, and I had to smile as I recognized the author's terrible dilemma in trying to square the facts in the case with his "class war" concept. The truth of the matter was that the "little people" were unanimous: "Hang the dirty bastards," and every taxi driver said: "I'd like to pull the switch myself on those Dagos." Of course. The stupidity of the unfair trial, the bigotry of the judge, the entire case itself was kept alive by a blue blood, an aristocrat, the corporation lawyer, Mr. William G. Thompson. This Mr. Thompson said quietly, "It is clear to me that they are trying those two people for their avowed anarchism instead of for the alleged murders." And Mr. Thompson decided to do something about it. (Always at his side was the young assistant defense attorney, my good friend and subscriber, Mr. Herbert Ehrmann of Boston.) For the next six or seven years they kept that judge busy answering a new writ every Monday morning. Mr. Thompson lost some of his corporation clients, he became unpopular with some of his fellow Brahmins, and earned the everlasting contempt of the taxi drivers; that is why he now sits on that parapet in heaven reserved for the men of dignity, honor, and fair play.

279

*Leadership* at the very top is lacking and this is reflected at every other level of our political culture of 1959. Everybody waits for the polls, or for the TV ratings, which are tearing the hearts out of so many of our most talented people.

Instead of leadership, we have samplings. "People" have become samplings, and it is all quite ridiculous, especially that 14 per cent that is always "undecided." Undecided— now isn't that something? The poll asks: "How do you feel about the new Paris styles?" And there are 14 per cent undecided. And yet everybody, from the top administration down, holds an ear to the ground and swallows whole the silly sampling culture.

Just suppose there had been a sampling or ratings system in Rome in the year 60 A.D. The results would have been as follows:

| | |
|---|---|
| For Jupiter | 63 per centum |
| For Mithras | 21 per centum |
| For Jesus | 2 per centum |
| Undecided | 14 per centum |

Now if Saint Paul had been a "sampling man" instead of a leader, he would have packed up and gone on back to Palestine, especially after hearing what every taxi driver was saying: "Let's hang that little bald-headed Jew." But, luckily for the Christians, Paul did not subscribe to any sampling polls, and so he just went ahead with his program, and conquered the whole works: the Roman Empire, Jupiter, and Mithras, including even the great Goddess of Vestal Virgins.

# We need the best man here

Down at Cape Canaveral, where the missiles are launched, live a whole group of scientists, psychologists, and doctors who spend their time trying to find the right man to launch toward the moon when the time comes. They have filed thousands of index cards describing top physical specimens and they have administered Rorschach tests to hundreds of volunteers. Machines constantly process these findings. The list of available candidates was narrowed down to fifty and then to seven; eventually this concerted hunt will select one man, physically sound, psychologically right, and smart. Truly, he will be a *mens sana in corpore sano*. But there is something absurd about the purpose of this team. Having found the perfect man, it seems the last place they should send him is to the moon. Rather they ought to keep him here, to help propagate the race. They ought to shoot off the *least* qualified man, because we *need the best man like we never needed him before.*

## "The Late Late Show"

You learn a lot about art, politics, and life if you stay up for "The Late Late Show."

As a man who sits up to watch the late movie, I have to ask myself, what was the black-listing crusade all about? Was it all a fake? To a reasonable man it would seem that if Gale Sondergaard was a threat to the American way of life while she was making movies in 1952, why isn't she a threat to us now on "The Late Show" in 1959? During the last five months I have seen her twice as a featured player in the movie *Anthony Adverse*. Does J. Parnell Thomas sit up to watch "The Late Show," too?

Gale Sondergaard is a competent artist and I'll not go into the merits of her case which resulted in depriving her of a livelihood. The point is that after publicly banning her, the TV network still shows her movies. Nor is this the whole story. A few months ago I saw on "The Late Late Show" a movie called *A Guy Named Joe*. Billed in letters bigger than the star's name was the writer—Dalton Trumbo. Dalton Trumbo was one of the "Hollywood Ten" and was supposed to be the kingfish of subversion. He, too, the movies publicly drummed out of the profession. But at Christmas in 1958 his movies were shown. More than that, I understand that under several pseudonyms he still writes scenarios. Even old Morris Carnovsky, another black-listed actor, is now as big as life, playing with Greta Garbo, no less, on "The Late Late Show."

What was it all about a few years ago? This black-listing process in which so many of the motion-picture and television writers and actors and producers were deprived of a living? Black-listing flourished. There were lists all over the place, several operated by fly-by-night free lancers.

Now we know the FBI was enough. We had *habeas corpus* during World War II. And after a considerable search I have been unable to find a single honorable excuse to criticize the FBI. The FBI is enough. I'll take my chances with them.

But God protect us from the vigilantes and the super-patriots, and the self-appointed guardians of the republic. Because as Martial, the Latin poet asked, "Whom do we get to guard the guardians?"

The black-listers, of course, were not solely responsible for the cruelty they caused. They gave impetus to a condition in movies and television. Television and the movies are highly inhibited. These two media refuse to trust their writers. They change the writer's script at whim or will. For many years, twin beds were *de rigueur* in movies for married couples, and Hollywood has always experimented with two different endings at sneak previews. Television is so inhibited that *Life* magazine refused to consider it as part of show business in one of its recent issues. The director changes script lines, and then the advertising executive, and then the sponsor. That is the reason television dramas are now all adaptations, because it is too hard and weary to convince a sponsor that an original script won't offend a middle-aged gas-meter inspector in Des Moines. Television executives issue a "forbidden sheet" to editors. You must not buy a script in which a man loses limbs. Never show a murdered body. Adultery is a permissible subject, provided it is not committed with the husband's best friend. (Whom do television executives think women commit adultery with?) Never show people drinking in the morning.

The black-listers took advantage of these inhibitions, designed to placate the public, and channeled them into a brutal and vicious persuasion.

All of it was silly. Gale Sondergaard and Morris Carnovsky and Dalton Trumbo are not subversive after midnight when everything is dark and quiet. Why did we deprive them of their opportunity to pursue their professions in broad daylight?

# The village atheist

ANOTHER great American institution is disappearing from the scene—the village atheist. Across the length and breadth of our land, in every city, town, hamlet, and crossroads, there was one stubborn man, the dissenter, the nonconformist, the fellow who by his atheism ennobled the character of those who wanted to "save" him, and strengthened the faith of those who were already "saved." He added interest and luster to his community, and he was as American as the Liberty Bell in Philadelphia, the whaling ships on the Gloucester coast, and as much a part of the American scene as the Baptist Church on each of the thousands of Elm Streets up and down this land. The village atheist entered our civilization at the very beginning of our country —from that first man whom old Cotton Mather sent into the woods with a one-day supply of water and bread to "think it over." The village atheist of America had about as much affinity with Russia as he did with Cambodia—probably less. But today he has been chased off the stage of our life.

This American, who harks back to the old days of America, when individualism was prized above all other virtues, even to the point of eccentricity, has become identified with ideologies which were completely foreign to him. Now that he is gone it is well to look back upon him as a part of the wonderful American scene of the past. He was the fellow that the high-school kid of another generation would seek out to ask about Homer and Shakespeare—that is, if the high-school kid's mother wasn't looking. But the kid's mother was not really worried—it was only that she didn't want the neighbors to see her son cavorting with "old eccentric Bill." And then finally, when the village atheist died, there was always one understanding clergyman in the town who would be sure to say, "Bill claimed to be an atheist, but he was one of the best Christians I've ever known." Thus, as the erosion sets in on our individualism, our great American institutions go, one by one, and one of the first to go was this noble product of the American soil —the village atheist.

# Rudolf Bing and Maria Callas

Now comes Mr. Rudolf Bing, the general manager of the Metropolitan Opera Association, and unquestionably a man of extreme talent. Not only does he not excuse or forgive rudeness and temperament and selfishness, but he refuses to suffer them as well. His predecessors at the Met, Messrs. Johnson and Gatti-Casazza suffered. Opera and concert impresarios are supposed to suffer. Not Mr. Bing.

On what meat does he feed that he has grown so great? That he refuses the right of artists to kick up a row? Mr. Bing should read the biographies of Gatti-Casazza or Sol Hurok. Both books are epics of suffering. Mr. Hurok has put his life toward one service—dragging the American public into the concert hall. He played cat and mouse with Feodor Chaliapin and what a run-around! And he stood in the wings the night Isadora Duncan, disappointed when a proper Boston audience gave her only indifferent applause, suddenly shouted, "You Bostonians know nothing about Art. This is Art!" And she bared her breasts.

Hurok and Johnson and Gatti-Casazza knew this was part of the job. Wilbert Robinson, who used to manage the Brooklyn Dodgers, knew it too when he saw three Dodger baserunners on third base at one and the same time. And John McGraw knew it when his outfielder Casey Stengel refused to chase a fly ball because he was undernourished. And Connie Mack, how he knew it when he had Rube Waddell! What would have happened to Pinky Higgins of the Boston Red Sox if he had fired Ted Williams the afternoon the slugger threw his bat into the crowd? Ted Williams spits at the stands. So what? Did you ever watch his rhythm as he swings his bat? How soon before we have another Williams?

And how soon before we have another Maria Callas?

The nerve of Rudolf Bing! His arrogance is aggravated by the fact that the Met has never earned a dollar—it is supported by public donation. In the old days it was supported by the millionaires who had boxes in the Diamond Horseshoe. When the income tax pushed these donors away, the general public became the Met's patrons.

Who is Mr. Bing to dictate standards of behavior and chase Lauritz Melchior and Helen Traubel and a few less famous stars, and now Maria Callas—the first great artist since Geraldine Farrar; Maria Callas who has brought excitement back to the opera with a gift of warming the bones of us who love New York and the Met?

Who is this Rudolf Bing?

# Long live the city

I HAVE always lived in cities. I was born in New York City and I have spent twenty years in Charlotte. For a few years in the thirties I did live in the suburbs. I convinced all my friends that I loved it and in convincing them, almost convinced myself. But I didn't love the suburbs. I wanted paved streets, taxis, buses, and business districts.

I love the sounds of the city, but lately I think the city is double-crossing me. When I last visited New York I traced the streets of my many joys. Of the happy places I remember, only Guffanti's, a fine Italian restaurant, is still there. Somehow the city of my youth has been pulled from underneath my feet. Well, people say, that's progress. Was it progress to tear down Mark Twain's home on Ninth Street? Is that thin-partitioned, ugly brick apartment an improvement over the rich brownstone where Mark Twain wrote *The American Claimant?* Was it progress when the old Brevoort Hotel came down to have saved every old gas jet and piece of red oak paneling to simulate in the new the charm of the old Brevoort? The authorities shrug and say, "Everyone is moving to the suburbs." But they are out of step, not me. More people still live in the city than anywhere else. *The Exploding Metropolis* (compiled by the editors of *Fortune*) has the answer. People aren't moving to the suburbs because they have given up on the city. They are moving to the suburbs because the city has given up on them. When I look at Charlotte and New York I wonder sometimes where the young lovers can stroll hand in hand alone. And I have seen a beautiful little plaza, where old men sat in the sun talking to the pigeons, torn down for a parking lot with a picket fence.

I think everyone who has an interest in the city ought to read the poetry of Baudelaire. He wrote of the city with its dust, grime, and poverty, but also with its excitement, color, and chance. Baudelaire took the city just as seriously as Shakespeare took heroism. Other than reading this poet, I would like to make a suggestion for all city planners which I shall adapt from Hippocrates, the Greek doctor who fathered medicine. Hippocrates said every doctor who treated a broken bone should have had a broken bone and every doctor who treated a fever should have experienced a fever. Hippocrates really meant that every doctor ought to consider the patient as well as the disease. I shall not be so extreme. But every architect who designs an apartment building ought to be made to live in it, and no realtor should be allowed to sell a city lot until he has occupied space on it for two years. This will convince architects, planners, and realtors that the people of the city are not just so many inconveniences, that as often as the people who live in a city are considered, just so often will the city be beautiful.

# How to make a speech

FOR me to make a speech is not as simple as it is for many professional speakers—and that's my hard luck. I just cannot make the speech twice. The first thing I think of when I stand up in front of an audience is that maybe there's someone there who had heard me a week before, or a year before, and that sends shivers down my back. I may conceivably explore the same idea or theme on several occasions, but I'd rather die than repeat the same arguments and sentences.

I find that most effective speeches (for me) are made in one of two ways—either I prepare very carefully for a week or two before the scheduled talk, or I make no preparation at all, not even think about it till I am ready to give the talk. A halfway preparation, thinking about it now and then, is no good for me. I either write it out, correct it, rewrite, and read it over three or four times, or dismiss the idea from my mind completely until I am introduced. Once you stand up in front of an audience, you realize that there is no escape, and you just bang away.

My entire idea is to leave the audience with some new idea or an original thought of some kind, which they can take away with them. When I am invited by a Gentile organization for the specific purpose of talking about "Jews" or the "Jewish Question," I invite them to ask me questions.

I inform them that if they wanted a fellow to get up there and say that "Love is better than hate," and "Let's put our shoulders to the wheel," etc., I am not their man. I tell them that in the interest of intellectual advancement there is no such thing as an "embarrassing question," and "Let's lock the doors and ask me anything." This has been highly productive, and I believe has resulted in a better feeling than the usual "interfaith" talks of benign vacuity. I have heard some very excellent questions, some which surprised me tremendously. I have them all written down. I intend to write a whole article on the questions and answers. In several instances the questions were so important that I was unable to cover the situation at the meetings, and I have promised those folks to answer the questions fully in my paper. Recently one man in Shelby, North Carolina, asked: "Mr. Golden, my grandfather came from Germany, but I am a Tar Heel—I have no affinity whatsoever for either Germany or Germans. I just never think of it. Why do the Jews retain their identity as Jews, and why did I lose mine so completely within one generation?" A schoolteacher at a meeting in Wilmington asked me: "Mr. Golden, is not the state of Israel following a course of nationalism, the same nationalism which brought such terrible disaster to your people?"

I am only mentioning two important questions. There have been many others. You'd be amazed at the fine minds you find around the Carolinas, but of course I am not amazed at all. It is just a matter of bringing this out, giving ourselves a chance to discuss these things openly, like gentlemen. I guess that is what Professor Oscar Handlin means when he says that basically there are no "minorities" in America. I am sure he doesn't mean that there are no separate and distinct cultural groups, but we do establish "the minority mood," when the Gentile is embarrassed to ask us something, or when we are fearful of answering anything he wants to know—a completely uninhibited relationship is still the only true road to mutual respect and fellowship.

# The Jayne Mansfield UJA

FIFTY years ago my Orthodox mother said that Judaism in America was doomed: the kosher butchers were too careless, the American rabbis were beginning to shave, and the men and boys were no longer saying their prayers three times a day.

My mother would be greatly surprised today. Fifty years later we not only have chocolate matzos but we also have Elizabeth Taylor. And not only Elizabeth Taylor. Marilyn Monroe too. Now all we need is Jayne Mansfield and we'll have it made. I am organizing a special UJA Jayne Mansfield Scholarship Fund.

# The boardinghouse

IN THE New York area alone there are close to fifty-five thousand licensed facilities for boarders, not counting the hotels. The total for the country must run into the many hundreds of thousands, which is an indication of the tremendous mobility and the rootlessness of our American society.

Before World War I, the boardinghouse was identified in the public mind with the split-week engagements of the vaudeville actors, or with the traveling troupe for carnival, fair, or opry house; and of course with the drummer, the traveling salesman.

Occasionally you'd find a permanent guest; an old bachelor, a spinster librarian, or a schoolteacher away from home.

Today America is on the move. Everything is temporary. "To grandmother's house we go" has given way to a mere place to flop, and when asked for his address the tenant has to open his wallet to find out where he lives.

## On beards

AMONG the Jews of Europe the beard was counted a thing of piety, wisdom, and male beauty. When these Jews came to America, however, they found all of the Yankees were clean-shaven. This was a terrible shock because soon all the sons of immigrants began imploring their bearded fathers to shave off the beard and look "American." In the process of Americanization the beard got lost. But almost as soon as the last beard was cut off, whiskers came back into popularity. The beard is used to sell Schweppes Quinine Water by Commander Whitehead, who sports a luxuriant, carefully tended hedge. Fidel Castro, the new leader of Cuba, and all his lieutenants have certainly done the beard no harm. And Ernest Hemingway and many other writers now have beards, behind which they peep at us from their book covers. Like my old father always said, "The Jews have no luck."

When Alexander the Great made his soldiers shave their beards the idea was handed down to us that he gave the order in the interest of "cleanliness." This is completely false, and undoubtedly the propaganda of the early razor-blade and shaving-cream people. Alexander had no such idea in mind. He knew very well the risk involved. He was willing to make the sacrifice; have his men surrender a bit of their manhood in order to become better soldiers. In those days there was much hand-to-hand fighting and one of the great tricks was to grab hold of your adversary's beard and pull. A man would much rather face a cleaver or an arrow than have his beard pulled, and many a battle was won by those who were quick to grab the beards first. That is the entire story behind Alexander's order and those who have made any more out of it during these past twenty-five hundred years are talking through their hats.

Then you have but to read the Burton translation of the *Arabian Nights,* one of the great treasures of our civilization, that rare document of a people who had made a true art of life and living. As you read it you shudder at every page and keep stroking your silly naked chin as contempt is heaped upon "the shaven." Even if you were forty years old those wonderful women of ancient days talked of you hilariously as "a beardless youth." They laughed fit to be tied; and as Fibber says, "It ain't funny, Molly." And seriously it isn't funny at all. There are millions of men who adhere sincerely to the fundamentalist concept that what God intended must be followed. Yet they shave and shave, and the more they shave the more it grows. Most of us, however, kick over the traces at least once a week, and there are a few hardy souls who assert their individualism oftener. What do you suppose we are doing every morning as we look into the mirror? We are actually weighing our chances. It is a daily battle—a deadly contest of nerves. "Can I get away with it today?" you say to yourself. You rub your fingers across your chin, you go up a ways on the side of your face, you rub with the grain and against the grain. You stand back a little and try to get a mental picture of how you'll look to others. Suddenly you say with great delight, "Yes, this is it." Once your mind is made up you hasten on for fear of altering your plans. You do not look in the mirror again and you try to act nonchalant as it were—eventually you even get a sort of chip on your shoulder. "There's nothing wrong with it, I look fine," and off you go, with the extreme satisfaction of having won a victory, which indeed it was.

Some months ago I visited one of the charming little cities of the Carolinas which was preparing for its centennial. There is a custom among the merchants and civic leaders of these towns to grow a beard for the celebration. They call themselves, "Brothers of the Brush," and they have lots of good clean Rotarian-Kiwanian fun. This custom is to bring back somehow "the old days" of one hundred years ago. The women join the celebration by wearing the clothing of the period. In this particular town I called on the two Jewish merchants, and lo and behold, each of them had grown a full beard! For a moment it looked to me like Ludlow Street, between Rivington and Delancey.

But every time I see a color advertisement now of the Schweppes man, I feel very sad. I am thinking of all the magnificent beards that went to waste on the Lower East Side when I was a boy.

## Exit the morgue

THE newspaper morgue is now called the library, if you please, and this entire development was inevitable, including the change in the personality of the custodian of these records. In the old days the morgue was in the charge of a tall and gaunt fellow who had answered, "This is the morgue," so often that after fifteen or twenty years he began to look like Boris Karloff. In fact, he began to think of those big filing cases as caskets, each one containing a favorite corpse which he would "replace" with city editors, advertising salesmen, and others who dared to argue with him.

It was inevitable that the newspaper morgue would become the library because of our tremendously expanding American middle class.

It was different in the old days. Mr. J. P. Morgan, standing on the gangplank of his *Corsair*, or Mrs. Cornelius Vanderbilt on the eve of a big party would say to the reporter, "I am in a hurry now, get the other details in your morgue." The elite were few in number and they knew the score.

Now we have millions of new people in the great middle class who are only beginning to enjoy the wonders of this very wonderful thing—status. The fellow pumped gas for eight years, then he became a contractor, and first thing you know he is a member of the highly exclusive Downtown Luncheon Club as well as program chairman of his civic club. Now you cannot tell a fellow like that to please give you a recent photograph for your morgue; why you would scare the guy half to death; as a matter of fact, he would hang up on you.

But when the rosy-cheeked little girl says, "This is the library," the fellow leans back and relaxes. But even "the library" may still be a bit too forbidding for some of the boys, and since the newspapers have only recently changed the designation I would suggest a better deal! Why not call it "The Peace of Mind Department"?

## The big worry

IT SEEMED that everyone—executives, laborers, editors, and actors—was terribly worried about Pay-TV. All of them were also worried about what was the best vodka mix, until Boom! The unemployment problem hit us smack in the face. Overnight Pay-TV and the proper vodka mix were dead issues. A big worry had banished them. The entrepreneur who leaves his office in a fret because he hasn't closed the big deal goes home and finds out his son has a sore throat and he automatically knows what the real worry of his life is. Many a man who's just found trouble has sat and wished like hell for yesterday's worries. A big worry always drives out the lesser. The only trouble is you have to keep finding big worries to rediscover this truth.

## What happened to debating?

HIGH-SCHOOL students report to me that there are no debates in their English, civics, and economics classes. In fact some of them never ever heard of debating. What happened? Is it part of the current fear of controversy or criticism? In the old days there was no phase of schoolwork which was more interesting, more valuable, and which left a more lasting impression on the students than a good old-fashioned debate. Ask any man who participated in classroom debates and he'll rattle off a whole list of subjects, and show a reasonable familiarity with all of them to this day. "Open Shop" or "Closed Shop"; "Protection" or "Free Trade"; "Resolved, That the Women Shall Have the Vote"; "Resolved, That Alcoholic Beverages Be Prohibited by Law"; "Resolved, That Immigration Be Restricted"; and dozens of other issues of the day that made going to school mean something more than learning how to sell football tickets.

# The church kitchen

Today when the rabbi or the Protestant clergyman shows you through his newly constructed edifice he shows you the kitchens first. Kitchens? In a church? A caterer tells me that the new churches and temples have better equipped kitchens than some of the biggest restaurants in town. Some institutions can serve as many as a thousand people within a half-hour. They are complete with steam tables for big affairs, short-order tables for meetings of the Couples Club, Sisterhood, Mr. and Mrs. Club, and the Women of the Church. The latter represents a development away from the Women's Auxiliary. This sounded too much like a labor union. All the auxiliaries are now the Women of the Church.

Five hundred years hence, people will dig up the churches and the temples built during the past ten years and they will conclude that this American decade was the most pious era in world history. But the steam tables, bakeries, and barbecue pits will puzzle them. This may send them off on a brand-new line of research—to find out the nature of the sacrifices we performed.

# The rabbis are on the go

AH, MY FRIENDS, it is not easy to be a rabbi these days, especially in the South. From pulpit to pedagogy, from pastorate to public relations, and the greatest development along these lines is visiting the sick in the hospital. But this is merely the beginning. The important thing in this matter is the timing. How soon after you are admitted to the hospital does the clergyman come? And the matter of a few hours or even minutes may very well be the determining factor.

Indeed, these pastoral calls have become so important that they now represent an important attribute of the rabbi's value—"Joe was in the hospital three whole days before our rabbi, his royal highness, bestirred himself." "He has requested a thousand-dollar increase but you have to drag him to visit one of the members in the hospital." "The only way I can get him to visit in the hospital is when my secretary—a Christian girl, mind you—keeps reminding him all the time."

But this story is part of the bigger story in terms of the almost desperate drive to reflect the mores and the values of the "majority" society. This visiting is a big deal in the Protestant fellowships, and of course adds to the woes of the rabbi. It all operates under a smooth-running system. The ambulance people call the clergyman involved the very moment the patient starts on his way to the hospital. This service is so efficient that there have been cases where the Protestant clergyman got to the hospital ahead of the patient. And since he is already there, it is a very simple matter for him to go in and see "one of my very good Jewish friends, Mr. Gottlieb."

Three hours later the rabbi comes and Mrs. Gottlieb gives him a terrible look. "He's already two hours down from the operating room," is the first thing she says nonchalantly, and this is followed by the coup de grâce, "Morris wasn't

here ten minutes before our dear Christian friend of the
Methodist church came in to see him—right away." I have
seen rabbis put through this ordeal and I know what it
means—but luckily the rabbinical students in the seminaries
will not believe me, and so there is no danger of adding to
the already overcrowded field of traveling salesmen.

The old traditionalist Jews had a better system. They
figured correctly the clergyman was already blessed of the
Lord, by the very nature of his calling, so it was unfair for
him to keep piling up the good deeds when he really did
not need them. His ledger was always in the black. Instead,
we turned this whole idea of visits to the hospital over to
the sinners, to allow them to accumulate these badly needed
credits. And thus we built up a whole professional class of
hospital visitors; they shook hands, said prayers, and there
was happiness all around.


# Clement Attlee and Dr. Kagawa

CLEMENT ATTLEE, the old Socialist, former Prime Minister, replacement for Sir Winston Churchill, has recently
toured America on a lecture series. Earl Attlee tells us
democracy is a good thing, and that we must put our
shoulder to the wheel, and that we will achieve great unity
in co-operation, and that England and America are blood
brothers and should live in peaceful amity. Earl Attlee, in
the chambers of commerce, at the women's clubs, in the
fraternal organizations, and in front of other audiences, is
saying nothing.

Earl Attlee's lectures remind me, in reverse, of the story
of Toyohiko Kagawa. During World War II, in back of the
*kamikaze* fanaticism and the treachery of Pearl Harbor,
many people still saw some honor in Japan in the figure
of Toyohiko Kagawa, a great Japanese Christian. Some place
in Japan, declared ministers from their pulpits, there was a
Christian spirit and eventually this spirit which Kagawa

stood for would triumph over the barbarity of Tojo. After the war was over, Dr. Kagawa came to America for a lecture tour. Many of his lectures were in the South, where he was particularly admired. He came to Charlotte in the late 1940's and spoke at the biggest and most respectable church in town. The nature of his sermon that night was that he was amazed that racial segregation existed in a Christian nation. In Japan he had heard of it, but trusting to the Christian spirit of America, he said, he had simply not believed it. I heard Dr. Kagawa deliver this lecture during his tour.

Almost immediately all the publicity about Kagawa ceased. No more editorials praised him. Ministers did not proclaim his goodness from the pulpit. Yet I still believe the great Japanese Christian was just that—a Christian.

Thinking of Dr. Kagawa, I wonder what is wrong with Earl Attlee. What is he afraid of? He has lived an honorable strife-torn life, must he conclude his public appearance dissolving in a mess of platitudes? Or does he look down upon us? Or does he simply not want to offend anyone so he can keep making lectures and if so, what for?

# Clothes make the revolution

APPAREL plays an important part in revolution. In the early days of the revolution the leaders make themselves as much like the people as possible. Lenin and Trotsky wore nondescript clothing and even on dress parades they wore shapeless cloth caps. There was a picture of General Marshall in China standing between Mao Tse-tung, the Communist leader, and Generalissimo Chiang Kai-shek, and this picture tells us the whole story: Chiang in his brilliant uniform and red-lined cape and Mao looking exactly like a Chinese truck driver who had just finished unloading fifty tons of galvanized pipe.

You recall the photos of the Korean armistice negotiations; the Korean general all dressed up with medals, epaulets, and the completely correct attire of a general officer, and the Chinese commander, representing one sixth of the earth's people, with that same black tunic, complete with cigarette ash and that same old shapeless cap at the back of his head.

When they are consolidating their power they wear a plain tunic, usually of a drab color, buttoned at the throat and with no adornments. They are usually seen with a cigarette down to its last puff and its ash dusting down the tunic front.

But once their power is consolidated the revolutionaries break out in finery. Remember Stalin wearing those red stripes down his trouser legs. Let us keep an eye on Khrushchev. Based on his apparel, he cannot possibly be satisfied with his position yet. But if we should suddenly see him with a new uniform and a Star of Lenin on his chest, then we can be sure that he, at least, thinks he has it made.

# The Reverend Mr. Cahill

LET me tell you about the life and times of my friend, the Reverend Edward A. Cahill, former minister of the Charlotte Unitarian Church, now of Atlanta.

Thinking about the Reverend Mr. Cahill, it occurs to me that maybe there should be an N.A.A.U.P.—National Association for the Advancement of Unitarian People.

In 1955, Cahill ran for a seat on the local school board. Cahill is a man who does not believe in lengthy political platforms. His had two planks:

1. Eliminate racial segregation.
2. Eliminate teaching of religion in the public schools.

That's all. Cahill, running in Charlotte, North Carolina, on that platform, was like the Senegalese prize fighter,

Battling Siki, who once fought Mike McTigue in Dublin, Ireland, on Saint Patrick's Day. The result here was similar to that achieved by Mr. Siki.

In the campaign, one group circulated a petition which declared among other things that the signers were "opposed to any man or woman for public office who denies the deity of Jesus Christ." A letter accompanying the petition said: "We must pray for the Reverend Edward A. Cahill, the Unitarian minister, that he may repent of his unbelief, be converted, and come to the saving knowledge . . ."

In addition, a chain-telephone campaign was conducted against him.

Cahill received 843 votes out of some 9,391 cast. We expected at least 2,500 votes, but, in general, the white voters frowned on his racial platform and the Negroes turned him down on his number 2 plank.

In other words, Cahill was in wonderful shape. He wound up with the Unitarians and *The Carolina Israelite*.

That's not the only interesting thing that happened to Cahill while he served here.

Several years ago, his Charlotte church desegregated its fellowship and gave public notice to the effect that Negroes would be welcomed to membership. Not a single Negro applied.

But what is even more to the point is the fact that very few Negroes have become converts to Roman Catholicism, despite the fact that the Catholic Church has assumed a sort of religious leadership in the fight to implement the United States Supreme Court decision, and has desegregated most of its own institutions in the South.

In the main, the Negroes of the South (with exception of lower Louisiana), belong to the several Protestant fellowships—Baptist, Methodist, Episcopalian, and Presbyterian. There are, of course, independent sects, as well as adherents to various fringe cults, notably the one that was led by Daddy Grace. The autonomy of the individual church organizations, aside from the spiritual benefits derived, is of

great importance to the vast Negro memberships. The
church is the outstanding social institution. It provides the
Negro with the only opportunity for self-esteem and self-
expression. The Negro is a truck driver, his wife is a
domestic, but over the weekend they are deacons, stewards,
elders, communal leaders, readers, Sunday School teachers,
and choir directors.

The open forum discussions of the Unitarian Church and
the Mass of the Catholic Church cannot, for a long time to
come, offer an equal opportunity for individual and family
status.

However, my good friend Cahill had an exploratory
luncheon with a Negro right before he was called to Atlanta.

But, historically, the final incident here that I associate
with Cahill is by far the most significant.

The Mecklenburg County Ministerial Association (Charlotte) voted to desegregate its organization. They invited the
Negro clergymen to join the organization on an equal basis.
The Ministerial Association desegregated "racially" but did
not desegregate "theologically," and the rabbi, the Roman
Catholic priest, and the Unitarian minister (what a parlay!)
are still not eligible for membership.

All this time the Negro clergymen had their own association, the Negro Ministerial Alliance, and they had ONE
white applicant. You guessed it. The Reverend Mr. Cahill,
the Unitarian. But Cahill asked that his membership application be held up, because, if he joined the Negro Alliance,
he feared he might be the stumbling block to the desegregation of the (white) Ministerial Association.

Well, when the Ministerial Association desegregated, the
Negroes went over in a body to the white association—leaving Cahill, the Unitarian, out on a limb, all alone, the first
white man in history to be segregated by both whites and
Negroes.

With such experiences in his background, you would think
that the Reverend Mr. Cahill would be a sad man. On the
contrary, he's as happy as a mouse in a cooky jar.

# Barbershop duet

WHEN I worked for a New York newspaper I patronized an Italian barber on one of the side streets near the water-front. I always liked to get the job over with early in the morning and I was usually the first customer of the day. The moment I entered, Vincent, the proprietor, pulled down the shades so no one else would enter during my stay. I got into the chair, Vincent went to work, and both of us sang Italian folk songs and arias from as many Italian operas as we could squeeze into half an hour. Neither of us was ever able to stump the other. Vincent knew more lyrics, of course, and I went along with tum-tee-tum-tum-tum; although I could follow with the Italian in such things as "La Donna è Mobile," "Vesti la Giubba," "O Marie," and "Mamma Mia."

They don't make barbershops like that any more.

# Today I am cuff links

THE old ghetto joke was about the bar mitzvah boy called upon to make his little speech about "becoming a man," and how he looked down upon the table where his presents had been spread out, and in the excitement of the moment began: "Today I am a fountain pen."

But no more.

Today he gets cuff links, and thus once again, in a few short sentences, we have the history of the Jewish people in America.

The fountain pen was the symbol of learning; and every cousin, uncle, and aunt delivered the same "few remarks" when making the presentation to the thirteen-year-old: "This is for you to write the prescriptions when you become a doctor."

Cuff links? Can you imagine cuff links on a thirteen-year-old kid on the East Side? As we entered the Rivington Street

Library we had to show our hands, both sides, to make sure
that they were reasonably clean before we handled those
books. Sometimes the lady librarian examined the hands,
other times an older boy, a monitor, made the examination,
and he was tougher.

There were no cuff links, but at least we read books; and
so "fountain pens and cuff links" offers the opportunity for
an interesting study for our sociologists and philosophers.

## Ivy League yarmulkas

Most of the religious supply houses now offer Ivy League
yarmulkas (skullcaps). These Ivy League yarmulkas come
in a dozen different designs: plaids and two-tones, reds,
grays, and blacks. Initials, frat symbols, or other designs are
embroidered in gold for a slight extra charge. The Ivy
League yarmulkas are well made with satin linings, and on
the average they cost four dollars a dozen.

And would Yossele Rosenblatt have been surprised!

## My favorite quotes

Eartha Kitt—quoted in *Ebony* on the trials and tribulations of her youth: "I didn't go out with boys till I was
fifteen years old."

Hemingway—In the Hemingway movie, *The Sun Also
Rises*, Ava Gardner goes through six reels saying, "I need a
drink." "Buy me a brandy." "I need a brandy." "Get me another brandy." "How about a brandy?" and, finally, at the
end of the movie, Mel Ferrer takes her in his arms and says:
"You are the first woman who said anything that made sense
to me."

Senator Alton Lennon of North Carolina in 1954—"I am
opposed to admitting either Hawaii or Alaska as a state.

They're both too far from the mainland, and the population has too high a proportion of *Orientals*."

These wonderful words can go without comment by me —except for Senator Lennon's reference to the *Orientals*.

Where did the three wise men come from, Senator—Virginia Beach?

# The finest store

I WENT to Tiffany's on Fifth Avenue to buy my first piece of ornamental jewelry for a girl. Tiffany's? Who ever heard of a boy from the Lower East Side going to Tiffany's?

But for some reason, which I still cannot explain, I learned this very early in life. In Tiffany's I was able to buy a piece of costume jewelry for eight dollars, tucked in a box marked "Tiffany," which was worth not eight dollars, but a million dollars.

The finest stores are, of course, the "cheapest," but unfortunately the poor people are "afraid" of the finest stores. They are afraid to go inside, and so they'll pay more for the same merchandise in the cheaper establishments.

I have seen this operate often in the matter of eating. There are inexperienced men, some of them even traveling men, who are afraid to go into the best restaurants, or even into the hotel dining room. They walk blocks looking for some flea-bitten joint, and the check comes to more than if they had gone into the best eating place. The finest store is, of course, the cheapest always!

# How to treat salesmen

HAVING sold advertising space for some years, I know what it means to sit and wait in outer offices of corporations and agencies. I know what it means to be a salesman, and I follow a rigid policy with the men who now call on me. The first thing I do is stand up and shake the fellow's hand. Then I offer to play him a game of darts on my dartboard. After that I ask him what he's selling and discuss the prospects with him. Whether I buy or not, I urge him to make himself at home in my office. Whenever he gets tired he can always visit here and read books, use the men's room, or just sit around and talk a bit.

# What shall I do now, Mama?

THE young people of America are having a tough time having a good time.

This boredom began when he was a six-year-old tot and asked, "What shall I do now, Mama?" And all around him were toys, railroad trains, teddy bears, and television.

How did we get along without the movies, TV, and all the wonderful toys that are available today?

The teen-agers who are having such a rough time of it trying to amuse themselves merely reflect the boredom which surrounds us all.

Visit a nice subdivision home of some young friends and they proudly show you their new washer, dryer, electric coffeepot, electric frying pan, electric toaster, electric deep-freeze, electric barbecue, and electric deep fryer. All in all, counting the house, furniture, and new car, they pay interest on twenty-five thousand dollars. They both work and so they hire a baby sitter for Junior, God bless his bored little soul.

Maybe they wouldn't be so bored if they had to throw a few sticks on a fire for the barbecue, and perhaps even slap a non-electric frying pan on the electric range, but this would be standing in the way of progress or whatever it is that is making everybody so nervous, and creating our crackling, sizzling, steaming civilization of Alka-Seltzer and sleeping pills. And tomorrow is another day to face up to the question: "What shall I do now, Mama?"

# Righties and lefties

HEBREW is one of the world's oldest languages. It was first written on stone, as witness the Decalogue. To write on stone a lithographer has to use both hands. One hand holds the chisel, the other the hammer. Most people are right-handed. Therefore, the writer holds the hammer in his right hand and by the simplest of calligraphic rules, he has to write from right to left in order to see what he is doing. Try it yourself. If you try to chisel from left to right, your left hand with the chisel blocks a substantial part of your view. The reason we write from left to right nowadays is because we use only one hand. If we tried it the way the Hebrews wrote, our right hands would block our view. Of course this proves that right-handed people have discriminated throughout history against left-handed people. I was overjoyed recently to see that banks have at last invented a check book for southpaws. The lefties have had a tough time of it.

# Don't look back

ONE of my sons recently sent me a book I had read as a schoolboy. It was Chapman's translation of *The Odyssey*. Looking through it I came across the passage which describes Odysseus's escape from Cyclops. Once Odysseus had blinded Cyclops and had led his men from the cave, he did not go back for his cape and sword. Once out of danger, stay out of danger. Don't look back, don't go back. This is not only good advice, but a principle by which human nature survives. The alcoholic who reforms never touches another drink. The wise husband does not look up the old flame.

## On eternity

ETERNITY scares me. What would I do with it? No trials and tribulations, Billy Graham says. I once went up to the mountains for three days with nothing to do and it drove me crazy.

## Vacations

THE enjoyment of a vacation is not based on the warmth and the sunshine to which you fly, but on the degree of cold and wind whence you fled. The minute you get to Miami you try to find out how bad it is back in New York. The first thing the vacationer does is find out the state of things in New York. If it's snowing up there, he's happy. If they are having mild weather, he suffers terrible agony. The worse it is back home, the better you enjoy yourself yonder. Vacationers in Florida spend most of their time trying to find out how deep the snow is in Chicago. They listen constantly to weather forecasts from up North. It is the same thing in the summertime when you go to the beach or the mountains. The best way to have a good time is to keep reminding yourself of how hot it is back in the city. Anyone at the seashore who reads that it is 102 degrees in the city is sure to have one hell of a good time. In Miami it has been discovered that the most money is spent on the night the television fellow says it is four degrees below in Chicago.

## The superhighway

I KNOW this is like throwing rocks at a church, but I do not share the wild, unrestrained, and ecstatic enthusiasm that people show for the construction of superhighways through the state. Nothing seems to bring such an out-pouring of pride among people as road building.

The secondary road program which the late Kerr Scott inaugurated when he was governor of my state was a wonderful thing. It could have gone much further. I'd love to see a paved road leading from the highway right up to the kitchen door of every farmhouse in North Carolina. This is good for the state, for the people, and for mankind.

But let us look at the superhighways a minute.

The whole idea seems to be to by-pass the cities. During the last fifteen years we have succeeded in by-passing most of the cities in the Piedmont, and the folks have a clear straightaway now, almost without a single obstacle.

So what? What conquest bring we home? What tributaries follow us to High Point, Greensboro, Salisbury, and Charlotte? The answer is—none.

The state of North Carolina (and the rest of them, of course) keep adding new taxes to build these superhighways so that the guy from Brooklyn may get down to the dog races in Miami ten hours earlier.

Somewhere in Virginia, the guy turns to the blonde and says, "Honey, that Carolina [he doesn't even say "North"] is sure a fine state. We can whiz right through—don't even have to stop once till we get to Georgia."

This is good?

Why should we provide him with this service? Is it coming to him?

On the contrary, what I would do would be to make that racetrack fellow go through every city, village, and hamlet of North Carolina. Let him get stuck in the traffic: "Honey, looks like we're stuck here for the night—let's find a place to eat." And the blonde says: "Don't forget, let's not have any more arguments; separate rooms," which makes it even better for our hotels and caravansaries.

We rush the guy through the state like he's going to a fire —and in exchange—he doesn't even buy a Coca-Cola in North Carolina.

# Too many by-lines

THE by-line used to be the mark of excellence. When the
time came for the reporter to have his story headed "by
John Jones," it was a "service stripe" which meant not only
unusual excellence, but influence in the community.

Today the by-line is meaningless. A kid comes out of
journalism school and gets his first job on a newspaper.
They assign him to cover the Y.M.C.A., Red Cross, and
March of Dimes. The next morning he sees the directors of
these agencies and discusses the new Y.M.C.A. building-
fund program. He jots down all the information. Then he
has a Coca-Cola on his way to the library to find out when
the old Y.M.C.A. was built and the name of the previous
fund-raising chairman. Now he is all set. The next morning
he sees his story: "Y.M.C.A. Drive to begin on March 20,
BY J. E. (BOOTSIE) PIPPICK." He has been raised to the
peerage—he has been made a journalistic Knight of the
Garter even before he has drawn his first pay check. By
the time he is promoted to covering the Kiwanis luncheons
he has already tasted of all the joys of this great profession,
and has a sated appetite for all its thrills and ambitions.
And his work must suffer since he has lost a sense of values.

# Anyone can be replaced?

THERE are several indigenous American platitudes, none
of which describes reality. Among these platitudes, now
grown to the proportion of myths, are "THINK"; "Does it
sell flour"; "It is later than you think"; and "The great
wisdom of the world comes from taxi drivers." But the
biggest hoax of all these platitudes is the cliché, "Anyone
can be replaced."

If there were an ounce of truth in this statement, life would spin itself out pretty stupidly.

The psychological force that the statement creates is engendered among the great mass who look hopefully toward an equality of mediocrity, helplessness, lack of initiative, and stupidity. It is for this reason that men of talent are usually pacifists. A war culture is a great leveler and makes everyone more or less alike. The tremendous acceptance of fascism, nazism, and communism in our generation is partly explained by the fact that these systems are extensions of the war culture into the everyday milieu. These systems effectively eliminate intellectual competition, and everyone thinks that it will be share and share alike. The decisions are made for the docile elsewhere and the fellow who never had an idea in his head becomes a captain.

Mediocrity breeds in a crisis. All too often politicians and demagogues perpetuate the crisis for the purpose of maintaining their jobs.

As far as we know, man is the only animal with a memory. No animal fights for its young with the scratching, tearing loyalty of the female Adirondack bobcat. But once the baby bobcat is weaned, the mother goes about her business and the little bobcat shifts for itself. It is forgotten.

Not with man. We remember, and because we remember we know that there are too many who can never be replaced and who will never be replaced—Mozart, Shakespeare, Beethoven, Thomas Jefferson. There are thousands of others. And, of course, there are your own father and your mother and your loved ones.

# Undoing of my diet

IF MY diet had not been so successful, I might have been in much better shape today. A few years ago my doctor gave me a diet which I followed religiously. At the end of two months I had lost twenty-one pounds, and I felt better

than ever. Because of the great success of this diet, I said
to myself: "If that is all there is to this I can do it any time,
so why not wait for a more appropriate moment?"

And that's where it stands now.


## Our representative?

I WAS a guest on the Jack Paar program and I thought it
was a good opportunity to make a suggestion about our
outer-space program.

The missile might land intact on Mars and we should
consider this possibility the next time we use a monkey in
the experiment. The occupant of our missile would jump
out and start scratching himself. The Martians would think
the monkey is one of us, wouldn't they? I think we should
equip the monkey with adequate information on microfilm
and with pictures of people, and we can duplicate this
information in all the known languages.

A fine thing if the monkey should land on Mars and the
folks there ask him some questions and he swings from tree
to tree. The Martians would immediately stop their own
program of trying to reach us.


## Why?

EVERY salesman, sales manager, and organization man
says, "We are doing better than this month last year." Why
must we always "beat this month last year"? This competition between this year and last year is carried to ridiculous
extremes. Every business report says that the first twenty
days of 1959 were 22 per cent better than the first twenty
days of 1958. I remember last year that we had two severe
blizzards the first twenty days. If you bring this conflict to
the attention of a salesman he will say, "It's the American

way." But we certainly do not hope that the drunkard is doing 22 per cent better the first twenty days of this year than last. Or do we?

# No one unites us

WHEN Enrico Caruso was at the height of his fame, it took two and a half weeks at best to cross the Atlantic. Yet the world over, those who loved music knew the name Caruso. When Charlie Chaplin portrayed the tramp, Chilean convicts digging guano in the Andes laughed at his antics. And Laurel and Hardy movies played in the smallest village in the Kashmir.

Individual personalities used to unite us. Across the oceans and the mountains and the plains we shared affection for them.

My team of such personalities—selected from memory of those who made their contributions in my time and leaving out statesmen, which is not the same thing, of course—is as follows:

> Enrico Caruso
> Lillian Russell
> John Barrymore
> Feodor Chaliapin
> Nellie Melba
> Ernestine Schumann-Heink
> Charles Chaplin
> Maurice Chevalier
> Al Jolson
> George M. Cohan
> Ethel Barrymore
> John McCormack

Today we brag about the five and a half hours it takes to cross from England to America by jet, but no one unites us.

No one is really interested in that five and a half hours, unless it be some harried diplomat on a state errand or a businessman hurrying to tie up some bauxite properties. No single image or voice or face gives us all a share in humanity. We just move faster.

# The individual

AT THIS precise moment there are one half million Hindus starving. Within this year, most of these Hindus will be dead. Dead children with swollen stomachs will litter the streets and their parents will collapse with dizziness and fatigue, pleading for a handful of rice which they cannot have. Yet these half million Hindus are only statistics to us.

Sometimes we hear people talk about the six million Jews who died in Nazi gas ovens and perhaps because he knows we cannot respond properly the speaker is indignant and rhetorical. And the man who talks of the half million Hindus does so with incredulity.

But the man whose little girl has been hit by a car is the least indignant and rhetorical of all men, and when he sees the crumpled body he is too all-believing.

The great sadness of our history is that the mortal imagination cannot summon the same grief for the casualties of an earthquake that it can for one little girl. It is too hard for the imagination to conceive of a half million Hindus comprising a half million different souls.

It is a lot easier for a college graduate to squeeze a button and release an atomic bomb from the *Enola Gay* over Hiroshima than it is for the same college graduate turned infantry sniper to squeeze the tigger on a lone, unsuspecting Japanese soldier. The people obliterated in the atom blast will not know who dropped the bomb, nor will the bombardier have to watch them die. It is much easier because a city is inanimate and cannot levy blame. But the Japanese infantryman will stand stunned and surprised and regret his carelessness before he sinks to earth. And there will be an instant when American and Japanese are each caught up in the significance of the deed. Because it is only to individuals that compassion and sympathy belong. The desperate fact is that we cannot will our sympathy to the group. Bitter though this truth is, we have not betrayed our heritage. We have made the individual supreme, because that is the only hope of exciting compassion and sympathy.

Perhaps the day will come when our imagination will not be surprised by vast numbers and we will be able to see every individual as integral in himself. If that day comes it will be because we placed such high value on the single individual.